Bowie & Me
Unparallel Careers!

Stephen Wyatt-Gold

Published by Reflex Books
(New Century Shows Ltd)

Copyright © 2019 by Stephen Wyatt-Gold

Paperback ISBN: 978-1-9161433-0-2
eBook ISBN: 978-1-9161433-1-9

Edition published 2019

The right of Stephen Wyatt-Gold to be identified as the author of this work has been asserted by him in accordance with sections 77 and 78 of the Copyright, Designs and Patents Act 1988

All rights reserved. No part of this publication may be reproduced, distributed, or transmitted in any form or by any means, including photocopying, recording, or other electronic or mechanical methods, without the prior written permission of the publisher, except in the case of brief quotations embodied in critical reviews and certain other noncommercial uses permitted by copyright law.

The author and publishers have made all reasonable efforts to contact copyright holders for approvals and apologise for any omissions in the form of credits.

Author's website
www.stephenwyattgold.com

REFLEX BOOKS

St Augustine's Business Centre
125 Canterbury Road, Westgate-on-Sea, Kent CT8 8NL
info@reflexbooks.co.uk

**to
Penny
without whom ....?**

Contents

Introduction 7
The Beginnings 9

Chapter 1 11
The Lower Third
(Class Of '62)
1962/1965
School's Out 16
London Blues - 1960s 24

Chapter 2 33
The Wilderness Years
1965/1969
The Cowboys 38
Real Showbiz 45
Go North Young Man 47

Chapter 3 55
A Big Fish
(The Jersey Years)
1969/1970
Back To Reality 64
A New Season 67
Affairs Of The Heart 70

Chapter 4 79
America
(The Cruising Years)
1970/1973
Don't Take Away The Music 87
A Bite Of The Big Apple 88
Some Private Enterprise 90
Buffalo 96
New York Nuptials 99
The Cracks Appear 101
Batten Down The Hatches 103
The Wilderness Again 107
Back Out West 109
Heart Over Head 112

Chapter 5 117
Trilogy
1973/1977
Military Manoeuvres 121
Filling In 127
Egypt 130
On The Record 134
Isle Of Man 138
The Holyland 141
The Doldrums 143
Nigeria 144
Eric & Ernie 146
Edwards versus Corbett 149

Chapter 6 153
All Change
(Achieving Gold)
1978/1979
The Summer Of Discontent 156
Ungentlemanly Conduct 159
Quintessential 162
Singapore Sling 164
A Short Break 167
Fighting Talk 169
Jellystone Park 171

Chapter 7 177
A Smouldering Flame
1980/1982
Up And Running 178
Cairo 180
The Italian Job 184
World Tour 188
Seoul 192
Gateway To The USA 195
Managing Expectations 199
Cologne 200
Barcelona 202
A Dark Cloud 205
Still Growing 206
India 208
The War Year 209

Chapter 8 — 215
Island Hopping
1983/1985
Wight Nights 218
Business Affairs 219
Around The World Again 221
Japan 223
South Korea 225
European Tour 227
Whitegold & The Big Idea 235
The Waltons 236
Another Japanese Christmas 238

Chapter 9 — 241
The Shipwreck
1985/1988
Teething Troubles? 245
The Final Breakdown 247
The Twilight Zone 249
New Delhi 251
Rich Records 252
The Little Man 254
Last Chance 256

Chapter 10 — 261
Sunlit Uplands
(The Theme Park Years)
1989/1995
Jollies 268
The African Interlude 270
Heroes, Fairytales and the BBC 277
The New Venture 280
Calling Time 281

Chapter 11 — 285
The Glory Days
(The Parkshows Years)
1996/2003
Adventure In A Small Country 287
New Orleans 292
Cairo Again 293
Hello Sailor! 295
Dubai 299
Moving On 300
Alice & Holly 304
The Lampies 306
The End Begins 308
Celebrate Good Times 311

Appendix I — 321
Out Takes

Appendix II — 335
The Complete Thorpe Park Years
1989/1995

Appendix III — 355
Important People

Photographs

The Lower Third	31
The Wilderness Years / A Big Fish	77
America	115
Trilogy / All Change	175
A Smouldering Flame	213
Island Hopping / The Shipwreck	259
Sunlit Uplands / The Glory Days	315

Bowie & Me
Unparallel Careers!

'Don't Take Away The Music'
because *'Music'* is my first love and
'I've Got The Music In Me' so
'I Write The Songs' because
'That's When The Music Takes Me'
so
'Don't Stop The Music'

Introduction

On a cold and blustery January day I was on an infrequent visit to the UK from my home in South West France. I was in Margate with my wife, Penny, visiting old friends and relatives and we had wandered into Waterstones bookshop at Westwood Cross Shopping Centre. As usual she headed for the health and well-being section and I passed by the history, war and travel sections before stopping at music where my eyes fell on yet another biography of David Bowie. On flicking through the early pages my own name leapt out at me. I showed it to Penny *"Hey look, I've got a mention." "Do you want to buy it?"* she replied. *"No,"* I laughed *"at £18.00 I can live without it."*

I remembered that an old friend had recently published a memoir of her years in show-business and, as we left the shop, I joked to Penny that if I ever wrote a similar memoir I should somehow have Bowie mentioned in the title. That way someone was bound to buy it!

That evening we were hosting dinner for my niece, her husband and my nephew who is a long time ardent Bowie fan. *"Have you heard the news,"* he said, before I had time to take his coat, *"David Bowie's dead."* In view of the earlier bookshop banter it was a weird surprise and, under the circumstances, something of a shock. It was January 10th 2016.

I never actually met David Bowie but, even so, he became a part of my life. He formed the centre piece of my conversational persona over most of my adult years. His name staunchly supported me while I waded through the muddy waters of a roller coaster life in show business. He never taught me anything and I was never particularly inspired by him. Whilst I may have envied his success from time to time, I was never a huge fan and I would have had difficulty naming, without reference, the majority of his many albums or songs. I did occasionally steal from him because, of course, I was familiar with his biggest hits and I used them often.

David Bowie died just over 50 years after our

Introduction

tenuous connection began and I must admit to having been slightly illuminated by the glow of publicity following this sad event. There were early similarities between us. We were both born in January within a year of each other, we grew up in the South East of England, we sang and played music from an early age, we both joined beat groups in Kent, we were hanging around the London R&B scene during the same era, we were both ambitious. The similarities ended decades ago but I will be eternally grateful for his success and his impact on the music world because of the very faint reflection that I have bathed in and shamelessly cultivated during my own musical journey.

The Beginnings

I was born on 17th January 1946 in Margate, a seaside town situated at the far eastern tip of the county of Kent in the South East of England. I was christened that same year Robin Stephen Wyatt. I was named Robin after the then famous BBC organist Robin Richmond. His trademark instrument was the Hammond organ and he had imported the first example to Great Britain from the United States in 1935. This was my one and only family connection with music – my mother was a fan of Robin Richmond!

We lived in a council house, 33 Addiscombe Gardens, Margate, and moved to a new council estate when I was six years old. It was there, in Giles Gardens, that my interest in music somehow took shape. I passed my eleven plus exams and went to Chatham House Grammar School in Ramsgate where the infrequent music lessons failed to get my full attention. However, I was picked to sing treble in the school choir, which was far more enjoyable than being picked for the rugby fifteen, which I often was, but only because I was very overweight and looked like a good forward. Choir practice soon ended when my voice broke which probably coincided with me hearing the first strains of Buddy Holly's *'Peggy Sue'* or Cliff Richard's *'Move It'*.

Chapter 1
The Lower Third
(Class Of '62)

Youth saw no boundaries
We took our chances well
Life was for the living
And music cast the spell
Stephen Gold (Music)

I guess it really kicked off on New Year's Eve 1961. It was a Sunday and the family had gathered at our home in Margate for an after Christmas get together. This was often the case after my elder brother had been killed by a drunk driver on my mother's birthday the 23rd December 1956. Since that date she had not been able to stomach her birthday or celebrating Christmas so we moved the family get-together to the nearest Sunday, which that year was New Year's Eve. Around four o'clock that afternoon there was an unexpected knock at the front door.

I was 15 and still dragging myself to grammar school where I had accepted the fact that I was not going

Unparallel Careers!

to do well academically. To the detriment of my school work I had, for the previous three or more years, been obsessed with the pop charts and assembled various tape recorders and other pieces of lethal electrical equipment in my bedroom in order to record the latest chart toppers from the weekly hit parade radio show, Pick Of The Pops. I idolised the American pop stars of the day – Buddy Holly, Eddie Cochran, Gene Vincent and, of course, Elvis who had been around forever by the 1960s or so it seemed to me. Then came the Brits copying their US rivals and I was absorbed by Cliff and The Shadows, Marty Wilde, Billy Fury and many of the one hit wonders long since forgotten.

At 13 I had taken my first summer job as a kitchen help in a small hotel in the then thriving holiday resort of Cliftonville. It was here that I felt my first adolescent stirrings ogling the hotel's well developed 16 year old waitress but I left the job, and the stirrings, as soon as I had earned enough to buy a guitar from Kennards, the local music shop. I learnt a few simple chords from Bert Weedon's *'Play in a Day'* guitar tutor and was able to sing a few of the Buddy Holly songs that I had been listening to – *'Peggy Sue'*, *'I Guess It Doesn't Matter Anymore'*, *'That'll Be The Day'*. Like everyone who picked up a guitar in those years I also attempted to play the tunes from the hit making guitar groups such as *'Apache'* by The Shadows and *'Walk Don't Run'* by The Ventures.

I travelled to Ramsgate each day on the school bus and often sat upstairs on the back seat where I met Roger Thomas, who was as passionate about pop music as I was, and we discussed our admiration for the pop singers of the time. He inspired me to listen to more American records like *'Walk Right Back'* by The Everly Brothers and *'Peter Gunn'* by Duane Eddie who I would have the privilege of meeting many years later. Roger was soon to become Roger 'Twiggy' Day. He embarked on a distinguished career in broadcasting by becoming a pirate DJ off-shore at Radio Caroline where he stayed until March 1968 when the law eventually ensured that the ship was towed away. He moved to Radio Luxembourg before a career in UK regional radio which still endures (2019).

Around that same time my Dad, who was a self employed decorator, announced that he had the offer of a piano from one of his customers and duly delivered it to my bedroom. Using my paper round earnings I quickly signed up to a series of piano lessons at the end of which I had not learnt to play the piano but had a pretty good idea what I wanted my future to be. I had, however, no idea how I could achieve it.

The two strangers on the doorstep that New Year's Eve would set me on a course that would shape the rest of my life. They were members of a rock & roll band that had a residency at a rather notorious Cliftonville nightspot called the Barbarian Club. They had had, the previous night, a serious fall out with their lead guitarist and desperately needed to find someone as a replacement so as not to lose the gig. They had called on a sometime mentor of mine, Michael Perkins, who played the guitar very well but who, due to his disability caused by polio as a child, did not leave the house. I had learnt a little more about the guitar and some extra chords from Michael and he had suggested they try me!

Unparallel Careers!

They told me it was very easy, it was just twelve bar blues arrangements in different keys. I had never heard of the expression 'twelve bar blues' and knew very little about keys. However, they were really desperate and persuaded me that I could bluff my way through.

So, at 15 going on 16, I found myself that night in the underground cellar, which was the Barbarian Club, hitting the occasional chord if I thought I knew it and purposely missing the strings if I didn't. Towards the end of the night the errant guitarist, who had walked out the night before, appeared in the club and somehow things were patched up enough for him to sit in and play. Denis *'teacup'* Taylor was to feature in my life for the next few years and it was from him that I would begin to understand how to play rock & roll and blues as a rhythm guitarist. The twelve bar blues was king from then on! I was paid something for that night though I cannot remember what. I guess that was my first professional gig.

Shortly after celebrating my 16th birthday I got a call from Denis asking if I would join a new group he was trying to put together. The musicians who had knocked on our front door that New Year's Eve were now just a memory but Denis had a drummer, nicknamed 'Duke', lined up together with an experienced singer called Glyn Jenkins and they were searching for a rhythm guitarist and a bass player. By coincidence both myself and the bass player they approached were pupils at Chatham House Grammar School although we had never met. Graham Smith was a sixth former while I was still in the fourth year. This highly successful and conservative school - one of the

The Lower Third

'Old Boys' being the future prime minister Edward Heath - would not take kindly to our involvement with a pop group. We both accepted the offer and joined the group which would then, to the disgust of the headmaster, inevitably take precedence over some important school activities.

The age differences in this fledgling group were very wide in teenage terms, with me at 16 and Denis Taylor at 21, but the first band practices seemed to go well and life got suddenly exciting for a young lad who hadn't had a clue how he was going to channel his interest in music.

Graham Smith's parents ran a small hotel in Derby Square, Cliftonville, and the dining room, cleared of tables and chairs, proved a perfect place for band practices during that first winter. Graham's father also ran The Orchid Room, a dance hall and functions venue situated over a small arcade of shops in Northdown Road. Although it had been dedicated to ballroom dancing, bingo and family weddings it was to become a regular summer gig for this new pop group.

But in the spring of 1962 we were a group with no bookings and no name and so it happened that I had a less than brilliant idea. It would be clever, I suggested, to use the word twist in the name because The Twist had become the latest dance craze. It was created on the back of Chubby Checker's hit record *'Let's Twist Again'*. What goes easily with twist? – naturally Oliver!! Glyn Jenkins, who was always full of witty expressions and phrases, had a long standing 'joke', which none of us understood, involving his old school class the Lower Third. Thus we became *'Oliver Twist and The Lower Third'* and for that first year we even wore exaggerated school uniform caps on stage.

After extensive rehearsals the group took up a two night per week residency at the Orchid Room in Cliftonville under the title *'Twist and Jive with Oliver Twist and the Lower Third'*. It quickly became popular and the regular fans paid two shillings and six pence (2/6d) each night to hear us play a repertoire that included material by Jerry Lee Lewis, Buddy Holly, Elvis, Chuck Berry and other American rock and roll and blues stars of the era.

School's Out

I was still at school and the late nights of gigs and rehearsals with these much older musicians inevitably took a toll on my studies. In May of 1962 Graham Smith and I were singled out by the headmaster, Mr Pearce, one Monday morning in school assembly for failing to attend the annual school Speech Day at Margate Winter Gardens on the previous Friday evening because *"These boys thought it more appropriate to be playing in a rock and roll group."* The words were spat out as though he had a nasty taste in his mouth and it certainly coloured his view of me over the next months. Of course it didn't help that I sported a 'teddy boy' quiff and wore what the headmaster referred to as a 'grubby overcoat' to a school which demanded strict adherence to uniform rules. In fact, as Mum and Dad could only afford to buy me one coat, I had persuaded them to make it a modern flashy overcoat rather than an old fashioned school raincoat.

Worse was to come. During the previous year I

The Lower Third

met my first regular girlfriend and the relationship lasted until December 1961 when we finally parted company. This relationship was to have an impact on my school life that I neither expected or was prepared for. Two evenings into my GCE exam week, while I was swatting in my bedroom, I became aware of anxious exchanges at the front door. I was called downstairs to be confronted by the mother of my ex-girlfriend who had just imparted the news to Mum and Dad that her daughter had given birth, that afternoon, to a baby boy. The baby had apparently come completely unannounced – she was 14 years old and had not recognised the warning signs. I was firstly shocked and confused and then relieved that my parents took it so calmly. It was probably due to the fact that my eldest sister had been born to Mum illegitimately in the 1930s when the stigma was even greater. She understood.

I never saw the child – I heard that he was christened Stephen. Some years later, after the girl had married, I received adoption papers to sign. Having never had children I sometimes wonder how his life turned out and if he ever knew who his biological father was.

This catastrophe precipitated my leaving school immediately after the exam week. In that era an under-age pregnancy was taken very seriously. I was subsequently given a *'caution by a uniformed police inspector'* at Margate Police Station. Luckily for me we were both under sixteen at the time of conception so no further action was taken. Had I been over sixteen it would have been a chargeable offence.

These events quickly threw me into the world of

Unparallel Careers!

work and I started at a local electrical transformer factory, firstly as a 'coil winder' and then as a trainee cost and works accountant – an education that would serve me well in future years, though at the time it was always secondary to my musical aspirations.

The group continued at the Orchid Room throughout the summer of 1962 but in August the drummer, Duke, announced that he wanted time off to go on holiday and this would mean cancelling gigs. After a serious row it was decided that if he took time off he was out of the group and would be replaced. Glyn Jenkins supported his friend *"That's it, if he goes then I go."* So Oliver Twist and his chum had resigned, thus ending the first line-up. We were now just *'The Lower Third'*.

The group had to be quickly re-formed and a very young highly talented local drummer, 14 year old Paul Pinder, was drafted in together with Terry Bolton, an excellent rock & roll pianist who had recently married Denis Taylor's sister. He had occasionally 'sat in' and sung a few songs with the group through the summer and was a perfect fit with his keyboard and vocal skills. We had lost the group's singer so it was decided that vocals would have to be shared. I was not considered as a singer because, up to this time, I had not sung at any gig or rehearsal so my vocal ability was unknown. One evening at a band practice I decided to suggest we try one of my Buddy Holly favourites, *'Peggy Sue'*, and, to the surprise of the others, I strummed the chords and sang it perfectly. I was soon singing leads with the group and my career as a singer had begun.

Terry Bolton played an electric piano and it was

from him that I eventually learnt enough to be able to play a small organ as well as guitar with the group. Terry was also a budding songwriter which inspired me to try my hand and we featured a few of our own numbers in the band's repertoire. There was no way to predict in those exciting days of the 1960s that Terry and I would cooperate on so many musical projects over the next 50 years.

About this time, at the other end of Kent, another aspiring singer and musician called David Jones was passing his time at Bromley Technical High School and in 1962 he joined his first group, The Konrads. We knew of them by reputation as both groups played the same West Kent halls from time to time.

During 1963 we continued to prosper. We invested in new amplifiers and microphones as well as buying recording studio time with local sound engineer Les Wake who worked mainly with Wout Steenhuis the Dutch multi-track guitarist. Wout had played with the famous jazz group of the 50s called The Dutch Swing College before settling in England and had regular appearances on radio and TV. He lived and recorded in what, to me, seemed an exotic 1960s modernist house in Broadstairs. It was a glass fronted building with a split level lounge and a studio built to one side. We recorded there several times by setting up the whole group in the lounge while Les engineered from the studio. We were amazed that Wout let a bunch of scruffy rockers loose in his lovely home - a place that we could only dream of owning. He was always very supportive of the group

Unparallel Careers!

and I took inspiration from him years later when it came to recording my own stage backing tracks.

In the summer months, when Graham's hotel dining room wasn't available, we practised every week in the front room of my house while my Mum and Dad were banished to the back room or bedroom. Looking back it's quite incredible that they, and the neighbours, put up with a rock 'n' roll group playing for several hours each week and then turning out loudly into the street around midnight. There would often be girlfriends and other hangers on at our band practices and it's hard to imagine now how we all crammed into the modest front room at 14 Giles Gardens and managed to achieve anything remotely musical.

We maintained our dates at The Orchid Room and at other local venues which included Margate's famous Dreamland Ballroom. In the 60s Dreamland regularly welcomed the top hit groups of the day - I can recall the thrill of seeing the late Buddy Holly's band, The Crickets, playing all his old hit songs in tribute to the great man. On one occasion we had won through to the final of a county wide rock group contest that was being staged at Dreamland. Two days before the final, I was involved in a motorbike accident on the way to my weekly college day at Canterbury.

My colleague from work, Colin Chapman, drove us to Canterbury each week on his bike and, before the fateful day, we had never worn crash helmets. In those days it was not compulsory. That morning he arrived to pick me up wearing a helmet because his father had nagged him. We returned to his home to collect a helmet for me and, wearing these for the first time, we set off again. Three minutes into the journey, on a section of dual carriageway at Westbrook, a van crossed our path and we hit it at full speed. We were thrown into the air and I remember nothing until I was lying dazed in the road, miraculously with nothing broken. We were picked up by ambulance and I could see that Colin was still unconscious. While being attended to in the emergency department of Margate General Hospital I was informed that he had died of his injuries. Some weeks later the van driver was convicted of 'driving without due care and attention'.

I was bruised so badly that the next day I was unable to walk without help and my face had been scraped raw by the road surface. But I was determined that the group would still be able to appear in the contest final and endured a painful band practice that night and prepared for the ordeal. In the event we came second to a group from Ramsgate called Flint Yates and the Vampires. Their bass player, Graham Rivens, would eventually become part of the final line up of *'The Lower Third'*. Press reports from that night state that *"The injured member was stoically playing his part."*

Towards the end of the summer Graham Smith decided to leave the group and go on to further education. Graham had continued at Chatham House Grammar School and, as far as I know, he then abandoned music for a successful career in electronics. Shortly afterwards drummer Paul Pinder also left. Records that I have uncovered show that this second incarnation of the group earned, from July to September 1963, £610.9.6 (610 pounds 9 shillings and 6 pence) which equates roughly to £12,000 in 2019. Each member took around £7.00 per week (£140.00 in 2019) and the rest paid for equipment loans, roadie costs and stage clothes. We thought we were coining it in!

The search for new members swiftly brought in drummer Les Mighall and bass player Graham Rivens who had been a casualty of the break up of The Vampires, our nemesis in the rock group contest. I took on more and more of the vocals and began to play less guitar in favour of fronting the group. This line-up quickly changed our musical direction and thereafter we were heavily into Rhythm & Blues, almost completely abandoning the pop music of the era and the original songs written by me and Terry Bolton. I bought a small Hohner organ and almost exclusively played and sang the twelve bar blues songs of Muddy Waters, Bo Diddly, B B King, Chuck Berry and other American blues giants. While this wasn't my taste in music the group began to reach a dedicated fan base and the gigs became more varied and away from the local East Kent area. We regularly featured on the Isle of Sheppey, particularly at a very established music venue in its time - the Sea View Hotel at Sheerness. Other well established and regular gigs were the Grand Hotel in Littlestone and the Grand Ballroom in Broadstairs which became a weekly date well into 1964. We still appeared in other local venues and occasionally as a last minute stand in at Dreamland Ballroom when a group with a top ten hit failed to make the date.

We often played the Riviera Club on Margate Sea Front and a photo of us rehearsing there is featured in one of the many published biographies of David Bowie. On one memorable night the club was raided by the

The Lower Third

police who were checking that all the drinkers had consumed a meal. It was the law then that to continue drinking after normal licensing hours drinks had to be accompanied by food. It killed our gig when all the working lights suddenly came on and police arrived in numbers from the foyer and the trade entrance at the back. The owner, a Greek Cypriot who ran restaurants in the town, was charged and narrowly missed having the club's license withdrawn. On another memorable night at The Riviera the world had just learnt that President Kennedy had been assassinated in Dallas, which rather dampened the enthusiasm of the Friday night crowd – it was November 23rd 1963.

In the early days we hired a van and driver/roadie who was a workmate of mine from the factory. He owned a Bedford Dormabile and we had a few hairy late night/early morning moments when he nodded off and sent the van careering across the road. Terrified shouts from the suddenly awakened passengers ensured the vehicle returned to its right side of the carriageway, thankfully without serious incident. Late one night in the severe winter of 1963 our way was blocked by heavy snowdrifts while trying to get to Broadstairs for a drop off after a gig. Our roadie, in his infinite wisdom, decided that the adjacent field looked passable as the snow had drifted onto the road. We set off across the field only to find a high bank on the other side. Wheels then spun and we dug into the ground, completely stuck. It was now two o'clock in the morning but somehow a couple of the lads managed, in the pitch dark, to find and knock up a farmer living nearby and he turned out in his tractor to drag us back across the field.

It was time to invest in our own transport and we bought an Atlas van which soon became covered in lipstick messages from fans. I had passed my driving test at the second attempt and bought, for five pounds, a monster of an old Humber Supersnipe of 1952 vintage complete with running boards and doors that opened from the front. But I was, for some reason, also left to care for the Atlas van. Both monsters parked in our little cul-de-sac.

London Blues - 1960s

This was the time to launch ourselves as a credible R&B band on the London scene and we did several trial gigs by knocking on the doors of West End music night clubs such as The Whisky Agogo, The Flamingo Club, The Scene and The 100 Club. We encountered the well known bands and personalities of the early sixties like Georgie Fame and the Blue Flames, Long John Baldrie, John Mayall's Bluesbreakers, Zoot Money, The Yardbirds and others who, like us, were trying to get established. Eventually we were offered a regular spot at the infamous La Discotheque Club in Wardour Street which was owned by the scandalous rent racketeer Peter Rachman, who gave his name to the misdeeds of unscrupulous landlords – *'Rachmanism'*. La Discotheque Club was so called because it was the first venue to play almost entirely recorded music and it employed the very first live disc jockeys. It was situated at the lower end of Wardour Street near to Leicester Square and was recognised only by a small door which opened to reveal a narrow staircase leading up to the club on the first floor of the building. The whole club was painted black – walls, ceiling and floor. There was no furniture save for some benches fixed to the walls and, at one end, several mattresses on the floor – also black. There was a bar which officially served only soft drinks and sandwiches – during a break one night I watched a cockroach crawl out of a cheese sandwich which was then bought and consumed by a saucer eyed kid. There was a disc jockey booth and a small stage where we played our sets from around midnight to 5am. We quickly learnt that the lack of alcohol in the club did not inhibit the dancers either on or off the dance floor and in the early hours, spiked by purple hearts/dexys (amphetamine), some of the mainly young teenage crowd made full use of the mattresses. I could not describe the atmosphere in the club better than these reminiscences I discovered online left by kids who went there at that time.

"***I made my way up the stairs*** *to La Discotheque and gave the nod to the bouncer whilst dropping some cash into his hand. We had sussed out some time ago that we could gain entrance for half price and made full use of the facility. The obligatory stamp went on the back of my hand and I was in. The door opened releasing a hot fug of fetid air mixed with cigarette smoke. The place was heaving as sweating bodies jostled for space to dance. Junior Walker's 'Shake & Fingerpop' was pumping out and I could feel my heart jump into overdrive. Locating the rest of the firm was easy. 'Haggis' and 'Big Roy' were giving it some on the floor. Roy was in a world of his own, dancing by himself, if that were possible in view of the close proximity of the bodies all around him. Terry*

was busy doing some business somewhere and Mac was sitting in a corner. He was completely stoned, staring at his clenched fists on his lap and chewing like crazy. I couldn't get any sense out of him. By now the combination of the music and the 'dexys' were really kicking in so I fought my way out to the others on the floor and let the music wash over me. Terry reappeared after a while. He had taken a few too many and his mouth had gone into overdrive. More 'dexys' were consumed. Every now and again a few more envelopes were distributed which meant occasional trips to the toilets. Still the music pumped out. Gradually the night wore on."
(Anonymous clubber)

The atmosphere in the club was intense and we were aware of the dealers plying their trade, especially in the toilets which were adjacent to our stage. The toilet facilities became so dreadful that even at 3am I would exit the club and walk to the public toilets in Leicester Square rather than run the gauntlet of dealers and overdosed individuals in the club toilets. The music we played at the time was pretty repetitive being mainly based on the good old twelve bar blues and on more than one occasion I actually nodded off while playing, quickly coming too when the discord sounded! We could not easily leave the club until it closed at around 6am and on several occasions the main entrance would be closed because the police were outside rounding up the under age kids. They took them to a police station and then called in their parents to collect them. On these mornings the club would let people out of the back trade exit until the police departed Wardour Street.

The Lower Third

*"**First went there in 1962ish**.... an ill lit hanger upstairs full of old mattresses on the floor. To the left was the small dance floor packed with Mod couples dancing the Twist. I was an innocent but I loved the ambience, the music and the dancing but was too wary so I passed on the purple hearts. Three or four dawns a week I walked the 5 miles back to Shepherd's Bush for a swift nap before catching the Tube to Photographic College."* (Anonymous clubber)

We would often travel into London for this Saturday all-nighter after an earlier gig somewhere in Kent. On one occasion we appeared on the stage at St Mary's Bay Holiday Centre as part of 'Big Bay Beat Festival' along with The Swinging Blue Jeans and Wayne Fontana and the Mindbenders, before jumping in the van and heading for the West End. On a couple of weekends we had to grab some sleep in the club after closing and we soon learnt that it was infested with cockroaches and also had resident rats, which were only in evidence when the working lights came on for the morning clear up.

We had been contacted by a minor record producer and asked to play on two of his projects so, after our uncomfortable slumbers, we drove down to RG Jones Studios in Morden, Surrey for the Sunday sessions. The first was with a singer from Kent called Dave Lee whose own band, The Rebounds, for some reason I do not recall, had declined to get involved. We recorded two tracks, an original song *'Time Passes Slow'* and *'High School Confidential'*. The next session was with the well known Carry On film actress Liz Fraser who recorded a song called *'Keep All Your Kisses On Ice'*. To my knowledge none of these master recordings were ever released.

I was still working, still doing the day job, but often in a less than efficient manner owing to the constant late nights and travel. I often drove to work in our Atlas van adorned with its lipstick messages and in this state it was not received well in the office car park. I somehow managed to get away with it and held onto the job in spite of the fact that I occasionally nodded off at the desk, usually when the hot sun was streaming through the accounts office windows.

In the autumn of 1964, while filling in time after setting up for another Sea View Hotel gig at Sheerness, Terry Bolton and I took a stroll along the windy promenade. We talked about our frustrations with the band, about songwriting, about the boredom that was setting in during gigs, especially in The West End at La Discotheque, and asked ourselves *"Do we want to carry on thumping out only twelve bar blues for the foreseeable future?"* We agreed that the answer was no.

This was to be the beginning of the end of my involvement with *'The Lower Third'*, the group that I had helped to form and in which I had spent three fantastic and exciting years. Three years that, as a teenager, seemed like a lifetime. The news that two of the group would like to quit did not go down well with the others but we continued to fulfil the remaining bookings into 1965 and then parted company with Denis, Graham and Les who had decided to press on with the R&B music. In April they set up auditions in London in order to find a new

The Lower Third

singer. Their efforts were rewarded when a singer and sax player called David Jones arrived to audition and they offered him the job.

From the book Ziggyology

By the summer of 1965 the Two I's in Soho was no longer the favourite hang-out of London's young and desperate musicians. The smartest mod heads and hem lines had shifted camp to an Italian cafe on Denmark Street, the small nucleus of pop publishers, agents and management offices known as 'Tin Pan Alley'. La Gioconda was the 'in' place where a band could form at any moment at any table over the steam of a few espressos. Where a beat group from Margate called 'The Lower Third' could come looking for a singer and find one called David Jones.
Copyright © Simon Goddard 2013. Publisher Ebury Press, London

They gigged first as *'Davie Jones and The Lower Third'* but by the end of the year David Jones had changed his name to David Bowie and the record of his time with *'The Lower Third'* is well documented in numerous books about his life. At the time I knew only that they had found a new singer and had decided to leave their day jobs and turn fully professional. My decision to leave the group, in those heady days of the early 60s, changed the lives of the boys I had spent so many good times with and, more importantly, it changed the life of the young David Jones. It propelled him on a path to his first minor record success and to the all important change from Jones to Bowie. What would have happened to my future, and that of David Jones, if I had stayed with *'The Lower Third'*? Who knows? Of

Unparallel Careers!

Course, at the time, I had no idea that the arrival of the newly named David Bowie would eventually have an indirect impact on my life.

Oliver Twist and the Lower Third - Original line-up at the Orchid Room
L/R Graham Smith, Robin Wyatt, Denis Taylor, Duke, Glyn Jenkins

L/R Robin Wyatt, Terry Bolton, Denis Taylor, Graham Rivens, Les Mighall

Recording at the Riviera Club 1965

The grubby entrance to La Discotheque Club

L/R Terry, Les, Graham, Robin, Denis

*Fronting the band
on stage at
Big Bay Beat
1964*

L/R Denis, Robin, Les, Graham, Terry

*Graham and Denis
with David 1966*

Chapter 2
The Wilderness Years

Lost in the confusion of life
Trying to find a way to be found
To turn it all around

So there I was, no longer into R&B and the sweaty smoke filled London club scene, but without a properly thought through new direction in music or in life. I first tried to improve my guitar skills and learnt to play finger style guitar to accompany myself singing folk songs and ballads, a complete contrast to the previous years of pounding rhythms and deafening sound equipment.

I contacted Les Wake, Wout Steenhuis's recording engineer, as I knew he supported some local charities, and he invited me to perform a short set of songs at a nearby Margate convalescent home – a truly captive audience. I shortened my name to Robb Wyatt and thus it would stay for at least the next decade. Though I sang rather nervously to my own limited guitar accompaniment I was invited back several times during that first winter and gradually gained confidence as a solo performer. Other cabaret type appearances followed at hotels and clubs in the area which was still a popular summer holiday destination.

After a short audition in the spring of 1965 I was engaged for some guest appearances with Les Shannon and his Music Makers in The Cliff Cafe at The Cliftonville Lido which, in the 60s, was an exciting place to spend the summer nights amongst its various shows and attractions. There was The Lido Theatre with its company of professional variety artistes and dancers, The Hawaiian Bar, The Dance Cavern (later called Hades) where I had played with *'The Lower Third'*, and The Golden Garter Saloon with its wild west show. Although I didn't know it in the summer of '65 that western saloon was to be my springboard into professional entertainment. I just soaked up the show business atmosphere and knew then, with absolute certainty, that it was what I wanted to do with my life. It is a sad reflection on the changing times that The Lido is no more than a ruin now (2019). Walking among the derelict buildings you can almost hear the ghostly sounds of its 60s heyday in the breaking of the waves over the dilapidated old swimming pool and promenade.

In the midst of that glorious summer I also signed my first publishing contract for five songs I had written and recorded earlier – I was elated that a London music publisher showed interest in my songs.

On January 14th 1966 my old band mates released their first record as *'David Bowie and the Lower Third'*. *'Can't Help Thinking About Me'* did not chart high but was played widely and was, at some radio stations, the 'record of the week'. After he heard the record my father didn't speak to me for several weeks because he was so upset with me for leaving the group. My pleading that *"Had I stayed then David Bowie would not have joined and the record would not have existed"* did not ease the tension. A stubborn man my Dad.

> *Question-time that says I brought dishonour*
> *My head's bowed in shame*
> *It seems that I've blackened the family name*
> *Mother says that she can't stand the neighbours' talking*
> *I've gotta pack my bags, leave this home, start walking*
> *Yeah I'm guilty, I wish that I was sorry this time*
> *I wish that I could pay for my crime*
> *I can't help thinking about me*
> *I can't help thinking about me*
> **David Bowie (Can't Help Thinking About Me)**

From the book 'The Age Of Bowie'

The single does not sell well and only makes an unofficial chart that can be influenced with some money in the Melody Maker music paper. He's on his own at the end of the month, walking away from 'The Lower Third' after one last show at The Marquee and then a miserable finale and an abortive cancelled show in his home town of Bromley where the group crumble without even a handshake let alone a hug. He had to break up the band. David and Ralph (Horton) drive off in the Jaguar.

'The Lower Third' have nothing left but their ambulance and a future of not making it into a history that David Bowie had taken control of.

Text copyright © Paul Morley 2016, reproduced by kind permission of Simon & Schuster UK Ltd

Unparallel Careers!

I had remained in touch with Terry Bolton and we worked together on recording demos of our own songs. Les Wake had taken over a section of a small industrial unit in Birchington to set up a studio called Stressa Recordings and I can recall his sound insulation was made from dozens of cardboard egg trays glued to the walls – it seemed to work! We also started writing a musical based on one of my favourite films *The Million Pound Note* which starred Gregory Peck. I found out that it was a story by Mark Twain and set about trying to find a copy of the book. I got nowhere at the library and local bookshops so took the train to London's Charing Cross Road and inquired in the various antique book shops *"Have you a copy of The Million Pound Note by Mark Twain?"* After several failures I finally found an old bookseller who had heard of the story and who lifted a trapdoor and disappeared down steps to the shop cellar from where he emerged, some minutes later, blowing dust off an old hard back book. It was a book of short stories by Mark Twain, one of which was 'The One Million Pound Banknote'. It was a first English edition from 1893 with a handwritten inscription inside the front cover by someone called J.B.Campbell. He had written *"Charing Cross for Paris June 8th 1893"*. I still have the book but we never finished the musical – perhaps one day! It did spur us on to write more and, whilst I only wrote songs occasionally, Terry became a prolific songwriter under his pen name of Gid Taylor and is still turning them out today.

We discussed trying a few songs together as an act, mainly because we both enjoyed singing close harmonies. I can't recall now whose idea it was but I set about looking for a girl singer to join us and I placed an advert in the local paper. After a number of auditions we came upon an excellent singer whose family managed a small Cliftonville hotel. Her name was Gillian Mason. We rehearsed throughout the spring of 1966 and secured a regular guest appearance for the summer season once again at The Lido's Cliff Cafe with Les Shannon's Music Makers. On the day of the first appearance we did not have a name for the act so before the show we wandered along the promenade to throw a few ideas about. Ten minutes before we were due on stage we still hadn't come up with an answer. At the last minute we decided that an earlier suggestion from Terry, that we had quickly dismissed, would have to be it. That night we became *'The Three Keys'*.

Terry Bolton *(2018)*
"The three of us stood overlooking the sea, and tried to come up with a name for the group, we were on stage in ten minutes! To my horror, I think it was me who suggested The Three Keys!"

The delight I felt in having found what I thought was a new and exciting direction was only surpassed in that July by the euphoria that swept the nation when England beat West Germany in the final of the Football World Cup. It was without doubt the most amazing moment when, watching the match on our black and white television, the commentator said *"They think it's all over – well it is now"* as Geoff Hurst banged in the last goal in the final seconds.

Unparallel Careers!

While World Cup fever gripped the nation we continued to work on the repertoire. We even recorded a couple of songs to promote the act. But after the 1966 Christmas and New Year season, appearing in a variety of mainly local hotels and theatres, the enthusiasm waned and Gillian, in particular, was keen to progress as a solo singer. I felt there was more to be achieved but the trio gradually and amicably fell apart. Gillian went on, a few years later, to head the Gilly Mason Band. In the 70s they toured widely in Europe and recorded several albums. But for me, in the winter of 1966/67, there was the no small matter of finding yet another new direction.

The Cowboys
Shoot straight and aim high!

The sign came in a tip off that Danny Arnold was looking for a local singer for the 1967 summer season at The Golden Garter Saloon – The Lido again. This was *'Sheriff Danny Arnold and his Wild West Saloon Show'* which had been running successfully for several years at the Golden Garter venue. I had seen the show a few times and rather fancied the idea of being a gun toting singing cowboy.

I was feeling rather good about myself that spring. I'd given up smoking and started a diet for a bet taken at my twenty-first birthday party. I'd been a tubby bloke since grammar school days and was always self-conscious about undressing or changing around others. I've never smoked a cigarette since and I lost three stones (42 pounds) in weight by the summer. So, with this renewed confidence, I travelled to London to audition for Danny Arnold.

The Wilderness Years

He was a Canadian who lived with his wife Lillian and son Danny Junior in a grand apartment in Great Russell Street, opposite the British Museum. I sang a couple of songs and it seemed like I'd cracked it. The rest of the audition consisted of Danny regaling me with tales of seasons past and of how he came to be an official Deputy Sheriff of Bexar County, San Antonio, Texas. He was a great raconteur as well as a tall and impressive figure in his stage outfit, smoking a large cigar and wearing his hand crafted six-gun.

The stories of seasons past and winter tours expanded immensely when the cast got together for rehearsals. Three of the team had worked with Danny for years and this was to prove difficult for me because the banter continued through all the so called rehearsals when I was desperately needing to work on the script – a script that wasn't written down anywhere. It just existed in Danny Arnold's head. *"When I say 'lets have a spin of the wheel' you say 'yep sheriff' and when I'm at the back of the saloon you shout 'hey, sheriff I think we got injun troubles – I can see a smoke signal', you got that Robb?"* Well I mostly hadn't got it. Moreover the group songs were all traditional cowboy ditties which the rest of the cast seemed to know by instinct while I had to scribble down the lyrics as we went along. In the month or so before rehearsals I had taken some dancing lessons at a well known dance academy in Canterbury. I fancied myself doing a kind of 'Seven Brides for Seven Brothers' routine and I did incorporate this, rather unsuccessfully, in my solo spot in the show. It was soon dropped!

Unparallel Careers!

***Coincidentally**, at about the same time, the ever ambitious David Bowie had also enrolled in a dance class. It was with the avant garde choreographer Lindsay Kemp and he appeared in Kemp's theatre production 'Pierrot In Turquoise'. I, of course, knew nothing of this at the time although I did know that 'The Lower Third' had finally broken up. David was, like me, searching for new directions and was trying dance and mime.*

Having decided I was not ready for dancing I fell back on singing old favourites like *'High Noon'*, *'Rawhide'* and other Country & Western hits which suited the theme. The essence of the show was simple - a night out in a wild west saloon. Members of the audience were thrown in jail, there was a trial with a predictable guilty verdict, then a hanging tree was paraded until the saloon was raided by bandits who came to rescue the poor convicted audience member. We all had revolvers firing blanks and a very loud gunfight ensued with the sheriff naturally winning the day. Add to this a cancan by the saloon girls and lots of rousing cowboy songs and you had the ingredients for a riotous evening. I would take advantage of this several times in future years by collecting all the good ideas and combining them into a proper show script long after Danny Arnold had hung up his spurs.

The show was staged every day of the week from mid June until the second week of September. I was paid the princely sum of £16.00 per week, which was a big addition to my salary at the day job, which I think was about £18.00. By the time I started on this first professional season I had begun to appreciate what the loss of weight and a fit and trim body meant for my personal well being and self respect. I must admit that I strutted arrogantly about in my cowboy gear inviting the world to love me. My Dad's favourite put down if I got above myself was *"You're too full of piss and importance!"* and he was right in that summer of 1967.

But I did learn a lot, from others, about how to present myself on stage and, more importantly, how to be respected off stage. Apart from Danny there were two other excellent influences in the show. Jimmy Grant was a very experienced singer who had kind of retired to Margate but kept his hand in doing Danny's show – I watched him perform and took on board some of his stage craft. But I didn't take his advice about my choice of girlfriends. We shared a dressing room and one night, giving me the benefit of his experience, Jimmy told me never to get involved with dancers. *"They are always bad news,"* he said, *"can't be trusted, they're all slags."* It seemed to me hardly fair on the two dancers in the show and those in the neighbouring Lido Theatre, one of whom I sometimes dated. I guessed he'd been painfully dumped by a dancer at some time in his life. I sadly never met Jimmy again after that season but I remembered this particular advice and ignored it on many occasions.

The Pianist, or Piano Player to use the saloon jargon, was Jack Freedman, who I admired greatly for his musicianship and for his sense of humour. He often entertained us after the show playing well known classical pieces while we relaxed with a beer or two. On several occasions after the season I visited Jack at his London flat which was minimalist but with excellent quality and taste. I first heard a superb Bang & Olufsen hi-fi system there as we listened to some striking orchestral pieces. He helped me with my vocal performances and had infinite patience while I practised new songs. When I last heard of Jack he was playing cocktail music and giving classical recitals on cruise ships.

I met and socialised with other entertainers who were working on the Lido complex and we often relaxed after the shows at The Caprice Nightclub, which was nearby, staying until it closed at 2am. They were all professional entertainers so while they slept on in the morning I was up and off to the accounts office. I tried to keep pace so as not to give away that I was still working a day job. How I envied them the freedom and wished I had the courage to go for it full time. While dating an achingly pretty dancer from the Lido Theatre I made endless excuses for not being available during the daytime for trips to the beach or drinks at lunchtime. I was too embarrassed to admit to Gwen Bleasby that I was not a 'professional'.

On Sunday mornings, to publicise the show, we took part in a 'hold up' on the terrace above The Golden Garter Saloon. Sheriff Danny Arnold would try to arrest the resident organist, Tony Savage, for not playing his favourite music. We would appear masked on the surrounding roofs and a gun fight would take place. This was a very successful publicity stunt which would produce an instant queue at The Golden Garter Saloon box office. We also judged the weekly Miss Golden Garter contest around the Lido pool where I got to eye up the talent in the hope that one of them might fancy a cowboy. I don't recall this as a great success.

The Wilderness Years

Towards the end of the season I was disappointed to learn that, after many years at The Lido, Danny was not going to renew his contract. For a while it seemed as though my debut in a professional show was also going to be my swan song. Then I was asked by the Lido general manager if I would like to return in 1968 when they planned to rebuild the show without Danny but with some new blood. I jumped at the chance.

My first attempts at the business side of entertainment started during this period when I put together shows for hotels and theatres, mainly in Margate, Ramsgate and Broadstairs. I set up my own agency, the Esquire Entertainment Agency, named after The Esquire Club, a nightclub in Northdown Road, Cliftonville. I actually managed the club for a few weeks and tried to build up the membership among entertainers and musicians.

In the mid sixties there were still plenty of theatres and concert halls in the East Kent area serving the thriving holiday trade and I took advantage of this. Presenting and performing in many of the shows myself I gained confidence in my stage presence and vocal ability. I often used a local dance team, The Emerald Four, as well as various novelty acts, one of whom was Norman Barrett who, remarkably, had a team of performing budgies. Norman later became the celebrated ring master for the Blackpool Tower Circus with many TV appearances. He was the foil to the famous circus clown Charlie Cairoli.

A decade later the East Kent resorts were in serious decline and the venues gradually began to close or morph into bingo halls but for that moment in time they served me well.

Even my guitar playing improved and at Easter 1968 I played guitar for a highly talented young soprano at a Canterbury Cathedral gala service. The singer was Linda Bumpstead (later Linda Jane) who had recently won a TV talent contest – she sang *'Were You There When They Crucified Our Lord'*. It was a moving experience in the vast cathedral packed with worshippers for what, I believe, was a scout and guide weekend event.

***I was still searching** for a new direction and I was trying my hand at producing shows in which I could appear as a talented artist! David Robert Jones aka Bowie was also experimenting with new ideas and he recorded a rather strange song called 'The Laughing Gnome'. We were both wading through mud and looking for a way out so that we could start running. He would soon run faster and further than me!*

Shortly after the cathedral experience my boss and mentor at the accounts office succumbed to a heart attack while carrying out the sad duty of telling several older workers that they would be made redundant. I did not like his replacement, and he didn't take to me, so one day, on the spur of the moment, I decided to quit. Before I could properly think it through or change my mind I marched into his office and resigned.

"Free at last, Lord God Almighty, free at last!"
(Martin Luther King)

The Wilderness Years

Real Showbiz

Overnight I became a fully professional entertainer and I was elated by the thought of arriving for rehearsals at The Lido with this new status. I don't recall feeling any apprehension about the future – I was sure I could make it work.

The show at the Lido started again in June with a new cast. Actor and singer Bob Blaine played the part of the Sheriff – he had appeared with Danny Arnold in other shows and knew the way the show was run – still no script but a straight copy of everything we could remember from Danny's time. The tall and glamorous Valerie Leon played the saloon hostess. She later became famous for her appearances in the High Karate adverts on TV and for roles in 'Carry On' films and in the James Bond classic 'The Spy Who Loved Me'. During that summer she acquired many fans among the older male members of the audience when they were asked to remove the golden garter from her spectacularly long leg. I was in cloud nine from the start of the season with my new freedom and took full advantage of it. I spent a lot of time at The Lido working on new songs and meeting up with other entertainers for various events and adventures. It all seemed so unreal after the years of nine to five working.

One evening in mid season I arrived at the saloon to find everybody in a state of panic. Bob Blaine, who commuted each day from London, had called to say he was stuck in the city for some reason and wouldn't make it for the start of the show. The venue was sold out that night and the general manager was proposing to cancel.

Unparallel Careers!

I stepped in and said I could link the show until Bob arrived and, with some scepticism, he agreed to let me give it a go. I bluffed my way through by making up a reason why the sheriff was delayed – chasing outlaws or something similar – and we carried on with the musical numbers until he eventually appeared and finished the show.

This impromptu stand-in set the seal on the year to follow. I heard a rumour that Bob Blaine was not interested in playing another season and that The Golden Garter Saloon was likely to stage a straight Country and Western music show. It would be led by a well known and excellent yodelling country singer called Ronnie Winters who had sometimes guested in the saloon. I decided to act quickly by writing a full script for the show, cobbled together from all the unscripted 'bits of business' that I had been involved in over the two seasons. I then presented the idea of actors being cast in the main roles working from a script instead of 'singing cowboys' making it up as they went along. The general manager set up a meeting with the chairman of Margate Estates who owned both The Lido complex and Dreamland with its famous fairground, art deco cinema and ballroom. Eric Iles was a formidable old character who struck fear into the Lido staff, especially if he arrived unannounced. He drove a big Bentley Continental which seemed to have a new dent each time I saw it. For a twenty-two year old upstart I managed to get along with him well and he seemed impressed with my proposals. I was able to square up to him in the contract talks and it was soon agreed that I would produce and appear in the 1969 show. I had taken my first steps into professional writing and producing. I now had six months to put a cast and a show together for the next season.

Go North Young Man

Into the unknown like a lamb to the slaughter
I outa know more about the unknown

That winter, without a day job, I needed some professional dates to keep the money coming in. Although I was still living with my parents I had to pay my way and I needed cash to keep going while I set up the new Golden Garter Saloon show. I decided to send my CV and publicity photos to agents who booked cabaret and social clubs in the North of England even though I had no real idea what to expect in the wild upcountry. I had never before had any reason to venture north of London.

I had put together an act of about an hour with songs linked by jokes which I had stolen from well known comedians I'd seen at The Lido Theatre or The Margate Winter Gardens. A local musician called Dave Corsby arranged my music for the backing bands and I headed north in my latest car, a little red and white Ford Anglia.

A Manchester agent had booked me, without seeing my act, into two cabaret clubs, starting on Sunday the 29th September - The Rosegrove Club in Burnley and The New Starlight Club in Blackburn. As in most other northern industrial towns, working men's clubs with live entertainment and cheap beer had sprung up during the middle of the twentieth century to cater to the factory hands, miners and other workers. Gradually, as the workers became better paid, some classier clubs began to open – the cabaret clubs of the sixties and seventies where well known artistes often topped the bill.

As I drove past Manchester for the first time that Sunday afternoon I suddenly felt very alone and a long way from home in what seemed to me to be an alien country. I booked into a theatrical guest house ('digs') for the very first time and then went to the Burnley club for a rehearsal with the band. It did not go well. According to the musicians my music was difficult to read. The pianist joked that it appeared as if a spider had walked over it with muddy boots! I later found out why. Dave Corsby was a great jazz musician but obviously not used to writing clearly and simply for the typical northern club trio. In later years I learnt to write all the band parts myself. The gig was known as a double – one performance at The Rosegrove Club at 9pm then rush off to the other club for 11pm. I went on stage in Burnley where my badly executed jokes and mediocre nervous singing meant that I never got to the second club. After that first appearance the club manager 'paid me off' - I was sacked!

I was miserable and embarrassed and got out of the club as soon as I could. I was a southerner trying to entertain in alien northern night clubs and I would learn in time that being a southerner, in those clubs in that era, was a cross I'd have to bear. However, I couldn't get away from the fact that I was pretty bad that night and realised that I was up against some formidable talent - acts that had learnt their craft in these clubs and knew

The Wilderness Years

how to handle the sometimes indifferent audiences.

I stayed on for a few days in the digs while phoning around desperately for any new opportunities. I did not want to return home to Margate and have to admit that I had failed. I secured an audition through a Blackpool based agent and I set off for the playground of the north. Blackpool, on the north western coast of England, was the holiday destination of choice for many thousands of northerners and was distinguished, not only by its enormous amusement park and its numerous penny arcades, but also by its many theatres playing host to the biggest stars of the era. Its great tower, reminiscent of the Eiffel Tower in Paris, was a stunning sight as I took my first cruise along the Golden Mile – the magnificent seafront road with its ancient trams dating from the pre-war years.

I stayed overnight in a guest house and went along the next morning to The Dolphin Bar in Thornton Cleveleys, just north of Blackpool, for a 10 o'clock audition. It was a Sunday and this was a well known cabaret bar with a popular Sunday lunchtime show. I sang a couple of songs and the manager asked me to do the show and to stay for the rest of the week because the singer who was due to start that Sunday had called in sick. The resident organist and the compere/drummer ignored my scribbled music and busked my songs superbly. They were excellent and greatly enhanced the presentation of all the acts for their mainly young and enthusiastic audience. I returned happily to The Dolphin several times. The compere was Brian Rossi who had previously found fame in Ireland with The Manhattan Showband and now held the Dolphin audiences in the palm of his hand. He was a great singer and mimic but he never attempted to upstage the acts that he presented. Needless to say this was a turning point for me in coping with 'The North'. I gained confidence, cleaned up my band parts, changed the songs, and dropped the bad jokes.

From the book Ziggyology
David Bowie was 21 years old. Now a singer-songwriter without a label, without a band. In bloody minded defiance he drew up a radical new master plan making full use of Kemp's training. He would re-launch himself as a mime artist in a one man show.
Copyright © Simon Goddard 2013. Publisher Ebury Press, London

I too was in the process of relaunching myself but it was not an enjoyable experience in winter, travelling alone and staying in less than comfortable digs. During one snow covered January week I read the whole of Dr Zhivago over two days in the bedroom of the guest house wearing an overcoat and gloves because the heating was switched off during the day. On another icy day I shivered my way to Belfast by ferry and train where I played a week in The Abercorn Restaurant. Some years later The Abercorn was attacked by paramilitaries in one of the more infamous acts of terrorism. In March 1972 it was devastated by a bomb which took the lives of two young girls and injured over 130 others.

Early in the new year of 1969, while booking artistes and revising the script for my new Lido show, I got a call from a Birmingham agent called Billy Forrest

The Wilderness Years

for whom I had auditioned some months previously. Billy was a principal agent for hotels and cabaret venues in the Channel Islands and the Isle of Man and was notorious for being a sharp negotiator, sometimes outside what might have been seen as strictly ethical, while not illegal. He was short and stocky and spoke with a strong brummie (Birmingham) accent which was often lampooned by artistes who worked for him. He wanted me to audition in London for a Jersey hotel director who was looking for a singer-guitarist. It was for the forthcoming season and, although I was already committed to The Golden Garter Saloon show, I thought it might be a useful contact for the future. I had visited Jersey with an ex-girlfriend, Joan Crane, whose family were from the island. I loved the atmosphere and the variety of entertainment. It had seemed rather exotic to me as it was situated just off the coast of France and sported French names for the towns, villages and roads. And yet it was British!

On the day of the audition I set off from Margate feeling rather depressed and unenthusiastic about auditioning for something I couldn't do and when I stopped on the way for petrol I was severely tempted to turn back. After telling myself that it would be poor form to just not turn up I carried on into the city. There were lots of singers lined up to do their bit, some of whom were very talented, but because I didn't need or want a job at that time I was relaxed and without nerves. I did a couple of songs and departed back to Margate.

As instructed I called the agent the next day and he informed me that the director wanted to book me as a singer/entertainer for the 1969 season at The Caribbean

Bar of the Hotel De La Plage starting at Easter. I was about to break the news that I was already booked when he asked me how much I would want per week. Knowing that I was to earn £25.00 per week at The Lido I decided to ask an impossible amount so that it would rule me out *"£40.00 per week,"* I said. *"I can get you more than that cocker,"* he said *"how about we get £55.00 and it's a bit for you and a bit more for me, you get £45 and I'll have the tenner."* £45 per week in 1969 seemed like a fortune to me and it was an offer I couldn't refuse, but what would I do about The Lido.

I had been seeing, on and off, an ex-girlfriend from my early teens called Gill Carter, who was a solicitor's secretary and therefore a pretty smart cookie! She agreed to manage my new show *'Way Out West'* at The Golden Garter Saloon while I took up the job in Jersey. I also had to find someone to stage the show and somehow, I can't recall how, signed up a Southern TV programme director called David Bellamy to take on that task.

While I was organising my show *for The Lido another project, unknown to me at the time, was underway at the other end of Kent. At Beckenham, at The Three Tuns pub, a folk club had been organised and run by one David Bowie and his local 'landlady'. Folk music lovers could hear acoustic delights from the future superstar in Beckenham while country music lovers could 'max out' on country standards at The Golden Garter Saloon!*

With a cast, director and company manager in place at the Lido I prepared for a new adventure in Jersey. Though I didn't realise it at the time this was the end of my wilderness years and would lead me in a direction that would shape my life for the next decade.

INTERVAL

Chapter 3
A Big Fish
(The Jersey Years)

When it's time to swim alone
Dive in and strike out
When your wildest dreams have flown
Go forth, don't doubt

On Saturday the 5th April 1969 I opened at the Caribbean Bar on Havre des Pas, Jersey. Three days earlier I had arrived on the island by ferry from Weymouth. I travelled as a foot passenger with my guitar, amplifier and luggage, having given up on the little Ford Anglia which I had sold for a few pounds. I found my way by taxi to the house where I had been able to rent a room and breakfast. The landlady was endearingly Irish with a very strong accent and I was at pains to understand all that she said. I can clearly recall the first morning when she prepared breakfast. She asked me if I liked my toast cut *"tick or tin"*. I think I went for 'tick'.

I found the island even more charming than

during the brief holiday some years before. I discovered a little of the history of this British Crown Dependency. Together with its neighbour Guernsey it became part of The Britsh Isles in the 13th Century when William The Conqueror became King of England. The islands had previously belonged to the Duchy of Normandy. By the 1960s Jersey was a thriving 'foreign' holiday destination that Brits could fly to before they discovered the costas in Spain!

It was a long walk through St Helier to The Caribbean each morning and evening, and it seemed even longer trudging back, so I quickly invested in an old Wolseley car. The seven day week and twice a day regime took some getting used to and took a toll on my voice, but I soon got into the swing of playing an hour every lunchtime and three hours every evening.

I realised, after a few days, that The Caribbean was the place to meet for the young seasonal workers, especially on weekend nights, and during the first few weeks I constantly heard from them how good my predecessor, Gerry Lochran, had been. Lochran was an accomplished blues guitarist and singer with, ultimately, several albums to his name. I, on the other hand, was a good singer of anything popular but a mediocre guitar player. However, playing for so many hours every day, I quickly learnt how to use the instrument in a way that covered my lack of guitar talent and the reminiscences the regulars had of great nights listening to Gerry Lochran began to fade away. I was the new flavour of the month and of the season. The Caribbean was so popular on Sunday evenings, for example, that it would be already full to bursting before

I started playing and the doormen would only allow people in as others left. There were often queues along the street at Havre des Pas, which was a great boost to the ego.

The atmosphere was so relaxed during the lunchtime sessions that it was easy to meet and talk to regular customers and I met some great people early in the summer who have remained friends down the years. Young members of one family came several times each week during the lunch break from their father's shop nearby. The Mallen family helped me enormously during my time in Jersey. Phil Mallen, who also ran a car repair business, helped me acquire a decent car after a few weeks struggling with the ageing Wolseley. I flashed about in a large pale blue Ford Corsair for the rest of the summer. Phil was also a devoted Bob Dylan fan and I tried hard not to disappoint him with my attempts at some Dylan classics.

Phil's sister Angela recalls (2018)
"This was Jersey in its heyday as a holiday attraction. It was buzzing like never before and its nightlife was a vibrant and big part of the summer season. Then a new face arrived at The Caribbean Bar. In the summer of 1969 we saw Robb for the beginning of his time in Jersey. Wow – a bit of excitement here!! Totally different to the last bloke! We were all impressed from the start by a totally different music style and, my god, not only did he play the guitar but he recorded his own backing tracks!! This was such an amazing new way for a 'one man band'. Add to this his repertoire of songs which appealed to all, he was an instant hit."

Unparallel Careers!

For a guy like me who had always found it difficult to approach and 'chat up' girls easily this was a job made in heaven. To use an expression of the era there was 'loads of talent' every day at the Caribbean and I was spoilt for choice. Some weeks into the season, after several short term and failed attempts at romance, a girl with golden blonde hair and a radiant smile charmed me with her soft Scottish accent and bubbly self-confidence. She worked as a kind of 'bunny girl' cocktail waitress at a popular nightspot called Les Arches which was on the other side of the island from St Helier.

Helen was from Clyde Bank in Scotland and had been in Jersey for several seasons. She was a year or two older than me – very pretty and self-assured and with the kind of life experiences that interested someone like me who had not really left the home comforts before. We started to go out together and she fitted in well with the friends I had made. After a few weeks I said goodbye to 'Mrs Tick or Tin' and moved out of my B&B to join Helen in a flat we found together in an old farmhouse at St Peters village.

It was really a studio, a very large downstairs room in one wing of this lovely old building. It had a cooking and sitting area at one end, a bedroom area at the other and we shared a bathroom with the landlady and her small son. She was a single parent and was renting out the room illegally, as did many people at that time. It was virtually impossible, as a seasonal worker, to rent a house or flat legally due to the stringent letting rules which favoured only Jersey residents.

The house was bordered by a small stream and the lane on which it stood led directly to open fields where cows grazed in the mostly glorious sunshine. For a townie like me this was a novelty and we would spend many off duty hours wandering the nearby lanes. It was also near to the Jersey airport perimeter fence and I could watch the aircraft coming and going while laying on the warm grass – I imagined they were bringing in my next audience – life was good. I don't know if I was in love with Helen - my only real love was music - but it was the nearest thing to love that I had experienced and I dived in wholeheartedly. Was it genuine and lasting or just a glamorous infatuation. Only time would tell.

> *Walking on through the park*
> *Holding hands in the dark*
> *Feeling just like summer sunshine*
> *Everything I do is free*
> *It's for you and me*
> *So come on and love me now*
> **Stephen Gold (All I Ever Do)**

My work at The Caribbean finished at 11pm, which was pub and bar closing time. Under the licensing laws in Jersey prevailing at that time it was not possible to enter a nightclub or hotel bar after the 11pm deadline. I was therefore reduced to sneaking into places through back doors in order to get a late drink and unwind after three hours of playing. This was not without risk for the obliging hotel owners or club managers who would have been prosecuted if caught. I was therefore very grateful to those who occasionally slipped me in. Often I would get word of a party taking place somewhere on the island but the news would also quickly filter through the grapevine and soon it seemed like the whole island had heard about it. So many people would turn up at the poor organiser's house that the street outside would soon be jammed with vehicles and the police would appear to turf everybody out.

The 'no entry after 11pm' rule obviously also applied to Les Arches where Helen worked until after midnight. On the occasions when I arranged to pick her up I was sometimes able to creep in through the kitchen entrance and join her for a drink but if the police were monitoring the car park this was too risky. Fortunately we made friends with the owner of a small hotel in Havre des Pas where we were able to spend a relaxing hour on the way home. One very stormy night, after drinks in the hotel bar, we drove home in torrential rain to find the ground floor of the house under a foot of muddy water. The small stream that ran beside the house had burst its banks and most of our possessions were floating about the room. In spite of this domestic setback, and the sometimes frustrating shared bathroom facilities, I still ended the season with very happy memories of the time we spent at the St.Peters farmhouse.

In 1969 Jersey was at the height of its tourism era and there were many show venues dotted around the island where artistes of varying talent and celebrity performed nightly. Some performers became Jersey 'household names'. A good example would be Simon Raverne. He and his band featured in various venues including Les Arches. Chico Arnez And His Cuban Brass were well known – Helen knew Chico and we spent some happy hours partying at his place after work. Another was Stuart Gillies, a popular Scottish singer who had already established himself after several

A Big Fish

seasons in Jersey.

There were also many celebrities who visited for a day or stayed for a season and that summer the American singer Solomon King was starring at The Watersplash, one of the principal island cabaret venues. The year before he had knocked up a smash hit single with *'She Wears My Ring'*. One lunchtime Helen was at the Caribbean when Solomon came in. He complemented me on my singing and chatted to Helen while I finished my set. He invited us to the house he had rented for a 'late lunch around the pool' the following day. When we arrived he was alone and wearing only a bathrobe which from time to time flopped open. It quickly became clear he was looking for a threesome – or maybe he wanted me to get lost! We took a drink and a couple of sandwiches and negotiated our way out. Unsurprisingly we never saw him again.

Ed 'Stewpot' Stewart, the Radio One DJ, was another brief visitor to the island who tried to get a 'scene' going at a party we attended. It's interesting to note that, although it was 1969 and the height of the 'flower power – psychedelic' era, I was never aware of any sort of drug scene or even pot smoking, which was probably due to the achingly strict local laws and law enforcement.

On the 11th July 1969 a single record was released *and began to be played on the main UK radio stations. When I first heard it I realised I knew of the singer – his name rang a bell with me. I hadn't heard the name since the day, in 1966, when I learnt that the remains of my group 'The Lower Third' had finally broken up after a dispute with their manager over an* *unpaid gig. The name I recognised was David Bowie and the single was 'Space Oddity', inspired by Stanley Kubrick's film 2001 A Space Odyssey. It introduced an astronaut called Major Tom who would return many years later in other Bowie songs.*

Ten days after the record was released *Neil Armstrong and Buzz Aldrin stepped onto the moon for the first time.*

"One small step for man, a giant leap for mankind."

By September, 'Space Oddity' had risen to number five in the UK pop charts and had heralded the arrival of a future superstar. I wasted no time in relating stories of my days with 'The Lower Third' to whoever cared to listen. I explained how a young David Jones had joined my group in 1965. I never lied, but was sometimes 'economical with the truth', which gave the impression I had played with him when in fact he had, in essence, taken over the singing from me as I departed. Henceforth this would be my defining conversation when I met new people and they asked me how I got started as a singer. "Hey, I was a founder member of the band who recorded David Bowie's first record."

During one lunchtime session in September a man arrived in The Caribbean and introduced himself as a director of St Annes Pier in Lancashire. He wanted to talk to me about my wild west show. He had recently seen the show at The Cliftonville Lido and wanted to discuss the possibility of having it for the next season at the St Annes Pier Theatre. It was a rather surreal meeting with me in my frilly blue shirt and white trousers and he in a dark business suit. Fortunately he seemed to have confidence in my ability to produce a show for him and

A Big Fish

it was agreed that I would visit St Annes as soon as possible after the season ended. This was an exciting prospect because at that time I did not know if there would be another contract on offer for the Lido show.

The season trundled towards its end and, surprisingly, I had not seen the agent Billy Forrest since the audition in London and had not spoken with him since agreeing to the contract back in January. He was often on the island as he had several shows running and numerous other artistes contracted. I would have expected a visit early in the season to check out what I was doing but it was not until the end of September that he appeared, unannounced, in the Caribbean. It was at the end of a lunchtime session and, whilst he didn't bother to listen to my performance or offer any compliments, he did bring news that the management wanted me to return for the 1970 season. There was, predictably, a bit more money for me and quite a bit more for him. I readily agreed as I was, by then, feeling a bit like a minor celebrity with the long queues at the door and numerous snippets in the local paper. A veritable big fish in a small pool!

Jersey Evening Post – October 1969
"Over the years The Caribbean at Havre des Pas has featured some first class solo entertainers. None more entertaining or with a bigger work rate than the present Robb Wyatt. Robb finishes his season on Sunday week (Oct. 11th) and if you haven't been down there, I can recommend it. Whatever your thing musically it won't be Robb's fault if you don't have a ball."

Back To Reality

After a big high came a reality check in that winter of 1969 – for a while I was no longer the Big Fish. And it wasn't only me who would have to adjust to a loss of status that year.

From the book 'The Age Of Bowie'

"As soon as his first hit single started to drop from the charts Bowie tumbled with it, falling back to Earth. He wasn't destined to be remembered because of 'Space Oddity', not at the time. For a while it seemed as if it would become his own tin can that he was sealed inside, drifting off into ultimate obscurity."
Text copyright © Paul Morley 2016, reproduced by kind permission of Simon & Schuster UK Ltd

I left the island by ferry a day or so after the season ended and took Helen with me back to Margate, arriving in the flashy Ford Corsair. I had already delicately inquired of my mother if it was alright to bring someone home who would share my room. This was a first. With this agreed we arrived and settled in to a warm family welcome.

I soon made contact with my old music buddies and discussed the possibility of recording an EP record which I could sell in Jersey during the next season. I was also able to tidy up any loose ends from my *'Way Out West'* show, at The Golden Garter Saloon, which had ended some weeks before and which Gill Carter had managed with her usual efficiency. The show had been very well received and the cast had enjoyed a great summer.

A Big Fish

Isle of Thanet Gazette - 20th June 1969 *"A flash of gunfire made sure everyone was very much awake and the 1969 Golden Garter Saloon Show crashed into life. But this was a very different show from previous years at The Lido's famous western bar. Gone was the ad-libbing of the past. It was replaced with a properly directed and produced show which the Friday opening night audience thoroughly enjoyed."*

In spite of the successful opening it had not been a roaring success at the box office and, therefore, neither was it with the management so I was not invited to pitch for the next season. In the event the Lido's Golden Garter Saloon became a country music venue for the next few seasons before closing for good in the 1970s. Nevertheless the experience had set the wheels in motion for several similar productions in future years. But for now it was time to think about the possibility of a new show on St Annes Pier.

During that winter of 1969/70 we drove to Scotland to visit Helen's family in Clydebank. It was an unforgettable experience for me to cross the border at Gretna Green, famous then for runaway marriages, and to see the mountainous landscapes and lochs for the first time. We stayed a few days and took in the sites along the banks of the Clyde, the centre of Glasgow and even the southern reaches of Loch Ness with its mythical monster. All places I'd read about as a child but, having grown up at the furthest reaches of southern England, had no chance of visiting before. After a few glorious days and a last meal of haggis, neeps and tatties I set off southwards towards Lytham St Annes, just south of

Unparallel Careers!

Blackpool, leaving Helen with her family for a few weeks.

A meeting at St Annes Pier Theatre cemented the contract for the next summer season and, following another week on stage at the Dolphin Bar in Cleveleys and a few unmemorable working men's club performances, I returned to Margate.

In the early days of 1970 I set about recording my EP. I had done very little songwriting since heading for Jersey and had no confidence in recording any of my earlier efforts so I opted for writing a new song especially for this record. I settled on three more songs that I could easily feature in my shows at The Caribbean. Terry Bolton had introduced me to the songs of Jimmy Webb and I became passionate about his music. I was particularly excited by a Fifth Dimension album called *'The Magic Garden'* which Webb had written and produced. I recorded my favourite song from the album *'The Worse That Could Happen'*. I also covered songs by Jose Feliciano and Glen Campbell. My own new song was called *'Brand New Heartache'*. Several other backing tracks were recorded at the same time for my live performances, including Herb Alpert's *'This Guy's In Love With You'* which would feature in a scary television moment during the season to come.

At about the same time *some other musicians were in another studio recording Bowie's first album. He called his record 'David Bowie' and I called my record 'Robb Wyatt At The Caribbean'. While his would be on general release mine would be on sale at a record shop in St Helier. This was when I became aware that our trajectories, at the turn of a new* *decade, were at an entirely different angle!*

With the record completed and the cast signed up for the show at St. Annes Pier Theatre it was time to plan my return to Jersey. Helen had joined me in Margate and we had arranged to rent part of a house at Havre des Pas which was to be shared by several entertainers. We set off for Weymouth with my guitar, amplifier, PA system, Ferrograph tape recorder, box of EP records and our substantial luggage all crammed into the Corsair.

At Weymouth, while waiting for the car to be craned onto the ferry (no roll on roll off ferries in those days) I had a rather bizarre encounter with a group of lads who insisted that I was Geoff Hurst, the footballer and World Cup '66 winner. The previous season in Jersey some boys had alluded to the fact that I looked a bit like Geoff Hurst, indeed one of them had insisted on calling me Geoff whenever he visited the Caribbean, but I had not seen the likeness and it had gone out of my head over the winter months. I tried in vain to convince these lads that I was not their idol but they were completely convinced that Geoff was trying to slip away unnoticed for a holiday in Jersey!

A New Season

We arrived on the island at the end of April 1970 and remarkably there was a dusting of snow on the ground. After a couple of nights in a small hotel we moved into the house which was walking distance from the Caribbean. It was a town house on Roseville Street with several large bedrooms. We shared the house with comedian Chris Carlsen and his beautiful wife Angie.

Unparallel Careers!

Chris was appearing for the season at 'Tams' cabaret venue in St Brelade. There was also a husband and wife vocal duo who were playing bar and cabaret venues around the island. To begin with it was an ideal situation because we got on well with Peter and Jo and hardly saw Chris Carlsen and his wife, who were at 'Tams' until after 2am. On Friday evenings, after The Caribbean closed, I did a short cabaret performance in the adjacent Hotel de la Plage and Chris Carlsen came to close out the show. Naturally I chatted to Angie while Chris performed and we all seemed to get along, which was great seeing that we were house mates. What could possibly go wrong?

I had started using pre-recorded backing tracks which enabled me to more easily promote the record and it was going well. Using backing tracks was virtually unknown in that era but I had picked up the idea from working with Wout Steenhuis's recording engineer and had even bought the valuable Ferrograph tape machine from him. But the guitar was still king and I pounded out three hours of popular songs each evening and drifted gently through some romantic ballads at lunchtime. It was still seven days a week lunchtimes and evenings. Helen returned happily to Les Arches for a second 'bunny girl' season and everything was going smoothly – until!

About three weeks into the season we were awakened one night at 3am by loud banging and shouting in the house and we quickly realised that Chris had locked Angie out of their room. She kept banging and pleading with him to let her in. Eventually the noise died down and we all went back to sleep. There was no

A Big Fish

sign of them for a couple of days and we thought they must be embarrassed by what had occurred. When they arrived at the hotel on the following Friday to prepare for the cabaret show there was a distinctly hostile atmosphere between them and Chris completely ignored me before going on to perform. As soon as we were alone I could see Angie was near to tears and I asked her what was wrong. *"He has accused me of having an affair with you,"* she said. I was stunned. *"How could that be, we've hardly ever been alone together – just here on Friday nights – is he mad?"* She didn't answer, but it was clear to me that he was an extremely jealous guy who must have looked for something happening with every man she spoke to. Flattered as I was by him thinking that this beautiful woman would succumb to my undeniable charms, it was completely irrational to have conjured up the idea of an affair taking place in the house when I had only occasionally passed the time of day with her. It was time to get out of there - as soon as possible.

By chance, soon after the problems had erupted, Helen bumped into our landlady from the previous year and learnt that the farmhouse rooms were vacant again. We jumped at the chance to move back in for the remainder of the season.

My performances at The Caribbean continued to go well, especially with the new songs I had introduced. I was able to promote the record and it was selling slowly but steadily. The Jersey Evening Post's entertainment section helped by printing little news items from time to time. I was contacted by Channel TV and asked to appear on their early evening magazine show hosted by a well known local presenter Mike

LeCoq – he preferred it was pronounced LeCoke! I was to sing one song with my own backing track and I decided on Herb Alpert's *'This Guy's In Love With You'*.

Scheduled before me on the programme was a pre-recorded interview with Warren Mitchell who played Alf Garnett in the very popular TV comedy *'Till Death Us Do Part'*. I sat on a stool mid-studio, slightly nervous, waiting for the interview to finish. Mike LeCoq gave me a splendid introduction and, as I raised the microphone, the sound of the Warren Mitchell interview came from the monitors again instead of my backing music. I tried to look cool while there was an obvious panic in the control room. They faded the interview soundtrack out and my music came in – but unfortunately not at the beginning. Now it was my turn to panic – there was no way to escape on live TV so I had to take a stab at it. The first words were over a repetitive two bar intro – but which two bars? I launched in and by luck and a quick jumble of the lyrics I found my place and finished the song with great confidence having sung it a hundred times or more already during the season. When the show ended the director and the sound engineer burst in with apologies and humble thanks for having got them out of a mess. That night at The Caribbean performing seemed easy in comparison.

Affairs Of The Heart

Life in the middle of that summer was going fine. I had good friends who I saw often, my music was flowing and the crowds kept on piling in to The Caribbean. I also got caught up in the excitement of the famous Battle Of Flowers, the highlight of the Jersey

A Big Fish

summer, because Helen had won through to be maid of honour to Miss Battle Of Flowers 1970. She looked fabulous on the magnificent floral trailer. The event culminated in a stunning carnival procession along the esplanade with all the other incredible creations entirely made from colourful blooms. Life was good - I was happy - *nothing needed to change.*

The Caribbean was always full of young people and I met many of a similar age to me who were on the island working for the season. A lot of them were there because they were running away from something at home, very often a broken love affair or problems with parents or siblings. It was always interesting to watch their lives change during the season. Some developed into strong independent characters but a few eventually succumbed to loneliness or homesickness and disappeared back to their former life. But some young people came to Jersey just for the 'crack', as the Irish like to call it, to get some freedom and have fun. One such person came into my life on an evening sometime towards the end of August. I was happy – *nothing needed to change!*

> *Out of a dream and into my day*
> *I didn't need it then*
> *Calling my name though I shouldn't play*
> *And it was not if but when*
> **Stephen Gold (Out Of A Dream)**

She was a striking nineteen year old who caught my attention as soon as she entered the Caribbean. Tall with long dark hair, great figure, long legs and a face full of interesting features. She appeared to be alone and

Unparallel Careers!

giving the right signals, so I made a beeline for her during my fifteen minute break and struck up a conversation. I unashamedly asked her to come in the next day to see my lunchtime performance and I suggested we could go for a coffee after the gig.

Sue was a freelance model and promotions worker taking time out to party – a truly free spirit. She was staying at a camp site at St Brelade's Bay, which was on my way back to the farmhouse at St Peters, and over the following weeks she would spend evenings at The Caribbean or I would visit her tent at the camp site on my way home or before I drove to pick up Helen from Les Arches. I was two-timing both of them, living with one and having an affair with the other – not something I had sought but I was excited by it. I felt very guilty about the lies and half truths I was telling – there was nothing wrong between Helen and me but here I was - truly hooked.

In early September I was disappointed to learn that I would not be re-booked for the 1971 season. Billy Forrest, the agent, promised he would find me something similar at another venue but the thought of performing again in Jersey at a less prestigious venue did not really appeal. I would no longer be the Big Fish!

I began to contemplate the next move – *'Way Out West'* at St Annes Pier had successfully survived the season but was not being repeated for the next year. I found myself with nothing on the horizon except the bitterness that would surely be the fall-out over my relationship with Sue Cockayne.

In desperation I answered two adverts for singer guitarists that were in The Stage showbiz newspaper.

A Big Fish

The first was for a similar job, as resident singer at a bar/nightclub in Hamilton, Bermuda, and the second was for someone to join a trio for a winter season on a cruise ship. I sent off my CV and photos and, on the strength of the reputation I had garnered from my two seasons at The Caribbean, I received a letter from a guy called Bobby Bigwood asking if I could join his trio on the Cunard ship QE2 at Southampton on the 20th September for the winter cruising season. How disappointed I was to have to turn this opportunity down – my contract at The Caribbean didn't end until the 7th October. Then in late September I received a reply from Bermuda and the chance to land this great job seemed highly promising. It was to take over from a resident entertainer at the beginning of December, subject to me sending references from the Caribbean Bar management.

As the end of the season loomed I was miserable, depressed even. Sue left Jersey for her home town of Sheffield in the north of England some two weeks before I was due to leave and I missed the excitement. Helen still knew nothing of what I had been doing behind her back, and neither did our good friends from the Mallen clan who had become close to Helen over the two summers.

At that point in time securing a contract for a job on the other side of the Atlantic seemed an attractive but cowardly way to gradually end the relationship. I had kind of done it to a girl once before. Back in the days after I left *'The Lower Third'* I was regularly dating a very pretty girl from the accounts office where I worked. I didn't feel that the relationship was going to be long

Unparallel Careers!

term and it must have shown. In order to get a reaction from me she announced that she was interested in going to Canada for two years on a special travel grant that was available from the Canadian government. Rather than the *"please don't go"* reaction that she wanted I didn't say anything to discourage her – I felt it was a way to end it without me having to be honest about my feelings. I drove Joan Crane to Heathrow Airport for a tearful goodbye and I never saw or heard from her again. I hope she found a good life in Canada. Now I was trying to avoid another bitter ending by running away myself.

Piling everything into the Corsair we left the island on the 9th October and headed back to Margate where we installed ourselves in my old room at the family house. I was soon in contact with Sue and she suggested we meet in London for a weekend. She knew nothing of my other relationship and I realised then that I had to resolve the situation properly. I was not going to get away with shirking the issue by leaving for Bermuda because a firm contract offer had not yet materialized. So, one night, with a lump in my throat, I told Helen that I had met someone else. Although over forty five years have passed since then I can still see her reaction and hear her words. It is with sadness that I have to say that Helen was the one person in my life I feel I really let down and hurt badly. It had been my first 'live in' relationship and I would not experience another for many years.

A Big Fish

Now it's too late for sharing
Too late to mend the lies
Just one night left to feel your warmth
And listen to you cry
Stephen Gold (Too Late)

I met Sue in London the next weekend and we checked into a small hotel near Trafalgar Square. The first time we'd stayed in a proper room! It was to be one of many similar hotel meet-ups which would form the basis of our future relationship, but this first weekend was difficult. I was in a turmoil, my mind was elsewhere, still feeling guilty about Helen and worrying about where my future was heading – I was without a job.

After a tearful Sunday night farewell at St Pancras Station I started chasing up agents I had worked for in the northern clubs and searching The Stage newspaper for new opportunities. I travelled to Northern Ireland for a week at the Imperial Cabaret Rooms in Belfast and arranged a week at a cabaret restaurant in Sheffield where I could see Sue again. Then one morning, at the end of October, the future finally came into view. I received a telegram from Bobby Bigwood who was in Madeira. *"Are you available to join the QE2 in New York on the 29th November?"* The singer guitarist who had joined them in Southampton had not worked out well and was being flown home. I was elated and excited by the prospect of a new challenge and a new way of life.

Recording with The Three Keys
Terry Bolton, Gillian Mason, Robin Wyatt

Going West

Sheriff Danny Arnold

A weekly chore was judging the Miss Golden Garter contest!

Golden Garter Saloon 1968 with me on the right and Valerie Leon (third right)

Robin becomes 'Robb' Wyatt

My great Golden Garter team in 1969 with Jimmy Rose left and Phil Brooks right

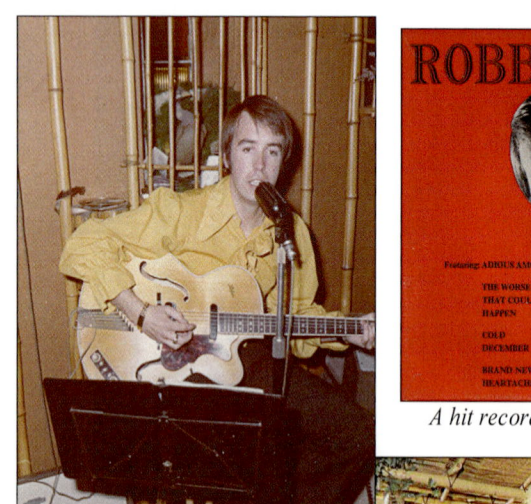

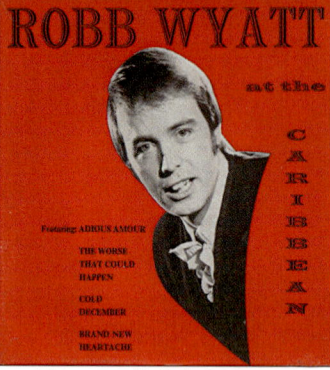

A hit record? Only in Jersey!

*At The Caribbean Bar
Jersey 1970*

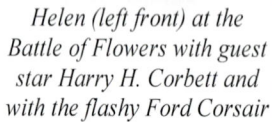

Helen (left front) at the Battle of Flowers with guest star Harry H. Corbett and with the flashy Ford Corsair

*The Hotel de la Plage
The Caribbean Bar is at the centre of the photo*

Chapter 4
America
(The Cruising Years)

New York, New York, they sang it twice
Because anyone can make it in this urban paradise
New York, New York, it's life at the extreme
Of the American Dream
Stephen Gold (The American Dream)

I boarded the flight at Gatwick Airport on the 28th November 1970 with my guitar, amplifier, personal luggage and a lot of hope for the future. I was joining an established trio. The husband and wife team of Bobby and Anne Bigwood had become a fixture with Cunard's ships and had worked with a number of 'third member guitarists' on several big cruise liners. They had worked on the old Cunard ship The Queen Mary before it was pensioned off and were now enjoying a second winter contract on the brand new QE2.

All musicians working for Cunard in that era were booked through the Geraldo Agency and I had been quickly supplied with a contract and details of my departure. It was to be by a crew replacement flight to Newark, New Jersey with Caledonian Airlines. I was to be paid the sum of £165.17s.6d per month - decimalisation had not yet happened - but with all accommodation and food supplied this was indeed a princely sum in 1970. I learnt later that there were strange extras to the fees, which had their origin in seamen's pay regulations, such as double pay for Sundays at sea. I was issued with a seaman's passbook – a kind of passport which contained a record of your time at sea. This pleased my Dad who turfed out a similar passbook from his time at sea in the 1930s. He approved of this career move!

I was met in New York by Bobby and Anne with news that the ship was docked overnight so we were going out to Long Island to party with some of their American friends. I lugged my heavy amplifier and guitar through the streets of New York, from one station to another, to get the train to Long Island. I was jet lagged, tired, confused and disorientated. This was my introduction to the city I would come to love.

Bowie was planning *his first promotional trip to America to publicise his second album 'The Man Who Sold The World'. Our schedules would cross unknowingly in New York during January 1971. I was there wholeheartedly embracing a new and fascinating way of life while he was there trying to create a new audience and break into the American music scene. How different for us both from the smoke filled sweaty clubs in Wardour Street where our paths surely must have crossed six years before. But he had fallen off the radar since 'Space Oddity' and, on Long Island, mentioning my old band and the* *connection to Bowie meant I had to explain who he was. Maybe the reflected glory was passing away!*

After a night in an impressive American home, complete with basement party room, we returned to New York City to join the ship at Pier 92. I was immediately overawed by the size and scale of the vessel but I had no time to dwell on it. *'The Bigwoods'* were scheduled to play at the embarkation point to welcome the passengers and their friends on board for the embarkation parties.

They first showed me to my cabin. It was on the lowest passenger deck, deck 5, and was an interior passenger cabin without a view of the outside world. It was modern and well furnished with a bed, wardrobe, shower and toilet. Cabin 5247 was to be my home for the next few months where, over time, I installed a unique record player with disco lights attached and a comprehensive bar facility!

After dumping my luggage in the cabin there was an urgent need for rehearsals. I had no idea what we would be playing for this session but soon learnt that it would be mainly Caribbean music as an introduction to this Caribbean island hopping cruise.

Bobby was an award winning accordionist who had migrated to a Cordovox which was an electronic accordion with all the bass and keyboard sounds of a Wurlitzer organ. I was at once impressed with Bobby. He was tall with a mass of long blond hair. His musical skills were many and varied and he sang tolerably well. Anne played drums and percussion in an adequate but certainly not exciting way. She was a slim and very attractive woman who often appeared slightly aloof which made her seem unapproachable to many men. Over time I warmed to her but was aware that she was the controlling partner in the couple's relationship. A relationship that I would eventually see disintegrate.

We quickly ran through some simple calypsos which I could quite easily play along with and they supplied me with a kind of pirate costume which vaguely corresponded with the music. It was a purely instrumental session and I muddled through. Crowds of passengers and their guests passed through the embarkation lobby carrying bottles, food and party streamers and we played on until the last guests had left the ship and it was closed up ready to sail. I cannot imagine that those sort of parties could take place in the 21st century with the security measures that are now required.

During my time on the ship I saw many drunken embarkation parties and even participated in a few when the embarkation music fell to other musicians. Frequently there would be guests, usually drunk, still on board after the ship had cast off from Pier 92. This in spite of the many calls for *"All visitors ashore – the ship is about to sail."* Normally the errant guests would be extracted from the ship by a New York harbour vessel somewhere down the Hudson River.

After the embarkation baptism of fire I had the time to return to my cabin to unpack and dress for the first dinner on board. Being totally unfamiliar with this vast ship and having, in the confusion of those first hours, forgotten my cabin number, I wandered up and down the seemingly endless corridors hoping

America

something would look familiar. Bobby and Anne had left me at the end of the session and I had no idea of their cabin number either. So there I was, on my first evening on board this famous and prestigious vessel, wandering lost from deck to deck and along endless corridors still dressed in a dodgy pirate costume. The wealthy passengers, who were now dressed for dinner, eyed me suspiciously. After some time I realised that I was not going to find the cabin and with acute embarrassment I accosted a steward and asked if he knew Bobby Bigwood, and if so how could I contact him? Luckily he did and my dilemma was resolved!

Life on board the ship far exceeded my expectations. We lived as passengers, ate in the passenger restaurants, had access to the library, the cinema, the bars and the nightclub. During the first few days, while the ship headed for its first port of call, we rehearsed hour after hour. I was to learn *'The Bigwoods'* extensive range of music which covered a number of themes such as Roaring Twenties, Irish, Caribbean, Italian and French as well as a good smattering of recent pop standards. We would be using all these themes at various times and in the beginning I lapped it all up and temporarily forgot my own repertoire and the image I had projected at the Caribbean in Jersey.

For a young guy on his first big trip overseas New York was the most exciting place imaginable. The sheer scale of the buildings, the famous landmarks, the music and theatre, Times Square, 42nd Street, 5th Avenue and all the other streets and buildings that I had only seen on the silver screen were there in front of me. And it wasn't just a fleeting visit. On the numerous stopovers I was able to experience the daily life of this fascinating but sometimes dangerous city. I was amazed to see the Broadway news stands selling copies of a tabloid newspaper called 'Screw'. I had never seen real pornography before and this featured pictures and articles alongside small adverts for any sort of service one could imagine. Crew members bought porno films quite openly in New York and showed them in late night drinking sessions, much to the embarrassment of the few females working on board.

I had never before been around a heavy gay scene either and was fascinated when the large community of gay crew members on the ship regaled us with lurid tales of their nights out at the many seedy gay night clubs in the city. One night several of us were invited to a party in an impressive apartment in Lower Manhattan where there was a lot of booze and plenty of puff. We were clearly out of our depth in this liberated New York environment and I recall my surprise when a busty blonde girl strode into the room and said in a loud voice *"Don't any of you Limeys fuck."* I'm sure we all did, but with proper British reserve!

***Proper British reserve** had not hindered Bowie who had married Angie the previous year and whose son was well on the way to being born. I had never considered marriage for one moment and saw it as a total career inhibition. I was surprised, therefore, that an artist on the verge of stardom had embarked on a route that might seriously hamper his progress. How wrong I was. Perhaps I should have married Helen – she might, like Angie Barnett was in the process of doing for David, have turned me into a star!*

America

Over the next days, weeks and months I experienced the sheer delight of the Caribbean islands - St Lucia, Martinique, Trinidad, Granada and many other ports of call all with varied and interesting characteristics. Every cruise visited St.Thomas in the US Virgin Islands where we took on board the duty free wine and spirits for cabin consumption. Barbados was a stand out favourite. A frequent stop where we stayed overnight so were able to spend the days on the exotic beaches and the evenings dancing in the open air nighteries. Of the few times in my life when I have been seriously drunk, one day in Barbados stands out. It was a combination firstly of exotic sun drenched luxury followed by hours of dreadful heaving.

Eight of us hired two speedboats and their drivers to take us to Paradise Beach for a day of eating, drinking and water-skiing. I declined the water skiing on account of my embarrassing inability to swim. We spent a glorious day on the beach and when the time came to return to the ship it was realised that three amongst us had not yet bought a 'round'. We were drinking planter's punch which is a lethal mix of several different rums tempered with fruit juice and topped with fresh fruit. The three rounds were purchased in one go and with only a few minutes to spare it was down the hatch with all three as we got dressed for the return run. When the boats came in close to pick us up I started to feel the effects of the overdose of rum. I scrambled onto the front of the lead boat which set off at a furious pace for the port which was about 20 minutes away. The sea had become choppy and as I tried to stave off the nausea we started to hit the waves hard. I was thrown around as I struggled to hold on. Water cascaded over the bow as it came down into the next wave soaking me completely and making it more difficult to stay in place. I was not only blind drunk – I was terrified of going overboard. When we arrived at the port the boat came up under the enormous bow of the QE2 alongside some steps that had recently been submerged and were covered in slimy seaweed. Terrified again I leapt for the steps and slipped onto my backside. I dragged myself up and in a semi-conscious state staggered the length of the quayside in order to enter the ship near my cabin. I was aware of voices as I weaved through the jostling crowd but I only had that one goal – get to the cabin before I passed out. I reached it covered in sea water and green slime. I threw myself into the toilet and remembered nothing until regaining conciousness the next day, still alive but with an almighty hang-over! I never touched a planter's punch again.

Although most cruises were out of New York we also called at various American east coast ports such as Boston and Port Everglades, the latter giving us time in nearby Miami. On one cruise we called into the US naval base at Norfolk in Virginia where we docked alongside the old blue ribboned ocean liner SS United States, the fastest ocean liner ever built. It had been 'mothballed' and was kept by the military for possible future emergency use as a troopship. On one of several stops at Nassau in The Bahamas I was amazed to see, docked opposite us, the ship that my nephew Peter was working on as a steward and we downed a few beers together. On a mini cruise we called at Hamilton, Bermuda and I was able to seek out the place where I might have been working had the QE2 offer not arisen. I took the opportunity to introduce myself as I still had an eye on the future. I did not know how long I would last with *'The Bigwoods'*.

Don't Take Away The Music

Musically the ship was exciting for me. There were numerous musicians in a variety of bands and several featured cabaret artists. There was a fifteen piece 'Big Band' which played in the main entertainment rooms and a trio that played in the various bars. There was also a solo pianist who played tea and pre-dinner drinks music. Count Basie joined us for two weeks of amazing music. The great man was wonderfully humble and members of The Count Basie Band were all exceptional musicians. Although big band jazz was not my bag I couldn't help admiring the excellent musicianship on display. When the brass section blasted out, in the confines of the ship, it knocked you backwards - louder by far than our amplified offerings. We fell neatly between the role of musicians and cabaret entertainers. We usually played a set in one of the main rooms before the nightly cabaret show and several times each cruise we would be the featured show in one of the bars on a particular theme – Irish, Roaring Twenties, Scottish. During afternoons, when the ship was at sea, we would occasionally play an hour of Caribbean music for the first class passengers in the beautiful Queen's Room.

At some ports local musicians or folk dancers would entertain on board and in Barbados we got to know an excellent 'caribeat'/calypso band called The

Merrymen who had released a number of albums of traditional calypsos and other local upbeat dance music. They were very successful and ran their own open air nightclub where they were the main attraction and where we spent some wonderful nights dancing under the stars.

The Double Down Room was the cruise class passengers' main entertainment area, so named because it rose over two decks with a sweeping staircase at one end. The staircase actually swept towards the exit doors rather than onto the dance floor and legend had it that this was an accidental design error. Although the first class passengers had an elegant separate ballroom most nightly cabaret shows took part in the Double Down Room where, naturally, the first class passengers were able to attend at any time. Of course the cruise class passengers were not permitted in the Queen's Room!

The cabaret shows were regularly enhanced by visiting American stars and meeting Victor Borge, who I had enjoyed laughing at when I was a kid in the 50s, was a real treat. Donald O'Connor spent a week on board – unfortunately he was far from the brilliant dancer he had been in his youth, starring opposite Gene Kelly, but nevertheless it was a thrill to shake his hand and listen to his stories about great Hollywood musicals and their stars.

A Bite Of The Big Apple

Life was pretty special for me during that first season. I relaxed into it easily and soaked up the hedonistic atmosphere of luxury travel. Cruising in 1970 was only for the wealthy and we certainly saw them on the QE2. All the Caribbean cruise passengers were American. We only saw British passengers when we returned to Southampton in 1971 for a short Europe and West Africa cruise.

The Christmas cruise in 1970 was an eye opening experience. It was the first Christmas and New Year's Eve that I had spent away from Margate and I looked forward to it with excitement. However, the passengers were almost entirely Jewish people who were escaping Christmas rather than embracing it. Naturally the crew, musicians and entertainers did throw themselves into the celebrations, but out of sight of the passengers. I have an abiding memory from that New Year's Eve. After all the shows and music had ended we retired to celebrate in the band rehearsal room. The ship's Scottish doctor, dressed in his full kilt and sporran and under the influence of too many whiskies, climbed up on a table and commenced a slurred rendition of *'Donald Where's Ya Troosers'* to the delight of the gathered throng. In mid flow there was a call for the doctor to attend the ship's hospital immediately. A passenger was suffering a suspected heart attack. I never did hear the outcome for the passenger but I know the doctor survived to celebrate another day.

Over that Christmas and New Year period we were twice in New York overnight and we went to see the show at the famous Radio City Music Hall. It was a traditional Christmas extravaganza with a grandiose finale. They staged the nativity scene with camels, donkeys and sheep on stage together with the shepherds, the kings and the Holy Family. It was augmented by numerous extras played by the thirty or

Unparallel Careers!

so dancers who made up the famous high kicking Rockettes. The stage was filled and the final scene continued along the sides of the vast auditorium – a breathtaking spectacle of its time but probably eclipsed in the twenty first century by the productions in Las Vegas. The show was followed by the film musical 'Scrooge' starring Albert Finney which had been released that November. With music by Leslie Bricusse and Anthony Newley it has become one of my favourite films.

After Christmas the snow fell in abundance. I had snowball fights in Central Park, drank hot spiced wine while enjoying the ice skating at the Rockerfeller Center and boiled up in Macy's, the famous department store, where the heating seemed to be at 80 degrees while outside it was well below freezing. I had been on the ship for only a month and it was still like living a dream.

Some Private Enterprise

I got on well with Anne and Bobby in those early days and in the new year of 1971, having talked about my Jersey experience with the sales of the record *'Robb Wyatt At The Caribbean'*, we began to explore the possibility of releasing an album for sale on the ship. We started recording in our free time using the ship's PA equipment and Bobby's wonderful Revox two track (stereo) tape recorder – the 'Rolls Royce' of tape machines in that era. We recorded the most popular songs from our numerous themed shows and it covered Caribbean, Irish, Greek and Israeli music as well as a smattering of pop. We called the album *'The Bigwoods*

Live' and it certainly sounded live given the limited facilities we were able to use! I wrote a song for the album called *'Paradise Beach'*, inspired by some of the blissful days relaxing at the Paradise Beach Hotel in Barbados, and this song would turn out to be a 'nice little earner' for us over the following year.

It wasn't possible to get the record pressed until we returned to England but remarkably, because we became so popular with the American audiences, we were able to take orders after our shows when people gladly gave us the dollars on the promise of mailing the album when it was available. We took orders for several hundred albums and mailed them all from England and New York later in the year.

We played what in 1970 was referred to as 'middle of the road' music - the ships 'real' musicians called it 'crap music'! It was all the late sixties pop hits of Neil Diamond, The Hollies, Mungo Gerry, The Beatles and many others. It was difficult for the big band musicians to accept or understand that we were so popular when two of us, myself and Anne, were not trained musicians. I played very basic rhythm guitar and she was only 'adequate' on drums. The big difference between us and them was that we worked at entertaining the passengers rather than trying to dazzle them with our musicianship. The passengers were mainly of later middle age and they were thrilled to find that they liked what they saw as a 'pop' group.

Over the course of that winter season many passengers approached us with congratulations on the shows. Some even booked us for private cocktail parties on board. We got into hot water on one occasion when

Unparallel Careers!

we agreed a fee for a party and were paid directly by the passenger. This upset the ship's hotel department because it should have been booked through them – there was a system of illicit back-pocketing from every event and the right people did not get their cut from that booking. This type of rip-off was endemic throughout the ship, everybody had to make an extra dollar or a hundred. Barmen bought bottles of spirits in St Thomas and put them up for sale on the optics, thus bypassing the ship's stock systems. They then shared the proceeds. This was one of many dirty tricks which seemed to go largely unchallenged by the Cunard management.

One approach from a middle aged couple, asking for our business card, was eventually fruitful. They explained that their nephew had a nightclub and that they would recommend us to him. They were sure he would want to book us for the club. We made the right noises, thanked them profusely and after they had gone did our usual sarcastic 'pigs might fly' routine. To our astonishment, some weeks later, we received a call from an attorney at law representing a client called John J. Piazza. He wanted to discuss booking us for the opening of his new restaurant and night club which was a renovated Mississippi riverboat. It was moored on the Niagara River in Buffalo, New York State. They arranged for us to fly up to Buffalo on our next overnight stop in New York. We met John J Piazza and agreed contract terms for the coming summer, subject only to us being able to get out of the agreement we had with Cunard to remain on the ship for the summer of Atlantic crossings.

The winter season ended with the voyage back to

America

England in April 1971. The ship docked at Southampton, the port on the south coast where all the famous ocean liners of the past century had arrived and departed and where the passengers had embarked on the Titanic before it set sail on its fateful maiden voyage.

Our arrival in Southampton was immediately followed by a cruise with British passengers which sailed down to Dakar in Senegal. I was delighted to find that the famous British guitarist Bert Weedon had joined the ship to give several performances. I had to tell him how my initial scrapings on a guitar at the age of thirteen were inspired by his book called *'Play In A Day'*. I was not alone in this admission because several superstar guitarists - Eric Clapton, Paul McCartney and Brian May – have all admitted to starting out with Bert's guitar tutor! I was also able to admit to him that, at the age of fourteen, I had obtained his autograph when he appeared at Margate's Winter Gardens.

The cruise stopped off at Lisbon, Las Palmas and Madeira where Bobby and Anne invested in some wicker garden furniture which was very cheap. It required some ingenuity in getting it back to the ship and secreting it onboard as well as getting it off in England without arousing the suspicions of vigilant customs officials. It was difficult to disembark in Southampton with any valuable items acquired overseas. The customs officers at the port were very hot on checking crew members. There was one particular officer who had assembled a keen knowledge of musical instruments and could tell if a musician departed Southampton with a British bought instrument but returned with a very expensive American one. The

Unparallel Careers!

import duty could be a killer. I had to duck and dive to get my Gibson EB330 guitar off the ship. I had dumped my old Hoffner guitar and bought the replacement at Manny's, the famous music shop on New York's Music Row (West 48th Street). It wasn't new but in perfect condition and cost me $130. I knew it was worth four times as much at home. (I sold it some years later for £1250).

After a few days off we were due to embark for the Atlantic crossing season. In the meantime I was able to visit my family in Margate and pick up the Corsair. Helen had remained in the town and we spent a few evenings together, but it was plain that the old sparkle had really gone. She had rented a flat and found some temporary employment to see out the winter before returning to Jersey. I also met up with Sue who took the train from Sheffield to spend a day and night with me in London. The relationship was unconventional because we had never had the chance to be a couple. It was just a passionate meeting now and again - more like a continuing affair – and that was probably why the attraction endured for a while. And also why it would eventually come to an end.

Before returning to the ship for the first Atlantic crossing I had written to Alan Fitzgerald, General Manager of The Paradise Beach Hotel in Barbados, enclosing a copy of the lyrics to my song *'Paradise Beach'* which we had recorded for *'The Bigwoods Live'* album. In May I received a letter from him asking for a copy of our album to be delivered to their New York office on 42nd Street. The hotel, it seemed, was part of the Cunard Trafalgar Resorts Company so also had an association with the ship. When next in New York we dropped the album off and this led directly to the release of our second album, aptly called *'Paradise Beach'*, which the hotel group agreed to finance to the tune of $4000,00 - a tidy sum in 1971. We would receive 8000 albums to sell ourselves while the hotel would have a quantity for sale and promotion in Barbados. We once again took orders after our shows and the albums were mailed out later in the year when they had been delivered to us. This record was pressed in America and the sleeves were designed and printed by the hotel's well known New York promotions company called Hannau Robinson. They took the initiative to promote the hotel with a sleeve design that lent slightly to the psychedelic era and featured great pictures of the hotel, the beach, and us.

Passengers on the Atlantic crossings were quite different to the winter cruise passengers and that required some changes to our shows. The ship was at sea for five days going west to New York and nearly six days on return. The passengers were a mixture of business people, politicians, celebrities and cruisers who were taking a holiday in New York. It was sometimes hard work entertaining such a mixed bunch but the good thing about this period was the time I was able to spend in New York and Southampton. It was mostly an overnight stop at each end. In New York it was great to spend time in a sunny Central Park, browsing around the now very over-airconditioned Macy's store or taking a coffee or a glass of wine in the Rockefeller Center Plaza where we had watched the ice skaters in mid-winter.

During overnight stops in Southampton I would often spend the night at Bobby and Anne's place in

Broadstone near Bournemouth, the holiday resort on the south coast. We would get our cars from the secure garage in Southampton and drive, late at night, to Broadstone - stopping off at The Night Owl in Branksome to get burgers and coffee before a good night's sleep. My Bournemouth days were spent discovering the area that my partners knew so well and that I would come to know and visit regularly in the future. On one Southampton stopover I received a letter from Helen who was still in Margate. She appeared distraught and in financial difficulties so I jumped in the car at midnight and drove the five hours to Margate - where I found all to be okay! The letter had been written a week or two before and her problems were already solved. That was the last time I saw Helen who then returned to Jersey. For some years she remained in touch with my friends on the island.

Buffalo

The contract with The Showboat was confirmed after we successfully arranged for a break from the ship. We disembarked in Southampton on the 31st July 1971 to prepare for the new adventure. Our contract was for six weeks playing six nights per week on the riverboat.

We flew from Gatwick to Canada's Niagara Falls International Airport on a charter flight with our instruments, amplifiers and luggage. We were met by Mr Piazza's lawyer who came in his Cadillac followed by a large pick-up truck. He drove us and our baggage over the Canadian border at Fort Erie into Buffalo and to the large apartment which would be home for the coming weeks. From the window we could see a large illuminated sign outside The Showboat announcing *"The British Are Coming"*. We opened on the 14th August 1971 and all went well with entertaining this American audience who were entirely different to those we had been used to on the ship. These were not wealthy cruisers, just locals having a night out and they knew how to party. The most enduring memories of this period are not to do with performing but with soaking up the atmosphere of everyday life in the USA. Buffalo was an unattractive industrial town but it was close to the natural wonder of Niagara Falls where we were to spend many happy hours.

We never knew how we had acquired our work permits for this contract – we did ask the question and were told *"it was fixed"* so we assumed John J. Piazza had influence somewhere! But it was a different story for Sue, who had agreed to fly over and stay with me for the last three weeks of the contract. I got a letter from her after we arrived in Buffalo explaining that she had been to the US Consulate in Liverpool to arrange a visitor's visa but it had been refused because she didn't have a regular job in the UK – she was still a freelance model and there would be a risk of her not leaving the US when the visa ran out. It was a great disappointment which I mentioned to The Showboat's lawyer who had now become a friend. He suggested that if she flew into Canada, where she did not require a visa, he could smuggle her over the border. So this is what we did – she flew into Toronto. I hired a car to collect her from the airport and booked her into the Fort Erie Motel for the night. The following day the lawyer drove over to meet her. He told her to pretend to be asleep when they arrived at the border and he made the crossing at rush hour when the border guards were very busy. Hey presto they arrived at the apartment. We now only had to worry about the departure!

After Sue arrived the owner of the restaurant, John J. Piazza, invited us on his river cruiser for lunch, his lawyer welcomed us at his home for barbecues and pool dipping, we spent lively days at the home of a Polish family who had become fans, and we had a glorious afternoon at Fort Erie Race Track watching and betting on 'trotting' horse races while drinking champagne in an owner's private box.

Three weeks later we packed up the equipment, said our goodbyes and headed for the crossing into Canada and the flight home. It had been a great experience to witness life in a typical American industrial town like Buffalo and to entertain ordinary American audiences instead of the idle rich. We passed the US border without incident – they did not check our visas so Sue got away with her illegal stay. Back in the UK it was time for some rest and recuperation. I spent a blissful week with Sue in Ibiza and then some days catching up with people in Margate before returning to Southampton and rejoining the QE2.

Paradise Beach is waiting for me
Heat of the sun and the cool of the seas
Back there where life is easy and living is free
Paradise Beach is waiting for me
Shade of the leaves on a coco palm tree
Hold on I'm comin' on back to you Paradise Beach
Stephen Gold (Paradise Beach)

America

After the crossing to New York we embarked on another winter season of cruises around the Caribbean. I entered this second season with an entirely different view of life working on board a ship. I had started to see different traits in people that I hadn't noticed during my first euphoric year when I was caught up in the glamour of it all. Now I started to see some of the downsides of ship life. It could sometimes seem claustrophobic. I began to feel a bit constrained and found myself wanting to do more with my days than sit about waiting for the next show. I wanted to write songs and record again but the atmosphere on board did not inspire me. I went ashore whenever possible and still enjoyed some fabulous days on these exotic islands, but I realised that long term cruise ship life wasn't for me. There were musicians and entertainers on board who were ideally suited to the life and you could easily imagine that they would be content to stay permanently on the ship. Others, like myself, got restless and this turned to moodiness and often to petty arguments which would have an effect on several relationships over the following months.

New York Nuptials

One situation, with the potential to foul things up, started to take shape early in the new season. Bobby and Anne had a 7 year old son who was at a residential school in Bournemouth. Feeling guilty about leaving him for so long, they had arranged for us to have a two week break in order to fly home for Christmas. This suited me as I could spend some time with Sue. It had been agreed with the on-shore head of entertainment,

Terry Conroy, who clearly hadn't communicated it to the QE2 cruise director Jon Butt. We began to realise that arrangements hadn't been put in place and it wasn't going to happen. We protested strongly and Jon suggested a compromise. He would arrange passage for their son to join them for the Christmas cruise if they arranged and paid for the flights. My girlfriend was not considered important enough to warrant providing her with a free cruise. It would obviously have pissed off other entertainers who would have been delighted to have their wives and girlfriends on the ship. I was furious. I had made arrangements to spend a big slice of the Christmas break with Sue in London and Sheffield. After some lively arguing Jon Butt came up with a cunning compromise scheme. If we invented a New York wedding scenario – that Sue and I would be getting married in a romantic ceremony in the Big Apple – he was confident he could get approval for a free cruise for my new 'wife'.

This was all quickly arranged and their son Mark arrived in New York with Sue on Saturday the 18th December 1971 to embark for the Christmas Cruise. In all the time I had worked on the ship I had never encountered the captain anywhere but on the bridge or at the captain's cocktail party. That was about to change rather alarmingly. As I walked with Sue to the cabin that we had been allocated I spotted the captain coming in the opposite direction. He proffered his hand and proceeded to congratulate us on our marriage – the problem was I hadn't got round to telling Sue how we had wangled her free cruise. A rather embarrassed silence ensued before the captain went on his way, probably thinking we had already had our first marital tiff. Fortunately our ruse was not exposed and the cruise passed without any further embarrassing incidents.

I strutted around proudly with this beautiful girl by my side but it was during the two weeks together on board that I started to doubt the strength of the relationship. I had arranged some tours which she declined to take up and she was occasionally moody. For the first time I had a feeling that some of the reasons why she was still attracted to me were to do with what I could provide – this cruise, Buffalo, Ibiza. But I dismissed these thoughts and I was sad when the cruise came to an end. I saw her onto the flight in New York and she promised that she would be in Southampton to meet me when the ship returned in April.

On Saturday the 29th January 1972 *'Ziggy Stardust and The Spiders From Mars' played their first gig in The Friars Club at Aylesbury. It was the start of a meteoric rise for the character from out of this world. Unknown to me at the time my exaggerated 'Lower Third' reminiscences were about to be given a boost.*

The Cracks Appear

Early in the new year the atmosphere on board started to turn sour. I suspected that all was not right between my two partners. It soon became clear that Anne was attracted to the bass player in the new trio playing the bars. He was a young good looking guy who, I imagine, was flattered by the attention of this very attractive older woman. Rumours started to circulate and questions asked of me about the affair that I could not answer. It was impossible for me to discuss

Unparallel Careers!

this with Bobby or Anne so I took myself away from them for most of the day, just meeting up for the shows.

Over the winter I had become very friendly with the girls who worked on board for Steiner's hairdressers and often hung out with one of them on visits ashore. Before we headed back across the Atlantic I heard that Bobby was attempting to start an affair with the youngest and most vulnerable of the girls who was quite naive and new to ship life. I felt compelled to warn her that she was the subject of less than flattering jokes by some of the musicians who found out that she'd spent time in Bobby's cabin – presumably while Anne was elsewhere with the bass player. I should not have interfered but it was unfair on a young person who was at the start of her career on the ship – she would carry her 'easy' reputation long after we had departed. All this confirmed my view that incestuous ship life was not going to be part of my future.

There were some other distractions during that winter of 1972. On one unforgettable stop-over in Haiti I took a taxi to the Jane Barbencourt rum distillery with several of the musicians, among whom was a sax player who everyone considered a pain in the arse. On our way back to the ship this 'pain' asked to stop so that he could take a photograph. He set off down a track and quickly encountered a mangy dog which took a bite out of his backside. Unable to contain ourselves we nevertheless took him to a local village doctor for a rabies jab. The place was filthy and so was the doctor who charged him a big wedge of US dollars for the privilege. He survived but not without some humiliation back on board!

Batten Down The Hatches
(Atlantic Hurricane)

On the 16th April we left New York on the return voyage to Southampton. Two days out in the North Atlantic the ship ran into a hurricane. This enormous ship began to be tossed around like a cork. On the first day, as the winds increased, it became difficult to move about safely but nevertheless all activities went ahead. We played sitting down and propped against a wall while we watched the cruise staff with amusement as they attempted to set up the big band's music stands only to see them fall like a pack of cards each time the ship rolled heavily.

After battling on for a day and a half the captain decided to sail south to escape the worst of the winds and then turn east towards Europe again. That evening dinner went ahead as usual but while the waiters tried heroically to carry on serving the ship began to roll alarmingly. Although the restaurant was on a high deck, as we rolled I could see the sea close to the restaurant windows and I panicked that one more severe roll could take the ship over. The next one didn't capsize the ship but it cleared the restaurant. Waiters were left running involuntarily before spilling their trays of food. Crockery and glassware slid off the tables and smashed, people fell from their seats and food from the buffet and servery poured onto the floor. I could hear the shouts of panicked and injured people and the sound of chaos in the kitchens nearby. Thankfully the rolling started to correct itself and after a few minutes the ship was comparatively stable again. I learnt afterwards that the

Unparallel Careers!

captain had attempted his turn to the east, thus putting the ship side on to the winds and waves! After this incident he had rapidly turned to the south again and halted to ride out the storm. A junior officer told me later that at the moment of the big roll the senior officers on the bridge were, in his words, shitting themselves. The ship was fairly new, only two years at sea, and had never encountered weather this severe before. A number of crew members and passengers were injured that evening. In one instance a grand piano tipped over and fell from the stage breaking the arm of a crew member who was trying to stop it doing more damage.

Over the next two days, while we rode out the storm, the passengers disappeared to their cabins and the main areas of the ship were deserted. It was not safe to be in the big public rooms where some of the large picture windows gave way against the gusts and shattered. The crew shored up the gaping holes with wooden panels. I was nearby when one window blew in and the noise was immense from the breaking glass and the howling of the wind. All doors to the outer decks were roped shut and the lifts put out of action. Ropes were stretched along the interior gangways to help anyone trying to move about.

I never once felt remotely seasick in spite of the constant rolling and pitching but hundreds of the passengers suffered and the doctor and nurses were kept busy for the rest of the voyage. On the third day of the storm I ventured up to the public rooms because I was going stir crazy in my cabin. In the almost deserted Double Down Room I saw a girl sitting alone and in passing the time of day we struck up a conversation.

America

Herta was a croupier in the ship's casino and, amazingly, I had never seen her during her months on board. She was a highly fanciable blonde German with immaculate English and I was instantly attracted.

The following day the storm abated slightly and the captain decided to get underway again and head for home. We were now several days late and would miss out a stop at Le Havre in France and go directly to Southampton where we would arrive two days behind schedule. The ship would have to turn around very quickly for the final Mediterranean cruise. Almost as I started to worry about having time to spend with Sue in Southampton I received a telegram via the ship to shore service which said quite simply *"Will not be at Southampton, best wishes, Sue."* I knew straight away that it was over – no point in replying. I saw her once again several years later when I was performing in Sheffield. We arranged to meet for lunch and afterwards we walked in the hills outside the city. She held my hand and acted as though no years had passed, it was quite bizarre. I was pleased that it was still clear to me that we could not have survived as a couple. I'd certainly loved her, but didn't really like her very much. I never saw her again.

On the last day of the voyage all the passengers were issued with a special certificate commemorating the adventure and on the last night the captain appeared in the showrooms to great applause and to the singing of *'For He's A Jolly Good Fellow'*. Little did they know that the ship had probably been endangered by the captain's decision to plough on through one of the worst North Atlantic hurricanes ever recorded.

Unparallel Careers!

The situation between my two partners did not improve but the young bass player left the ship in Southampton which eased tensions during our final cruise to Mediterranean ports. After receiving the *'Dear John'* telegram I met up with Herta during the last days of the Atlantic crossing and we decided to enjoy the last cruise together. We visited the apes on The Rock of Gibralter, took a ferry to the Isle of Capri and climbed the steps of the Acropolis in Athens. I felt somehow liberated because deep down I had always known that the relationship with Sue would not survive and I am eternally grateful to Herta for filling in the void at that sensitive time. I saw her just once more after the cruise when she visited me in South Devon the following summer.

As we disembarked for a final time in Southampton I knew that it was the end of an exciting and unforgettable experience. I had been to places that I never dreamed I would visit. I had experienced performing in the real America, wondered wide eyed at Niagara Falls, partied on Long Island, thrown up in Barbados, 'married' in New York, met up with my nephew in The Bahamas and lots more besides. But I knew I would never want to return to ship life.

Another close encounter? *Soon after I sailed from New York for the last time on the QE2 the ship carried another ex 'Lower Third' member in the opposite direction. Ziggy Stardust was among the passengers travelling to The Big Apple. Bowie was afraid of flying, because of a dreamed premonition of a crash, so he'd elected to go by sea. He had, ironically, chosen a ship that had almost come to grief battered by 100 m.p.h winds and 50 foot waves in the great hurricane!*

America

The Wilderness Again

I remained with *'The Bigwoods'* and we secured a contract for the summer of 1972 touring Pontin's Holiday Centres in South Devon where we staged a two hour show with our own lighting and sound system. It was primitive by today's standards, but nevertheless very successful at each venue we played. We invested in a Volkswagen van for the touring and also took our own cars. I had, by then, bought a Mark 2 Jaguar from the manager of the Royal Exeter Hotel in Bournemouth where we had appeared a few times before the season started. I passed on the Ford Corsair to my Dad. Bobby drove a Triumph Spitfire and between us we looked a right pair of flash gits! We rented a farmhouse near the village of Stoke Gabriel and spent a pleasant summer in the countryside.

*'**Ziggy Stardust and The Spiders From Mars**' played a concert at the nearby Torquay Town Hall on the 16th June and I was able to tell anyone who was prepared to listen that Ziggy was David Bowie who sang with my band 'The Lower Third'. I never missed an opportunity!*

While in Devon the relationship between us started to falter. I wanted to try for a record deal and in the meantime I arranged a trial recording session at the BBC in London. We recorded two songs at Broadcasting House and were added to the 'approved list' of bands available for live music shows, which were still broadcast regularly in 1972.

The irony! *It only emerged in 2018, while I was still writing this, that Bowie had been rejected by the BBC after a similar* *trial recording when with 'The Lower Third'. The BBC panel had been scathing about his voice saying that he sang "wrong notes and out of tune" and "he was devoid of personality." Wow!*

However, 'The Bigwoods' never made another recording for the BBC whereas Bowie made dozens on both radio and television. A good definition of ironic?

I contacted agents I had worked for previously and pulled in some dates in northern clubs to follow the summer season. My colleagues weren't happy with that, or my attempts to develop other projects for us, and it resulted in an almighty row in which I was criticised for being 'too ambitious' and was called a 'stupid little businessman' by an irate Bobby. In retrospect they were probably right. I was trying to change them into something they were not – they had established themselves as the popular trio and were happy to stay that way. I couldn't argue with that, but it was not my view of the future.

Over time the atmosphere improved between the three of us. I gave up trying to manage the act and decided to look for a new direction as soon as possible. The winter of 1972/3 was not a happy period for me. After dates in the North East we spent a month in Nottingham at The Black Boy Inn. To help pass that dreary winter period I had occasional after-show nights with a travelling bank representative. She visited Nottingham frequently, for two or three days at a time, and was interesting and attractive but with no intention of creating any ties. It suited me that way. I got to Margate for a family Christmas and was joined by a girl

America

I'd met in a Newcastle nightclub a few weeks before. That didn't last beyond the New Year celebrations!

In January *'The Bigwoods'* took up a residency at the Royal Exeter Hotel in Bournemouth and I rented a luxury flat in Westbourne. I was bored with the shows which we were playing to small, mostly unenthusiastic audiences – it was a bleak January. Bobby and Anne returned to their house in Broadstone every night and I wandered back to the flat. I had no friends in Bournemouth and spent the days watching daytime TV and reading books. It was broken only by a couple of dates with girls I met at The Exeter, one of whom, and I remember it well, stood me up which added to my misery that winter.

Back Out West

Searching for a new direction I hit on the idea of offering a touring version of my wild west show to Pontins for the 1973 season to cover the slot that *'The Bigwoods'* had filled the previous summer. To my amazement the offer was instantly greeted with enthusiasm and I quickly signed a contract for 5 months starting in May. I set about re-writing the script so that the show would work with a cast of six, three of whom would need to be musicians as well as singers. I arranged auditions in London and recruited a guitar duo (The Circles – Bob and John). Next was a pianist with a wife who could sing and dance and an American lead female singer (Cathy Cota). I was to play the sheriff and the guitar duo would be the deputies. Cathy played the part of the saloon hostess. My deal with Bob and John included the use of their sound system plus the use

Unparallel Careers!

of their transit van to transport all the stage equipment, costumes and bits of scenery.

I had arranged all this while still playing each evening with Bobby and Anne who, meanwhile, had accepted a further contract for *'The Bigwoods'* to remain at The Royal Exeter Hotel for the summer season. I had to break it to them that I was leaving. I did it one night after the show and it was an ugly scene. We didn't get on so well by then so I was surprised that they felt so disappointed and thought I was being disloyal. But as the song says *'Breaking Up Is Hard To Do'*. We had been together for over two years and had experienced some good times together along the way so I was sad that we didn't end on the best of terms. I'm pleased to say that we met from time to time in later years and only talked about the good things.

Before the new season began I got together with The Circles and Cathy Cota at a studio in Broadstairs and recorded an album of the popular western songs that we would feature in the show. I also designed a souvenir programme based on the original Danny Arnold programme from The Golden Garter Saloon. The records and programmes were on sale at each performance and added greatly to my income.

Summer 1973 was hard work. I rented a couple of rooms in a house at Paignton but did not see much of it except to sleep. We travelled every day in time to set up the sound system and bits of scenery which consisted of a jail house that bolted together and a 'hanging tree'. It was a two hour show which featured well known western songs such as *'Ghost Riders In The Sky'* and *'Wanderin' Star'*, plus medleys from the musicals

'Oklahoma' and *'Annie Get Your Gun'*. It was a hard slog and there were no 'understudies'. We could get by if we were one man down, but that man could not be me! I developed a bad cough mid way through the season which I couldn't shake off and one particular night, when dosed up with Benolyn Expectorant cough syrup and several 'medicinal' whiskies, I noticed that the audience were out of focus. I had difficulty gripping the microphone let alone delivering coherent words. I somehow made it through and did not miss one performance during the whole season.

As the summer neared its end I started to think about what to do next. Through my undying devotion to the songs of Jimmy Webb I had become a great fan of the five piece American vocal group The Fifth Dimension. I had also heard a few tracks by a British group called Blackwater Junction, with a similar line-up of three guys and two girls, who were all session singers. With the Pontin's contract fees and the sale of programmes and records I had accumulated some, not inconsiderable, funds over the summer season and decided to embark on an ambitious project to set up and finance a similar vocal act which would be able to tour and make records.

Over the season I had formed a good relationship with Bob and John both personally and on stage, where our three part harmonies blended well, so it seemed natural to approach them about the new group. They were immediately enthusiastic so I set about advertising for girls to join the group. We auditioned several girls who were working in the Devon area and one of them, who was dancing in the summer show at The Princess Theatre at Torquay, fitted the voice and image I was seeking. I offered her a place in the group beginning with rehearsals in November. Her name was Linda Turtle (stage name Lynne Lacey and later Linda Quinton-Jones).

About ten days before the season ended Bob and John told me they had changed their minds about the new group. They had been offered immediate work as The Circles and decided that it was safer than starting something new with me. It was necessary to have a long hard think about my next move. I had committed to Lynne Lacey and felt I needed to let her off the hook as soon as possible so that she could find another job. But I hesitated – I needed more time to think.

Heart Over Head

The summer had been a barren time socially so I was excited, during the last week of the season, when I noticed a gorgeous girl with long blonde hair sitting with an older couple in the audience and beaming radiantly every time I glanced in her direction. I plucked up the courage to corner her after the show and discovered she was visiting her parents for two nights while they were holidaying at Pontins. She lived in Thornton Heath near London and worked for Hertz Car Rentals at Gatwick Airport. We shared a couple of drinks and went on to a late night bar. I saw her again the next night and persuaded her to come down to Devon for the last weekend for Pontin's end of season staff ball.

When you're near I get a chill right through my body
Melt you down and light a fire inside you baby tonight
Stephen Gold (Cool Lady)

She stayed in my flat at Paignton and by then I was seriously besotted. But there was a bizarre twist to come. After I returned to Margate I went to see her a few times in London and was getting heavily involved. Trudi told me she had been having an affair with a married man for some time. He had promised to leave his wife but, as is not uncommon, had not gone through with it. I was just beginning to see her as the start of something wonderful when, out of the blue, she turned up in Margate in the Mercedes of a wealthy estate agent who she introduced as her boyfriend and said *"I've told him that we had a couple of nights in Devon but that it's all over now."* He said *"I believe her but I need you to confirm that it's over."*

She sat beside him with pleading eyes and I thought, *this isn't real – I was with her in a hotel room two days ago and now this.* I looked directly at her and agreed it was over. They left and I never saw her again. Two or three years later when flying out from Gatwick I wandered, out of curiosity, to the Hertz desk and asked for her - she was not on duty!

> *Here I am again right back where I started from*
> *I really don't know what went wrong*
> *Here I am again back in the same old place*
> *I hear your voice and see your face with him*
> **Stephen Gold (Here I Am Again)**

I quickly came down to earth and realised that I was never going to run off and start a new life with someone I hardly knew and who was still attached to her married lover. They had saved me from myself! I made up my mind there and then that I would keep my promise to Lynne Lacey. The vocal group I had planned would not be five but three, myself and two girls. Could it be the perfect trilogy? This was to be the start of a project that would see out the 1970s and open all sorts of new and exciting avenues in the future.

The Bigwoods

'The British Are Coming' Buffalo 1971

On Paradise Beach with my favourite hairdresser 1971

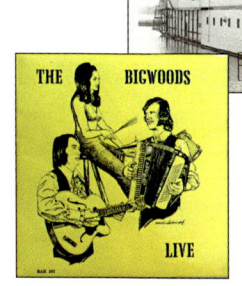

The Twin Towers under construction from the deck of the QE2 in 1970

Count Basie Band - QE2 1972

Senegal 1971

Roaring Twenties!

Sue on board and skiing under the bows of the QE2 Nassau, Bahamas 1971

QUEEN ELIZABETH 2

STORM CERTIFICATE

This is to record that on her North Atlantic voyage, leaving New York on the 16th April 1972, for Southampton, England, **RMS QUEEN ELIZABETH 2**, of 65,863 gross tons, encountered exceptionally severe weather in position Latitude 42°18′ North, Longitude 55°52′ West.

During this storm, winds reached speeds in excess of 100mph. Combined with a heavy swell, waves were encountered of 50 feet in height.

This weather caused even the **QUEEN ELIZABETH 2**, with her exceptional size and sea-keeping qualities, to lie hove to for 21½ hours between 17th and 19th April 1972, until the storm abated.

I commend all passengers in sharing this unique experience with great cheerfulness and calm.

Captain

Chapter 5
Trilogy

An artistic work in three parts
A triple whammy or a threefold disaster
Who knew, who cared
Except the servants and the master?

Ziggy Stardust had announced his retirement *on stage at the Hammersmith Odeon. 'Life On Mars', 'The Gene Jeanie' and 'The Laughing Gnome', Bowie's odd little song from yesteryear, had all charted and he was the best selling UK artiste of 1973. And me? I had managed to get some money together and was about to form an exciting new act – our careers had spectacularly diverged by this time!*

By November 1973 I had decided on a name for the act and auditioned a number of possible candidates for the third place. At one London audition I offered the place to a girl from Manchester called Carole Wallwork (stage name Carole Seton and later St.James and later still Jardine). She attended the audition having taken a train down to London and, after I offered her the job, she asked if I could lend her the train fare back to Manchester as she'd only had enough money for a one way fare. It was an inauspicious start to the partnership and a story that I would embarrass her with over the coming years.

Earlier that year I had taken on the lease of a small cafe in Margate and my Dad had tarted it up for my eldest sister Jean to run. My justification for such a move was that it was 'something to fall back on' if the showbiz failed. There was a small flat above the shop and this enabled me to move out of the family home and also accommodate the two girls.

We started rehearsing in a nearby church hall and the first version of the *'Trilogy'* act was with me playing guitar and electric piano on most of the songs. The instruments were soon dropped. It was a hassle I could do without when travelling in a car with the costumes, our personal luggage and my newly acquired sound system. Also quickly dropped was my beloved Mark 2 Jag as it was patently unsuited to the job. I acquired a large Mercedes with an enormous boot and this would serve us well for the next few years.

After dropping the instruments my vision for the act was to have each song fully choreographed and that was how I approached it - with me putting in the least effort, being a poor dancer, and the girls making me look good. I stole this technique from the well known dancer of that era, Peter Gordeno, who, as he got older and I suppose stiffer, got his girl dancers to do all the work while he just looked cool in the centre. My reason for using his technique was not down to advanced age or stiffness but to a glaring lack of dance ability.

Trilogy

We worked on up-tempo songs such as *'Love Train'* (The Ojays), *'Swinging On A Star'* (Big Dee Irvin & Little Eva), and *'If It Feels Good Do It'* (Della Reece), interspersed with big ballads - *'Bridge Over Troubled Water'* being one we always featured.

My deal with the girls was pretty simple. I would finance the set up period, including the cost of their daily expenses, and pay for all stage costumes, photographs, music and transport. For this I would take half of future earnings while they shared the rest. This arrangement worked for us throughout the 70s. I had several costume sets made and incorporated costume changes into the act. All had to be photographed to produce the initial promotional material which I circulated to all the agents that I knew.

Lynne Lacey was from Cramlington, near Newcastle, in the heart of the North-East club circuit and it was to there that we went in the spring of 1974 after contacts with agents in the area proved fruitful.

It was a year of strikes and power cuts while the Prime Minister, Edward Heath, the 'Old Boy' from my grammer school, tried to wrestle with the unions. I didn't give politics a second thought at the time and, in spite of the occasional disruption, just soldiered on regardless and avoided the worst of it.

I can't recall many of the clubs we played or how it went on those first dates because it all went by in a blur, but I do recall staying with Lynne's parents and venturing out each evening to discover a different working men's club in the pit villages or industrial areas of the region. It would sometimes be 'a double' – dashing from one club to another without the aid of a SatNav!

Sometimes we needed Lynne, whose accent reverted strongly to Geordie when we were in the area, to translate for us when asking directions.

The influence of the northern working men's clubs as a fertile breeding ground for artistes and musicians who became household names is well documented, as are the idiosyncrasies of the clubs' 'concert secretaries' who booked and introduced the artistes. A number of comedians of that era based their acts on parodying these and other club officials from whom there were endless funny examples. I remember one amusing instance in a club where the concert secretary concluded all his announcements with the words '*mighty fine*'. "*The snack bar is now open, mighty fine.*" - "*Welcome on the stage Trilogy, mighty fine.*" - "*Get your bingo tickets now, mighty fine.*" On this particular Sunday lunchtime, just after he had introduced us and we had started into the first number, he interrupted us to say "*Important announcement – will the owner of car number HXY 93R go to his vehicle as the windows have been smashed and the radio stolen, mighty fine.*"

So much for the North-East where we played several weeks during that first year. The drive up the M1 and A1 from the south was always tedious and my heart would sink every time we approached the spot on the A1 where the industrial chimneys of Middlesbrough came into view over on our right.

Mist floats in from North Sea winds
and makes the outlook grey
The people with their narrow lives
impress me the same way

Trilogy

> *The grime of ages past remains*
> *on buildings there to see*
> *And tells me this is just a place*
> *it's better not to be*
> **Stephen Gold (Sunderland 1972)**

After all I was a softy southerner and, whilst the people were always good to us, it felt like an alien place and an alien way of life after my years in Jersey and on the QE2. The upside was that we were able to hone the act by working with different musicians at every club, some excellent, most mediocre and the occasional real bummers – it was always a challenge and we sometimes lost!

Military Manoeuvres (CSE)

During the spring and summer we performed several 'promotional shows' for which we didn't get paid – let's call them auditions. One such performance was in a little private theatre near the Thames Embankment in Central London. It was here that we first met Derek Agutter, whose daughter Jenny was the star of the 1971 film 'Walkabout' in which she had managed to stir many male juices.

Derek was the director of CSE – Combined Services Entertainment - the modern incarnation of the old wartime armed services showbiz organisation ENSA. His bearing and personality was every bit the ex-army officer while his deputy, Johnny Harris, was every bit the civil servant – at least this is how they appeared when sober. The agent who introduced us to Derek and Johnny was Al Heath, and he called me the day after our appearance at the little theatre with some dates for our first taste of CSE touring. So it was that in September 1974 we travelled to British bases in Germany and then for the first of many times to Northern Ireland during the height of the 'troubles'. The fee was £175.00 for each of these first tours plus travel and accommodation costs.

On the visits to Northern Ireland we stayed in a hotel either on the outskirts of Belfast or Londonderry depending on the tour itinerary. The schedule was always tight – just three days in which there were four or five shows in different locations. Some were in permanent army barracks and others in makeshift outposts which were often set up in old warehouses or factories.

Travelling to and from the bases by road or by helicopter was a little tense and on the tour coach we were usually accompanied by armed soldiers in civilian dress. Sometimes there would be an escort of armoured jeeps front and rear. The tours were always managed by either Derek Agutter or Johny Harris and by the end of each evening they were invariably somewhat inebriated. At this point safety often went out of the window. The personalities of the two men were poles apart when drunk. Derek became the jovial prankster while Johnny got morose and abusive. Fortunately, in my experience, they were never both on a tour together.

When fully charged with alcohol Derek would quite often forgo the escort, especially if it was delayed for some reason, and we would set off from the last base at around midnight in a hurry to get to the hotel before the bar closed. He had a party piece which he performed on the coach now and again, especially if there were new people on tour. Its reputation went before it and it was anticipated on our first tour. He had oversized testicles which he would suddenly display on a large glass ashtray - hardly a stunning sight but in an alcohol fuelled moment it seemed hilarious coming from someone who was so correct when sober. On one such unescorted late night drive, while bantering with the coach driver about the quickest way back to the hotel, he threw his overcoat over the head of said driver and shouted *"Now find your way back."* We all experienced a moment of panic before someone grabbed the coat.

Tours with Derek were always fun but not so with Johnny Harris. He would get very drunk and I suspect he was well on the way to being an alcoholic by then. He would often fall out with the base personnel who were in charge of the set up for the show. This would make it very awkward for us and it was always necessary to apologise for his behaviour. He would be last on the coach when leaving and, slurring his speech, he would castigate and abuse us all about anything he could think of. We took it all with a false seriousness and it was difficult to keep a straight face when he was in full flow.

The regular coach driver in Northern Ireland, Alf, usually got a tongue lashing and late one night, when we had waited too long on the coach for Johnny to appear, Alf was anticipating the worst. When Johnny started up the front coach steps with a tirade of abuse Alf suddenly pulled away causing him to fall back into the stairwell where he remained trapped, legs in the air, until we reached the hotel. Sadly, and inevitably, Johnny died some years later from alcohol related problems.

Unparallel Careers!

The CSE set up was interesting to say the least. Apart from Derek and Johnny there were full time road managers and technicians and some office staff based in London. I think their salaries were augmented by various financial deviations. One such was known by artistes and musicians as 'The Fiddle Sheet' which was produced in Northern Ireland during the coach ride from RAF Aldergove to the hotel. We all had to sign for expenses which were for rehearsals the previous day at the CSE headquarters in London. Rehearsals that never took place and expenses we never received. In return we would be given a great lunch with drinks on arrival at the hotel. I assume these expenses, being paid out in cash, went into the CSE management 'retirement fund'.

Apart from the sometimes fraught, but always fun, trips to Northern Ireland during the 70s there were further interesting CSE tours to Gibralter, Germany and Ben Becular in the Outer Hebrides where the army had a missile testing range. The highlight of the Ben Becular trip was discovering the rugged wind swept terrain and visiting a small converted crofter's cottage which boasted over 100 different whiskies for sale. I was able to sample several of the wonderful old single malts.

But by far the most exciting of all the CSE tours was to The Middle East in 1977. It started with a night flight from RAF Brize Norton to the RAF base on Masira Island which is in the Indian Ocean off the coast of Oman. The flight was by an RAF VC10 aircraft mainly carrying freight for resupplying the base and it was disconcerting to sit facing the rear of the plane as was apparently the norm on RAF passenger flights.

We were flown immediately from Masira Island to

Trilogy

Salalah, in the south of Oman, by an RAF Hercules Transporter. I got to spend some interesting time on the flight deck during the journey. It was surprising how relaxed the aircrew were in comparison to today's stringent aircraft security. They even briefed one of the girls to call the control tower on the landing approach to announce the aircraft's imminent arrival - much to the air traffic controller's surprise. We did two shows at Salalah where RAF personnel were on secondment to the RAFO (Royal Air Force of Oman). They trained Omani recruits and helped to monitor aggressive rebels on the border with Yemen.

Heading up our show was The Terry Lightfoot Band – a well known traditional jazz band of that era. There was also a dance group, Charade, and comedian Jimmy Marshall. This tour was, unfortunately, under the direction of Johnny Harris. As usual he proceeded to get very drunk and abusive on the first night which, understandably, did not go down well in the RAF officers' mess.

Before leaving Salalah I had a long and very interesting session on the live firing range with several types of lethal weapons and a kind officer, Squadron Leader Tony Wilkinson, took two of us for a flight in a four seater helicopter. We soared over the barren landscape and down near to the Yemeni border where we hovered a while to gain height so as to avoid being fired on by rebels in the hills. We returned low along the beaches watching the traditional dhows fishing off the coast. I was exhilarated by the experience and on a high when we boarded the Hercules for the flight back to Masira Island.

Unparallel Careers!

The base at Masira was on its last few months of service before the RAF pulled out for good and handed it back to Oman. As it was already partly closed down when we arrived the remaining personnel had very little to do. This meant that they entertained us almost more than we entertained them. Three nights of shows were followed by three days of unique experiences when the RAF officers and men, who had maintained a number of World War 2 vehicles, provided us with some unusual adventures.

We crossed the desert in old wartime Jeeps to search for fossils and took a land and sea trip in a DUCK (WW2 American amphibious vehicle). They had also restored a railway line from the 1930s that was used to supply the base with drums of fuel from the nearby port and we enjoyed a journey on the old diesel powered train down to the sea. On the last day we had a spin in a helicopter of the Royal Omani Police Force. This was a fourteen seater and a very different experience to the previous helicopter flight.

There was to be a final addition to the excitement of this tour. The night before our departure for the UK we were informed that the VC10, which had arrived to take us back, was being diverted to Nairobi in Kenya to pick up the then Defence Secretary, Fred Mulley. We went with it and spent a great night in Nairobi. We had a short tour of the city, drinks at the New Stanley Hotel and dinner at The Jacaranda Hotel where we spent the night. The following day we took off with the Defence Secretary and his entourage on board. The flight then landed at Akrotiri RAF base in Cyprus where we were stuck for a few hours, while Mr Mulley held meetings, before the final leg back to Brize Norton. A diary reminds me that we eventually reached Margate at 4am the next morning – exhausted after driving through fog and snow. What a trip!

Filling In

A breed that everybody loves
because of laughs they get
From living under roofs of those
who do the weekly let
The heat that turns on by request
at just a nominal charge
The shower where you hardly wet
and toast adorned with marge
The telephone with coinbox
situated in the hall
She gives you keys for late night life
but an early morning call
But though I knock these ladies fair
with husbands under thumb
We always come to think of them
just like a second mum
Stephen Gold (Landladies)

The act soon became fully established on the cabaret club circuit and we travelled from town to town each week staying in 'pro digs' – the showbiz name for guest houses that catered for us wandering minstrels. It was always good to return to familiar places and to meet other acts and musicians. A time to swap news and the usually highly embellished anecdotes about clubs, acts and not so welcoming digs.

Unparallel Careers!

This conversation was, of course, always my chance to somehow bring the chat round to my background in 'The Lower Third' and to the band's singer who was now a superstar and living in America. It never ceased to impress people but I always qualified it by saying that the band had broken up years before he made it big, so there could be no regrets on my part! It is a fact that Bowie was, by 1974, firmly addicted to cocaine. I, on the other hand, was never seriously tempted beyond alcohol and our similarities ten years on from 'The Lower Third' could not have been less numerous.

I started to get contracts for *'Trilogy'* to support top line artistes of that era and during the summer we appeared with the American singing star Jack Jones at The Commodore Banqueting Suite in Nottingham. Jack was big business in 1974 and all the more so because of his affair with actress Susan George. She had starred in the 1971 film 'Straw Dogs' with Dustin Hoffman and the famous rape scene was astonishing for its time. Men drooled over her and I was one of them! One night she suddenly appeared backstage and my drooling turned to amazement to find she was quite the normal 'girl next door' and not the sex symbol from the film – always a pity to break the fantasy. The next time I saw Susan George was about twenty years later in a supermarket near Windsor – that really broke the magic. I was particularly pleased to work with Jack Jones because I had sung one of his hit songs every night for two years in Jersey - *'Seeing The Right Love Go Wrong'*.

A month in Malta was a welcome break, just being in one place for a while. I needed to take stock as I was not completely happy with the act – it was not accurate enough with the vocal harmonies and not consistent in performance. There was still a lot of work to do to find the best formula between the three of us who, it was now clear to me, had very different talents. Lynne was streets ahead in the choreographed routines, I was struggling with movement but streets ahead with the singing, and Carole fell somewhere in the middle. Not an easy mix but, given the time I had spent working on it, one that I hoped would endure and improve. We needed to be vying for chart success not wallowing in clubland. It was time to make progress not least because I needed to make money.

I heard it reported in 1975 *that Bowie was existing on 'a pittance' due to legal disputes with his sacked manager which had cost him millions in compensation. His lawyer took over as his manager and also took him for a tidy sum a year or so later. I can't say I felt unduly sorry for him – I imagined by that time 'a pittance' to him was probably akin to my income for the decade! Well, at least it gave me another talking point.*

Early in 1975 my old agent from the Jersey years, Billy Forrest, was looking for acts for various summer season clients. I had sent him the *'Trilogy'* publicity and he responded by suggesting we appeared in a showcase he was organising at a club near Birmingham. When we arrived I was disappointed to see that there were dozens of other artistes and musicians in the club. With the arrogant confidence of believing that *'Trilogy'* was already more successful than the other contenders I decided to approach the great man thinking my two long seasons in Jersey, paying him lots of commission, would give us a head start. I strode towards him through the waiting acts with my expensive sheepskin coat draped stylishly over my shoulders trying to look pompously superior to the others. As I drew near one sleeve of my sheepskin swung around and cleared a large number of beer glasses and their contents from a table onto the floor more or less at his feet. I apologised profusely and, to make my embarrassment even worse, he didn't recognise me – I had to explain who I was and where I had worked for him back in 1969. He then nodded in recognition, but it clearly didn't mean much to him. It kind of summed up the man!

By this time I felt like telling the girls to pack up our gear and load the car but, fortunately, I swallowed my pride and we eventually went on stage. The outcome looked positive and the possibility of a long and lucrative season on the Isle of Man emerged. It was there where I would meet our future manager.

Egypt

I had secured a contract to appear at The Sheraton Hotel on the banks of the River Nile in the heart of Cairo. This first visit to the fabled Egyptian city was an experience like no other I had encountered. The hotel was excellent but the apartment we were allocated to share with three girl dancers was large but basic and dirty. I managed to persuade the hotel general manager to have it decorated but almost immediately after the painters arrived I got food poisoning. I was stuck in bed, with the strong smell of new paint invading every part of the apartment, while the army of painters wandered around with their rollers and brushes ignoring the

Englishman throwing up in a bucket.

Before leaving England I had reluctantly agreed to arrange a couple of songs for us to perform with the dancers. But the general manager wanted more and, after my complaints about the apartment, things quickly deteriorated between us. He seemed to want to change the format of the show, something I could not agree to. After a few difficult days I decided to take the pragmatic route. We would grin and bear it - but it was not to be a happy showbiz month!

Cairo was a fascinating city. Naturally we visited the nearby pyramids and the fabulous Cairo museum to see the Tutankhamen treasures but for me the most interesting thing was watching the daily life unfold outside the hotel. The Sheraton was situated on the banks of The Nile next to a very busy and chaotic six lane road which led from the city to the pyramid area. Directly outside was a junction boasting traffic lights that everybody ignored. This made it a life threatening act every time we needed to cross the road to get to the apartment. It was necessary to look for the slightest gap in traffic and then just make a run for it, hoping the cars, trucks and buses avoided you. The mix of vehicles was fascinating. Old 50s American jobs, modern taxis, horse drawn carts, clapped out trucks and the ever entertaining buses which would have people hanging out of every window, clambering on the roof, standing on the back bumpers and jumping on and off as the vehicle passed. All this would be accompanied by a cacophony of noise from the car horns, police sirens, broken exhausts and the population shouting to be heard.

Unparallel Careers!

The Cairo experience included an early morning drive over the desert road to Alexandria in order to spend a day there on a Mediterranean beach. We also took afternoon tea at the celebrated Mena House Hotel, within sight of the Great Pyramid, where many famous people had stayed in the early 20th century – Winston Churchill and Rudyard Kipling among them. In addition we made frequent visits to the various smaller pyramids which, in 1975, you could climb on and walk into at will.

There were the inevitable hawkers selling everything from postcards, souvenirs and sometimes even their own sisters. I can vividly recall a camel owner at the Great Pyramid who would entice clients by naming his camel. For French visitors *"My camel he called Maurice Chevalier"* and for the Brits *"My camel he very good, he called Noel Coward."* For an American victim *"Ten dollar please for picture with my camel, he called Al Jolsen."* The unsuspecting visitor would be invited to pose for a photograph on the sitting camel which would then rise up with visitor on board and on the way to an unwanted and expensive promenade around the desert! I was a keen photographer and in the habit of developing and printing my own photographs and Cairo offered magnificent opportunities to bring back some stunning images for the darkroom.

We were heading up the European show in the Sheraton Nightclub but the real star was an Egyptian belly dancer who followed us each night. Nagwa Fouad was a superstar in Egypt and her band were superb players of highly rhythmic Arabic music. She would sweep in with her entourage of minders, dressers and various hangers on just before her show. On stage she was brilliant at working the audience, who clearly loved the music and her celebrity. It was due to Nagwa that we were privileged to entertain some top American diplomats because she had become a firm favourite of Henry Kissinger. He was engaged in the Egypt/Israel peace mission and he visited the Sheraton Hotel to see her every time he was in Cairo.

One night, after we had performed the song *'Everybody Gets To Go To The Moon'*, an American woman approached me to say we had just sung a song written by her good friend Jimmy Webb. I was thrilled to meet someone who was close to my song writing idol and to chat about his songs and his success. The woman was with a delegation from an American entertainment company who were in Cairo to discuss building a theme park around the pyramids! I thought this laughable and a typically crass and barmy American idea. Twenty-five years later I was to be in Cairo myself on a similar mission!

> *Jimmy, why can't I put them down like you do*
> *Why can't I take them to the top*
> *You must have been born to be great*
> *To write classics at any rate*
> *I wish there was a little of your magic in me.*
> **Stephen Gold (Jimmy)**

Near to the end of our stay I turned down a request, from a chap who had befriended us, to illegally take £2,000 of his money to England – Egyptians could not take more than £70 out of the country at one time. In return he offered to change our Egyptian Pounds to US

Dollars on the black market, but it didn't seem to be a risk worth taking. Contractually we had to take half of our fee in American dollars and the rest in Egyptian pounds that had to be spent before we left. My cash was exported as carvings, costume materials, general tatty souvenirs and a splendid chess board inlaid with elaborately carved ivory and mother of pearl which has sadly not survived the ravages of many moves and much time in storage.

At the end of four long weeks we did the last uneventful show and followed it with a final blast at The Auberge des Pyramids, a disco style nightclub where we had already spent many late nights. We partied until dawn, packed our bags, and checked out of the Cairo Sheraton Hotel with some good memories and a few bad ones. The general manager did not come to see us off!

The early morning flight offered us a magnificent view over the sands of the Sahara, a sight that I would experience several more times in later years. The journey was from the bustle of Cairo to Margate via Beirut and London. Quite an abrupt change of cultures!

On The Record

Dear Mr DJ,
Won't you let this record play
I know it's not your favourite song
But you see it moves along
Gid Taylor (Dear Mr DJ)

A lucky meeting early in 1975 had put me in touch with an independent record producer called Bill Crompton. At the end of the previous year we had recorded some demos with my old friend from *'The Lower Third'*, Terry Bolton, who was then writing solidly under his pen name Gid Taylor. He had offered us two great songs, *'Dear Mr DJ'* and *'Raincheck'*. The demo of the two songs found its way onto Bill Crompton's desk and he called to say he wanted to record and release *'Dear Mr DJ'*.

Over the following weeks we spent several busy days at Bill's studio in London and emerged with a potential hit single only to hear from Bill that an American record had just been released called *'Mr DJ'* and that his distributors, Pye Records, had decided to shelve our *'Dear Mr DJ'* to avoid confusion. Panic, what else did we have?

Terry came up with another cracker called *'Summer Song'*. Back to record again, this time to Weir Sound Studios at Swiss Cottage. Several days later we had completed the new recording and a release date was set for the 18th July – right in the middle of our possible summer season on the Isle of Man. We were still completing the recording sessions for *'Another Just Like You'*, the B-side which I had written in a hurry before leaving for Cairo, when we got a call from Bill Crompton to say his car had been broken into and our master tapes stolen! We would have to re-record *'Summer Song'* from scratch. Starting again at that stage was depressing to say the least, especially as we had dates in the diary that took us away from London for several weeks. We managed to do it by dashing back to London for sessions between dates.

The record was finally released, as planned, on the 18th July and we did whatever we could to promote it from the Isle of Man. It attained the playlist for BBC Radio Two so was heard on a number of programmes over the first weeks of release. Unfortunately it was too 'middle of the road' for Radio One so its chances of success were diminished. Our original single *'Dear Mr DJ'* would have had a much better chance of breaking through.

Coincidentally *'The Lower Third' single with Bowie, in 1966, had also been on the Pye Records label and that didn't sell well either – did that mean anything? Comedians who introduced us on stage often said "It's good that Trilogy's new single is on the Pye label. If you don't like it you can eat it!" That same year (1975) a re-issued single,'Space Oddity', gave Bowie his first number one in the UK. But not on the Pye label!*

At the time I still hoped that a second single would soon follow but it was not to be. Bill Crompton disappeared from view quite quickly and our new manager was not able to secure another record deal quickly enough to capitalize on the exposure of the first single. I found out later that Bill Crompton had moved to Canada in the late 70s and, some years later, had fallen on hard times. He had sold his publishing catalogue and master tapes, including mine, to a Canadian publisher who made contact with me in 2015 – forty years later. A bit late for a re-release!

The spring of '75 had turned out to be a frenetic period. I was in talks with several agents and managers who offered lots but produced little. They were interested because of the impending record release. I was desperate to get a break but the offer to tour with Dukes & Lee, the husband and wife team who were very big business in the clubs and just breaking into TV, wasn't how I saw the act developing. So we kept moving from town to town plying our trade and in the main I was enjoying the search for stardom – I still believed it could happen.

It was exactly ten years since I had left 'The Lower Third'. Life and work had certainly been varied. Unfortunately, no single thing that I had achieved had really captured the enthusiasm of the public. Certainly not in the way that Ziggy Stardust had for Bowie. I sometimes dwelt on that.

Occasionally something did capture the public's attention but not always for the right reasons. For example, in Manchester an amusing incident took place at The Broadway Club where we were playing a week. I had arranged the song *'Bridge Over Troubled Water'* to enable a very quick costume change half way through the show. The girls went off stage to change while I introduced the song and sang the first verse – they then re-emerged with the new costumes and I exited to change while they did the second verse. I, of course, returned for the big finish! But at the Broadway Club the dressing rooms were accessed through a door at the side of the stage and when the girls were due to return they found the door firmly shut against them. The band played on with a 'till ready' phrase while the girls struggled and I tried to remain looking cool. Eventually Carole panicked and banged on the door, thus alerting the audience to the predicament and turning the number into a comedy sketch. I walked to the door and pushed from the stage side and it opened immediately allowing the girls to stumble on trying to keep their dignity while the crowd laughed. When we finished the routine I told the crowd that I would be sending the girls for door training next morning! I noted in my diary that *"I spoke to Carole about it after the show and she got hysterical and shouted at me."* Sounds like a good night all round! Thankfully such incidents were few and far between.

Isle of Man

With the re-recording of '*Summer Song'* in the bag we shipped out to the Isle of Man and to The Palace Hotel & Casino Show Room in the capital Douglas. The island lies between mainland Great Britain and Northern Ireland and, like Jersey, it is a British Crown Dependency known the world over for the The Isle Of Man TT motorcycle racing event.

The season was largely successful for us, even allowing for the fact that I had fallen out with Billy Forrest over his insistence on an ill thought out finale to the show. We played seven nights per week so there was no day off until it was over. But with most of the shows being at midnight our days and early evenings were free. I managed to see many concerts and attend all sorts of events and still get to the Casino in time for the show.

There was another venue in the Palace Hotel complex called The Lido, which brought back memories of those great days at the Cliftonville Lido in the 60s. It was big enough to host major concert appearances and it also had a resident summer show which we watched on its opening night. The compere and comedian for that show was Dave Ismay who we got to know well and who introduced us to his manager Bob James.

Trilogy

Bob watched our show one night and we began talks on a future management deal. He had been the manager of Dave Dee, Dozy, Beaky, Mick and Tich in the late sixties at the height of their success and I was instantly encouraged by what he had to say and the fact that he didn't make over-grandiose claims about what he could do for us. Meeting Bob re-lit my enthusiasm for promoting the record and I started to chase up Bill Crompton for news. When the record was released I knew there would be a limit to what we could do to promote it from the island. I did several interviews with Manx Radio who played the record regularly but in reality we could only wait patiently to see if it would take off with the major radio stations. It didn't!

The rest of the summer went by without too many hitches. We sometimes battled with the sound system and one night the Hammond organ broke down half way through our act and dropped a semi-tone, which was an interesting problem to overcome. At weekends the crowd could be rowdy, but overall I managed to keep positive while looking forward to the future with Bob James at the management helm.

I also had the pleasure of seeing and meeting some of the acts I had admired over the years when they appeared at The Palace Lido. I saw Duane Eddy and Del Shannon from the 60s and Hot Chocolate, The Rubettes, Marc Bolan and Status Quo from the then present 70s. Rik Parfait of Status Quo had just invested in a brand new and very expensive Range Rover and proudly took us for a spin around the town.

Unparallel Careers!

I remembered that, earlier in the decade, Marc Bolan with T.Rex had often vied with Ziggy Stardust for their placings in the record charts and he had once counted Bowie among his supporting acts. Sadly Marc Bolan died in a car crash two years later - 16th September 1977.

I left the Isle of Man on the 22nd September 1975 with great optimism for the future. We now had a very experienced manager who I hoped would take *'Trilogy'* to new heights. I was totally immersed in my ambitions for the act to the exclusion of any other life. I was almost thirty years old and I had no real friendships other than with the two girls. I jealously guarded the three of us from any outside influences and, with hindsight, I can see how corrosive this attitude was. It would become even more so later in the decade.

Back home the little cafe was up for sale and we had a buyer. At the same time I was negotiating to take over a Margate High Street premises to turn into a coffee shop and pizza restaurant modelled on those I had seen in America – I was thinking big and imagining a future chain of such coffee shops! It had a very large flat above which was ideal for accommodating me and the girls as well as providing an office and storage. Carole agreed to be involved with the new cafe project. We had formed a relationship early on and, although by this time it was mainly platonic, we remained close. The idea was still, as with the previous cafe, to have something substantial to 'fall back on'. Unfortunately it would not turn out to be so. How naive I was not to see that the coffee shops (we opened another in the nearby seaside town of Herne Bay the following year) would end up being a mill stone around my neck within a few years.

Trilogy

The Holyland

That autumn we were on the road with more dates around the UK before flying to Israel on the 25th November 1975 for a run at the Haifa Theatre Club which would take us into the new year. The club was well equipped and, apart from some initial problems with the band, the shows went well.

We topped the bill supported by a magic act, an Israeli girl singer and an Austrian stripper. The Austrian girl's poor command of English was always a good source of amusement for us. For example, one night, after having a costume malfunction during her act, she announced *"My shoe, she is falling down the stage."* On another occasion she arrived at the club to announce that she'd been to the market to buy food and *"The chickens, they were not good looking."* This last pronouncement has stayed with me and I'm still inclined to use it myself from time to time!

Over the month we were in Israel we had the good fortune to be able to visit many of the legendary sites. We took a bus to Jerusalem, some two hours away, and visited the Mount of Olives and The Garden Of Gethsemane before walking the Via Delorosa and visiting The Holy Sepulchre. After a fine lunch we saw The Wailing Wall, Mount Zion and King David's Tomb. Not bad for one long day.

After a good night's sleep we picked up the bus to Hebron where we saw the tombs of Abraham, Isaac and Jacob, then on to Bethlehem and the church of the Nativity.

On another occasion we drove up to Nazareth and on to the Sea of Galilee, visiting Capernium, before enjoying a lunch of St. Peter fish from the River Jordan at Tiberius. All this seemed quite surreal – mythical places recalled from my childhood.

One Saturday we were lucky enough to be invited to attend a gala performance by the Israeli National Ballet featuring Valery & Galina Panov who had recently defected from the Soviet Union. They were the Russian ballet stars of the day. It was staged at the Haifa Auditorium at the top of Mount Carmel which was reached by a kind of mountainside tram or railway. These opportunities were easy to enjoy as our show did not start until after 11pm.

On Christmas Eve we took a taxi to Nazareth which, being a predominantly Christian Arab town, was decorated for the celebration and Christmas music was playing in the streets. We went to a carol concert at the Anglican Church which turned into a bit of a disaster when the organ broke down. The singing went ahead unaccompanied but unfortunately the many nationalities present seemed to know different versions of the carols. What followed was a a very non Christmas like cacophony! On leaving the church local youths jostled and catcalled the churchgoers which I assumed was because of the display of comparable wealth in this very poor town.

We saw in the New Year and did our last performance on the night of January 1st 1976. I had the usual Middle East battle to get all the money but, after a few wrangles over the rates of exchange, I came away quite happy with cheques in pounds and a fistful of dollars. We flew back from Tel Aviv to London stopping over for a welcome night out in Athens.

Trilogy

The Doldrums

I arrived back in Margate to learn that my offer to rent the shop and flat in the High Street had been accepted and the sale of the first cafe had gone through. I had decided to call the new place El Ranchero and I started work on the very vaguely Mexican style interior with the help of my Dad and his various building trade friends. We moved into the flat above the coffee shop and were quickly back on the road to Bristol, Southampton, Chesterfield and other far flung places.

El Ranchero opened on the 1st March with my sister Jean at the helm and myself and Carole assisting when we could. It seemed to be well received in the town and the flat above was a major improvement to living conditions. To fill that summer I was excited by the prospect of two months in Rhodesia and South Africa. Bob James had been negotiating the contract for some time and it was to be a vital boost to my finances. In late May he dropped a bombshell – the Rhodesia contract had fallen through!

We now had no work for the season, which was a disaster given what had been spent on the coffee shop. After confirming with Bob that it was already too late for any possibility of a replacement contract I decided that we had to take over the running of El Ranchero for the summer to save on staff costs. I also arranged to let out rooms in the flat to artistes appearing at Margate's Winter Gardens and Lido Theatres which paid some of the expenses. This was a serious setback which certainly dented my pride and the dreams of stardom seemed ever more likely to remain unfulfilled. Most weekends we travelled to other seaside resorts to do 'Sunday Concerts' performing with the variety stars of the era - Frankie Vaughan, Rod Hull, Leslie Crowther, Dick Emery, Jimmy Tarbuck and others who are long since forgotten by today's public. This at least kept me in contact with real show business.

Nigeria

I was greatly relieved when, at the end of August, we flew to Nigeria, courtesy of a Spanish agent called Francisco Bermudez. We were appearing for a month at The Federal Palace Hotel in Lagos. In the 1970s Nigeria was still sometimes referred to as *'The Arsehole Of Africa'* and even as we arrived it was easy to see why it had gained that reputation. On the drive from the airport to the hotel I spotted a body floating in a filthy river that was also home to numerous abandoned ships. A glimpse of the sea revealed many more rusting hulks anchored offshore – these had apparently been used to bring 'imports' to Nigeria for corrupt politicians and businessmen and then abandoned.

The hotel was supposedly the most luxurious in the city and, on first viewing, looked genuinely first class. Unfortunately the electricity failed regularly and water often dried up. Other breakdowns that affected the restaurants were frequent, which made us concerned about the safety of the food. The hotel's Spanish band leader was so hung up about it he rarely ate anything but bananas.

Luckily we met an English ex-pat called Rex who took pity on us and, when the hotel was at its worst, he would pick us up after the show and take us to his house. But travelling through the city at night was fraught with danger and on one occasion we were stopped by police for no apparent reason other than we were white Europeans. They hauled Rex from the car and started to rough him up and demand money. In the ensuing argument he dropped the name of a well placed politician which luckily had the desired effect on the two scumbags and they let us go. Rex had built up his successful electronics business from scratch, and still ran it, but had been forced to sell it for a pittance to a local chief when the government brought in an indigenisation law which banned foreign nationals from owning assets in the country. One night he arrived at the hotel to celebrate the signing of a major contract and announced that this deal had made the chief a millionaire. So much for colonial influence!

We sometimes wandered down to a nearby beach until a frequent visitor told us something of its recent history. She had been trapped at the hotel during the previous year's coup and saw captives being marched down to the beach where they were executed by firing squad or hanging. It lost its charm after that!

Although the show was a success and finances were boosted I was somewhat relieved when we reached the end of that contract and boarded an aircraft for the flight back to civilisation. There was one more surprise however when we learnt there would be a stopover for twenty-four hours in Upper Volta - a country I'd never heard of. There was no explanation given and I put it down to the hazards of travelling in darkest Africa! We were given day rooms for a few

Unparallel Careers!

hours to get some sleep before re-embarking for Paris and then London.

Eric & Ernie

In December that year we played the first of three big annual Christmas charity concerts supported by the now infamous Jimmy Saville and featuring several headline artistes. There were two dates at the Victoria Palace Theatre and a final one at The Old Vic in Central London.

Before the first one there was an afternoon party for mentally and physically disabled children at The Hard Rock Cafe. It was hosted by Saville and I now know that he was already offending when we were photographed alongside him at that party. It kind of concluded what was not my most successful year!

During that same year *I recall watching a Russell Harty chat show on ITV when he attempted to interview an incoherent Bowie. I did, of course, point out to those watching with me that I was in 'The Lower Third' – Bowie's first band! Nevertheless, it was sad to learn that he had reached a low point with drug addiction. He dropped out for a while and resurfaced in Berlin. He then began work on the first of three albums soon to be known as 'The Berlin Trilogy' while I battled on through another year with 'The Margate Trilogy'!*

After our return from the aforementioned CSE tour in Oman *(see Military Manoeuvres)* our illustrious manager, who had clearly never looked at a map of The British Isles, fixed up a tour of Scotland and The Orkney Islands which was only surpassed in distance by the following summer when we covered even more miles during endless weeks trudging around the South of England. The Scottish tour was a disaster and I never got to see The Orkneys!

I was getting increasingly frustrated with the lack of positive progress for the act. After the disappointment of the previous year's cancelled South Africa contract I was attributing it to our manager's lack of initiative, which was in contrast to the way I had felt when we first met on The Isle of Man. Bob had been based at offices in Upper Street, Islington, London when I first met him and then he moved several times in a comparatively short period. Each time he joined another established entertainment agency and took his acts with him. For me his most positive move was to London Management which, in the 70s, was the biggest and most prestigious agency in the UK representing a majority of the big named television stars of the era. I was greatly encouraged by this and for a while it led to *'Trilogy'* sharing the stage with most of these stars. But I soon realised that Bob was a 'serial mover' because he quite quickly parted company with London Management as well.

I began to have some difficult conversations with him about the direction we were heading, which to me seemed in reverse. He arranged for us to record some new songs but I was unhappy with the results. There were cancelled appearances, mix ups over dates and problems with musicians at several clubs. Then, in the midst of it all, my dad had a stroke and was hospitalised for several weeks. It hit me hard because I thought that he was indestructible.

The only bright spot during this period came in

April when we supported the true showbiz legends Morecambe & Wise at The Bristol Hippodrome. It was a great feeling to run on stage knowing that the audience were already conquered – if you were appearing in *'The Morecambe and Wise Show'* you must be somebody. Backstage the pair had separate dressing rooms. Ernie Wise played host to visiting friends and local dignitaries while Eric sat quietly in his room telling us,*"He loves all that does Ernie – and he's welcome to it."* We found Eric unpretentious and friendly – he even charmed one of the girls into ironing his shirt! After the packed houses for every show we unashamedly wallowed in the reflected glory from these true icons of showbiz, especially as we exited the stage door and pushed our way through the waiting autograph hunters.

In 1970s Great Britain *I considered that Eric & Ernie were probably more famous than Bowie but it didn't change my dinner conversation completely – I name-dropped all three for a while!*

In May *'Trilogy'* started a long summer appearing at Pontin's holiday centres. We drove from Margate to Weston-Super-Mare on the west coast every Monday for two shows and then to Weymouth on the south coast for two more the next day. We stayed overnight in Bournemouth before two more shows at Chichester and then on to a show at Camber Sands in Kent, after which we drove back to Margate. After the weekend the whole routine started again. This went on for months and was only broken up by several Sunday concerts, happily in proper theatres with good musicians and big name artistes. The only remarkable thing that is lodged in my memory from that season was hearing on the radio, while driving from Weston-Super-Mare to Weymouth, that Elvis had died. It was August 16th 1977.

While I was touring Pontin's Holiday Centres Bowie was promoting his album 'Low', the first of the 'Berlin Trilogy'. The album was not received well by the critics and his former manager, Tony Defries, tried to stop it being released. In spite of this the single 'Sound And Vision' made number three in the UK charts. It seems we were both desperate to find a new way!

Edwards versus Corbett
(Middle East Tour)

To close out the year we flew to Bahrain for a Christmas season organised by a promoter called David Mills whose previous claim to fame had been as a member of The Temperance Seven, a 20s nostalgia band that had notched up several hits in the 1960s.

Headlining the first few shows was a famous old radio and television comedy actor from the 50s and 60s, Jimmy Edwards. He played the euphonium as part of his comedy stage act and always carried a small hunting horn in his pocket which he would toot amusingly to lighten the mood, especially when we were travelling between venues.

I recall waiting in a frustrating line at passport control in Doha, capital of Qatar. Seeing Jimmy looking rather glum, I suggested that a quick toot on the horn could lighten our mood considerably - to which he replied *"I never use it at passport controls, no fucking sense of humour!"*

After the shows in Qatar we returned to Bahrain

and Jimmy left us to do some appearances in Sharjah, another of the city states in the United Arab Emirates.

We took a flight to Abu Dhabi together with the tour band plus all the stage equipment, instruments and costumes. We were to join up with Ronnie Corbett for a show at The British Club. On arrival we were immediately barred from entering the country and locked in an office, from where we were deported on the next available flight back to Bahrain, leaving all the equipment in a heap in Abu Dhabi airport.

The promoters had cocked up the visa applications – we had passed through Abu Dhabi the previous week with Jimmy Edwards and the visas were for a single entry only. We found ourselves that night at The Hilton Hotel, Bahrain and we soon heard from Jimmy Edwards - *"Mission aborted, I'm returning to base."* His show in Sharjah had been cancelled due to the death of an important emir. *"Wait up for me chaps – keep the bar open."* Thus we had one last hilarious night with Jimmy.

He was on top form when he arrived in the Hilton bar where the few late night stragglers included two German guys who, on being told he was a famous English actor, asked to be introduced. *"Jimmy,"* I said, *"these chaps would like to meet you - they're from Germany."* *"Good God"* he cried *"I spent five years trying to kill you bastards."* He had been a World War Two RAF pilot – Flight Lieutenant Edwards, DFC. They laughed along with him and he carried on entertaining them and us.

After several more rounds of drinks had been consumed we finally called it a night. It was the last time I saw Jimmy. I was saddened to see, some time during the following year, that he had been 'outed' as gay by a

Trilogy

Sunday red top. He was from a different era and had always maintained his image of the big macho man while, it seemed, keeping his private life private. It was a pity that in his late seventies he had to endure the humiliation of his private life being spread across the front pages of a Sunday paper.

Fortunately the visa problem was a temporary setback which was solved the next day by the intervention of some mysterious Sheikh, of whom we had no knowledge. We joined Ronnie Corbett in Abu Dhabi for a successful show and then returned with him to Bahrain to see out 1977.

The final show of the tour was in the ballroom of the Hilton Hotel. It was a disaster. The audience were almost all local and visiting Arabs with only a smattering of English speaking ex-patriots. They had been supplied with party poppers, hooters and polystyrene balls which they used to great effect in disrupting the show. We managed to get through reasonably unscathed but poor old Ronnie lost the battle – apart from the noise disruption it was obvious that most of the audience didn't have a clue what he was talking about. To rub salt into his wound Ronnie told us, when we next shared a stage with him, that he hadn't been paid! David Mills and his organisation had come to an abrupt end, fortunately after I'd banked the dollars.

We flew back to Heathrow via Beirut on the 4th January to be met by Bob James with the news that there was no good news about anything. It was to be the start of a tumultuous year that would eventually lead to the big changes in my personal and working life that were long overdue.

INTERVAL

Chapter 6
All Change
(Achieving Gold)

Gold, live for it strive for it
Gold, keep hope alive for it
Gold, hold on for gold it's the colour of dreams
Stephen Gold (The Colour Of Dreams)

The year of '78 started with the last of the alcohol fuelled short CSE tours for the troops in Northern Ireland. On the last night Derek Agutter, true to form, repeated his 'gigantic bollocks' party trick on the coach and, back at the hotel, he and Nigel Hopkins, the *'Boy Wonder Trumpeter'*, enticed the show's girl singer, Verity (sorry Verity – can't recall your surname) into a hotel room where they were standing naked. She left quickly with a shriek followed by hilarity in the hotel corridor which took some time to die down. This was the last of the riotous and sometimes outrageous CSE tours that I experienced. Shortly afterwards Derek retired and a far more sober and disciplined management was installed. Overall, much safer but much less fun!

Unparallel Careers!

The return from Belfast next day, the 11th January, was marked by heavy gales causing the flight to be diverted to Birmingham where we experienced a frightening landing in the high cross winds. After a dreary coach ride back to Heathrow to collect the car we eventually arrived in Margate in the late evening to find the seafront closed to traffic due to gale force winds and waves crashing over the road. That night most of Margate's old entertainment pier was destroyed leaving the Margate Lifeboat stranded in its housing, which was halfway along the pier. There was flooding and damage throughout East Anglia and it evoked my childhood memories of the great storm of 1953 when the Margate lighthouse was toppled and the old town flooded.

In an effort to revive our recording career, which had stumbled at the first hurdle due to the lack of success with *'Summer Song'* and the disappearance of the record producer Bill Crompton, we went to Sound Suite Studios at Camden Mews, London to record new songs. Terry Bolton had written two songs just for us - *'Sugar Daddy'* and *'Devil's Angel'*. Securing a new recording contract was surely the job of our manager but I had completely lost confidence in Bob James to accomplish this. His management style was no longer proving successful for us. Moreover, I was becoming more and more frustrated about all aspects of my life.

The finished recordings were quite good but to me they only served to emphasise what I saw as a lack of solid vocal ability in the act. Lynne, being a trained dancer, had brought enormous benefits in the early days with the act's choreography but her vocal strength had not improved very much over the years. Carole's voice was solid but she needed a stronger vocal partner if we were to make any further progress as a viable recording group. I began to feel that some kind of major change was necessary.

The general feeling of frustration was not helped by other bad news. I had opened a second 'El Ranchero' in Herne Bay in partnership with an old friend, Peter Jefcoate. He now wanted to leave the coffee shop for 'personal reasons' and he wanted to leave with a cash settlement for his share of the business, which I could not afford to pay. The arrangement with Peter had lasted less than 18 months and left me with a big dilemma. The shop was not making money yet and I had nobody in mind who could run it day to day. This enterprise had been a big mistake and would be a constant irritation throughout the year. I soon encountered financial problems trying to keep the two coffee shops afloat and had to take out several bank loans which were a further burden during this 'annus horribilis'.

Then even more disruption. My Ford Granada was stolen from the car park of the Excelsior Hotel at Heathrow Airport. Luckily we had removed our luggage and costumes before it disappeared. It was found some days later in a sorry state at Penge in South London. This was the first of two occasions in 1978 when that car was stolen – the next was from Manchester some months later when it was eventually dumped in the car park at Manchester Airport.

In late March I received a call from Bob James to say he had secured a record deal with DJM records which called for two singles per year for three years and came with a substantial advance. We were ecstatic and our spirits were raised, only to be dashed again when the deal failed to complete for reasons he never explained and I never learnt.

A brief and disappointing trip to Stavanger in Norway only served to add to the discontent I was feeling and this was to be the last hurrah for *'Trilogy'* because, in my increasing frustration, I had been playing with the idea of a name change and decided that now was the time. I had calculated that if I assumed a separate identity to the girls it would give me the flexibility to make more major changes to personnel in the future. I decided to have a new and more sophisticated surname and use my own second name. Robb Wyatt would henceforth be known as *'Stephen Gold'*. The girls became known as *'Flame'* because I thought the photo opportunities and publicity would be easier with that kind of evocative name. Indeed the first photographs of the new entity featured a flaming background.

The Summer of Discontent

In April I signed a contract for a welcome summer residency as *'Stephen Gold with Flame'* at the newly renovated Pier Theatre at Cromer on the North Norfolk coast. The producer was an ebullient Irishman called Dick Condon who had already earned a reputation for vastly improving the fortunes of the Norwich Theatre Royal and was turning his hand to restoring good old seaside entertainment on Cromer Pier. It was to be a bitter sweet period. Whilst the shows were successful and thoroughly enjoyable my personal life was to change completely and I would find myself close to financial disaster and even bankruptcy.

We arrived in Cromer on the 21st June and took up residence in a spacious rented apartment which belonged to a lovely family with whom we would spend many lazy hours eating and drinking, mainly on their boat moored on the Norfolk Broads.

The show was headlined by a singing duo called Millican and Nesbitt who had enjoyed fame on a TV talent show and scored a couple of top ten hit records. The comedy was supplied by veteran Scottish comedian Denny Willis and his straight man Johnny Mac. They performed a couple of classic comedy sketches that I was lucky enough to participate in. I remembered seeing Denny perform his classic sketch, The Quorn Quartet, on TV's Sunday Night At The London Palladium when I was but a kid and it was now great to be part of it every night.

Soon after the show opened I had to deal with the problems in Margate and Herne Bay. I had luckily persuaded my nephew Peter, who had restaurant experience, to run the Herne Bay coffee shop for the summer but it was still losing money. I found myself writing to various suppliers and the landlords asking for 'time to pay'. I was sending money from Cromer to help keep things going and was soon faced with a dilemma. We were constantly being chased for unpaid bills and I had to decide if we could carry on or whether I should declare bankruptcy.

The pressure was huge because the shops were in my name and bankruptcy would be personal. I knew that could seriously affect my life in the future. There were days when I avoided phoning anyone in Margate or Herne Bay so that I could get a rest from the bad news. In the midst of this my sister Jean, who ran the Margate coffee shop, walked out on her husband and, without asking me, moved into the flat above the shop. I had let out rooms to entertainers working the season at Margate Winter Gardens and I had to talk to the tenants to smooth things over because I couldn't afford to lose their rent payments. On the 4th July I got the news that my cat, who had been part of the family for ever, had died. I was feeling pretty miserable and, while surrounded by lots of happy friendly people, I was feeling alone.

Luckily the takings at the two coffee shops started to improve over the high summer period and, together with the cash injected from loans and my show earnings, I managed to pay the rent and placate the creditors. In August my nephew decided he would not stay with the Herne Bay coffee shop after the season was over and it was clear I would have to find a buyer as soon as possible.

In the meantime, to take my mind off the financial woes, I threw myself into all that the summer had to offer. There were after show parties, long lunches on the Norfolk Broads and several special events including an award presentation for Morecambe & Wise. It was at Anglia TV in Norwich and many of the principal comedians of that era attended. Larry Grayson, Lenny Henry, Frank Carson, Norman Collier and several others were there to celebrate with this most famous double act.

In the middle of July we were drafted in to play parts in the new Spike Milligan TV series Q8. Series director Ray Butt arrived in Cromer with Spike and a full BBC production crew and soon got into the habit of visiting us at the theatre. They stayed at the Hotel de Paris where Spike demanded that he was given a room in the impressive tower atop the hotel roof, which was not really habitable. The bewildered hotel management obliged by kitting out the tower for his stay. This was just one of his many eccentricities that we witnessed.

His co-star, Bob Todd, was invariably on the booze before shooting started in the morning and pulled some hilarious stunts. One morning we arrived to see him chaotically directing the vehicles on the road outside the hotel dressed as a traffic warden, which was his costume for the day's shoot.

In the midst of all this we were still managing to do Sunday concerts in various parts of the country. Long drives usually followed the Saturday night show or we would set off early on Sunday morning. Blackpool, Bournemouth, Skegness and an epic seven and a half hour journey to Weymouth, through bank holiday traffic, were all part of the hectic schedule.

Ungentlemanly Conduct

Towards the end of July we threw a party at our flat for the show cast and the Spike Milligan Q8 crew for which the BBC caterers kindly supplied the food. It was a great night but it was to have an unexpected effect on the last weeks of the season. The show featured four dancers who I had naturally got to know quite well over the summer. Three of them were married and the fourth was a dizzy 19 year old. As the party got late I found myself in deep conversation with one of the girls. Her husband was a member of a well known comedy act who were in a summer show elsewhere in the country and therefore away from the family home. We had both consumed quite a lot of wine, she wanted to talk, she was unhappy, we talked some more, she stayed the night.

__In Bowie's song__ 'An Occasional Dream' he talks about nights so close but with eyes open and gently crying under summer skies of blue. I felt this beautifully summed up our situation that day.

As well as dancing every evening she was also looking after her two year old son. But over the following days, thanks to her sleep over baby-minder, we were able to hang out together after the shows. It was clear to me she was looking for a full blown affair to take her out of her depressed state of mind and I guessed that I was just someone available at the right time. I liked her a lot but couldn't see where it would go because I would not have got involved with the break-up of her marriage – I was too much of a coward for that. I didn't want to cause her even more unhappiness by diving in and then buggering off at the end of the season – a typical showbiz summer fling.

However, one night in early August, she confided in me that she had been having back pain and had been told she might have cancer of the spine. She had not told her husband or anyone at the theatre but was to undergo precautionary sessions of radium treatment straight away. I decided I would give her all the support I could but was struggling to find a way to help other than be a shoulder to cry on. She was desperately unhappy and would come back to the flat with me, sometimes in tears, self confidence gone, frightened she would not be able to dance anymore and saying she felt useless. Fortunately the treatment went well and her health and mood improved over the last few days of the season.

The show ended on the 5th September and after a last night together I headed for Margate with her promise that she would come to visit me in a week or so. The following week she called me from hospital to say she had passed out in the street and doctors had told her she had pleurisy and had suffered a collapsed lung. A week later she had recovered sufficiently to be back at home and I drove up to Norfolk and stayed with her overnight. She then dropped the bombshell - she was pregnant! My mind leapt to memories of my sixteen year old self and the terrible night that I found out I had suddenly become a father! Another shock!

She was terrified that her husband would find out. He had not been home since early June so it could not be his. I was a little terrified too and I left the following morning full of despondency. She called a couple of days later to say she had seen a doctor in Norwich and arranged a termination which would cost £100.00. It took place in early October. I agreed to contribute but I could not send money to her at home for obvious reasons. I managed to send the money by other means and that was the last time I had contact with this lovely person. I ran for the hills - what a little shit I was.

(As a postscript to this story some 39 years later, with the help of Facebook, I made contact with her and discovered she had eventually parted from her husband after 24 years. She was in good health and living in Spain. That was good to know).

Unparallel Careers!

Quintessential

Back in Kent I discovered a recording studio near Herne Bay run by guitarist Graeme Quinton-Jones leader of a band called Quint. We recorded a number of new tracks and then Graeme asked us to record two master tracks for him. He had secured a deal with a record company run by well known music entrepreneur Terry Noon. *'Lay Love On Me'* and *'It's Much Better Now'* were the results. This turned out to be another dead end as Terry Noon, having heard the original American version of the main track, didn't like the arrangements Graeme had produced and swiftly dumped the deal. At the same time I had been asked by A/R manager John Rose of Sunbury Music in London to produce a track for submission to the BBC for Eurovision. I wrote a song, partly in French, called *'Je Reviendrai' (I Will Return)*. Unfortunately my attempt at Franglais for Eurovision did not become the UK's 'Song For Europe'. Worse than that, because I wrote the line *'I'm posting my love to you my French lady'* the song became known as *'The French Letter Song'* among friends and colleagues. It was truly f....d!

We hitched a ride to old Marseilles
You showed me places that you knew along the way
We drank champagne from paper cups outside a small cafe
And lingered there until the setting of the sun
Believing life had just begun
Stephen Gold (Je Reviendrai)

The meeting with Graeme Quinton-Jones and his band mates inadvertently led to the beginning of the break up of the act. I was fiercely protective of our image and reputation as *'the top UK singing dancing act'* and I was especially, and unjustifiably, protective of that image in Margate and East Kent. I'd built up a kind of local mystique around the act, keeping up a veneer of success in show-business and with the coffee shops. The financial troubles had all been well hidden.

One night, completely unreasonably, I objected to the fact that Carole and Lynne had been going out with Graeme and drummer Roger Diamond. Whilst Carole was reasonably sanguine about it Lynne was affronted and some days later an almighty row erupted between us which soured our relationship over the weeks to come. It was a big factor in my decision to bring the partnership to an end as soon as I could and to find another way forward. (Lynne became Mrs Quinton-Jones in the summer of 1980 and we have remained good friends.)

With emotions back in check we took to the stage at the Old Vic Theatre, London for the last of the Jimmy Saville Christmas Charity shows and then shipped out to Portugal to see in the New Year during a month long run at The Casino in Estoril. While there we had the pleasure of performing in a Gala Spectacular in front of various European royals including, as guest of honour, Princess Grace of Monaco. I was corny enough to say after one song *"Well did you ever, what a swell party this is"* which were well known lyrics from her hit film 'High Society' in which she starred with Bing Crosby and Frank Sinatra.

The end of 1978 came with deep reflections on a difficult year. My head was full of ideas about the long overdue and necessary changes. Inevitable changes that

Unparallel Careers!

would happen in the year to come. It started slowly with the usual club dates around the country and in March we decamped to the exotic splendour of Singapore.

Singapore Sling

We flew to Singapore on the 5th March 1979 for a three week run at the Shangri-La Hotel. The hotel was a heavenly oasis of calm in the bustling city. Each luxury room had a balcony from which tumbled cascades of colourful bougainvillea. There were several restaurants and a fabulous free form swimming pool surrounded by palm trees and tropical flowers of all kinds.

Unfortunately the show did not open as scheduled since, at the appointed hour, I was in the local hospital recovering from a severe bout of food poisoning. It had started the day before, shortly after I had lunched on a Reuben sandwich in the hotel coffee shop. Beef, Swiss cheese, sauerkraut and Russian dressing between lightly toasted rye bread – delicious. Mid afternoon, during rehearsals for the show, I began to feel nauseous and it worsened as time went on. Back in my room, suffering from stomach cramps, I began to get scared and called the girls for help. I was losing the feeling in my lower limbs and at one point it felt like paralysis was creeping up my body. I remember thinking, quite irrationally, that if it reached my heart I could die.

The room was soon filled with people – the Duty Manager and Assistant Manager, the room maid, Carole and Lynne and finally a doctor who decided I needed to be hospitalised. The emergency ambulance crew arrived and I was strapped to a wheelchair. Then the comical farce began.

All Change

The reputation of the hotel immediately became paramount and, as I was now the responsibility of the ambulance crew, the hotel managers set about dealing with damage limitation. They scanned the corridor outside my room until it was clear and then gave the nod to wheel me out – not to the guest lifts but to a scruffy service lift. This descended to the depths of the building behind the kitchens where I was abandoned among the bins while the medics retrieved their ambulance which was still parked at the front of the hotel. When it arrived I saw that there was already one patient in the back and the poor woman had to wait while they loaded me in and then watch me throwing up as we drove to the hospital.

I was taken to the local free hospital and quickly given a bed in a large open sided ward and put on a drip. There were many people in the ward with the beds close together. In my hazy state I was still able to see the various tropical birds that flew freely through the ward. I began to feel better and eventually fell asleep, only to be woken in the early hours of the morning by a commotion around the bed closest to me where doctors and nurses were attempting to revive the patient. They failed. The poor chap was covered up and taken away before the sun came up in the morning.

By now I was feeling okay and desperate to get out, but frequent checks by the doctors seemed to confirm that I needed to stay another day. I put my case - *"I have a luxury hotel room at the Shangri-La Hotel and will recover much better there than in this ward full of sick people."* Eventually they agreed and I was released that afternoon. At that time in Singapore the free hospital,

Unparallel Careers!

which seemed to provide an excellent service, was for the poor. Other people, especially foreigners, paid for the excellent private hospitals. We had travel insurance and, back at the hotel, the girls were just arranging for me to be moved to a private hospital when I emerged, white faced, from a taxi. The hotel did not officially accept that I had contracted the poisoning in their coffee shop but they nevertheless coughed up for any expenses we had incurred and paid us for the no show nights.

In spite of this inauspicious start I fell in love with Singapore and all it had to offer. It was clean, safe and prosperous. The multi racial population, Chinese, Indians and Malays, rubbed along side by side without any noticeable discrimination.

There still existed, in 1979, many examples of the traditional old shop-houses where you could buy pretty much anything at any time of the day or night. (When I visited again twenty years later sadly much of this had been torn down). There was also Bugi Street, where you could eat and drink from the many food stalls late into the night and be entertained at your table by conjurers, fortune tellers, musicians and, most celebrated of all, the beautiful 'Ladyboys'. They had been introduced over decades to unsuspecting first time visitors to Singapore to trick them into thinking they were on a promise – what a shock!

To top it all there was the famous Raffles Hotel – a little piece of empire nostalgia where you could still sample a Singapore Sling in The Long Bar or take afternoon tea in The Tiffin Room. Scones with jam and cream, various cakes and all kinds of exotic teas were on offer while a pianist played gentle soothing melodies – bliss.

Before leaving Singapore we appeared in a local TV show singing our old single *'Summer Song'* and were interviewed for the Straits Times by a journalist who found it amusing to compare us to Andy Capp and Florrie. They were the working class cartoon characters featured in the 'red top' newspaper The Daily Mirror in the 60s & 70s. I must have struck her as a domineering misogynistic brute in my relationship with the girls – perhaps she spotted something there?

A Short Break

On our return to the UK the act finally broke up. I was both relieved and excited for the future but nevertheless a little sad – the three of us had been together for six eventful years and that could not be dismissed lightly. Lynne went home to Cramlington and later moved in with Graeme Quinton-Jones. I suggested to Carole that we should get a replacement, strictly on an employee basis, to fulfil some contracts that were still on offer.

We auditioned several girls for the role and we employed an excellent singer called Sandy. We soon had the act up and running again with a much stronger vocal sound and we started to play some dates. But there were soon warning signs that all was not well in the camp. Sandy was prone to unfathomable and instant mood swings. This personality defect began to manifest itself during the first few weeks but we thought we could live with it.

During this period we did a showcase

performance for an agent called Geoff Davey. It was on the US Air Force base at Lakenheath in Suffolk and it would turn out to be pivotal in shaping the future direction of my career. This was also the first time we performed to pre-recorded backing tracks that I had produced in Herne Bay. At the time this practice was frowned on by musicians who, quite reasonably, thought it endangered their work opportunities and were opposed to it being introduced into venues where musicians were normally employed. For me it was picking up on the experience I had with pre-recorded tracks during my years in Jersey. It gave me a previously unfulfilled freedom to arrange new numbers for the act which would never have been practical when relying on limited rehearsal time with live musicians of varying ability.

There was still the financial stress of the two coffee shops hovering in the background but by mid July the Herne Bay shop was off my hands and the Margate El Ranchero followed in October. With the cash raised I bought a large house near the seafront at Margate which would become the centre of my showbiz operations for the next few years. The three storey property boasted a self contained flat on the top floor and there was a sitting tenant on the middle floor who rented a kitchen and bedroom. For this reason the selling price was just £12,500 which was almost exactly what the Margate coffee shop business had sold for. The estate agent informed me, rather indelicately, that the tenant was an old lady with 'one foot in the grave' who was living mostly with her daughter in London. I'm pleased to recount that she did not die but instead, without any pressure from me, decided to give up the tenancy shortly after I moved in.

Fighting Talk

I took a booking from a Dutch agent in that summer of 1979 and we arrived in Amsterdam to find that the venue was a strip club in the red light district of the city. The club manager wanted us to perform a couple of numbers in between each stripper's routine – not on my watch!

The agent apologised and booked us into an alternative venue in The Hague. It was a striking old building with no indication on the outside that it was a place of entertainment, but I soon learnt that we were not the only ones doing a turn. During the first show I noticed that the audience were constantly coming and going and the truth soon revealed itself – it was a high class brothel and we were entertaining men on the waiting list. It was an unusual but educational week and I guess our fee was paid by the proceeds of prostitution!

In late October we played an altogether different kind of venue. At the Pavilion Theatre, Glasgow, we were supporting a well known Scottish country singer and broadcaster called Sydney Devine. Completely unknown in the rest of the United Kingdom he was mobbed at the stage door each night by his legions of mostly female fans. We bathed in the reflected glory as we had with Morecambe and Wise at Bristol two years before.

With Sandy by then firmly integrated in the act we embarked on a comprehensive tour of Norway which

Unparallel Careers!

took in the five cities of Boda, Narvik, Allesund, Tromso and the most northern city in the world, lying above the Arctic Circle, Hammerfest. Here we played a week in a showbar/restaurant owned by a charming and attractive couple, Gunner and Britt Larssen. Hammerfest in November was fascinating in that the days never really got light. It would be a kind of half-light around midday and completely dark again by 2pm.

Gunner took a shine to Carole and I got the impression that Britt would have turned a blind eye to that if I had surrendered to her charms. With this in mind I was quick to accept when they invited us both back to spend a weekend with them at their country hotel at Skaidi about 40 miles from Hammerfest. We danced the night away in the hotel disco and I ended up slow dancing with Britt. I'm sorry to have to admit that, not able to get over the embarrassment, we all retired to our own rooms. One night, six months later, I was awoken in my Bahrain hotel room at 4am by a phone call from a tiddly Britt who said they were enjoying some drinks in the warm sunshine and thinking about us – it was midnight in Hammerfest. As a memento of the city I still have my certificate, signed by the mayor, that confirms my membership of the Royal & Ancient Polar Bear Society – very proud!

During the last week in Norway Sandy's unpredictable mood swings peaked alarmingly. One night a minor mishap in the audience led to one of the spotlights being misdirected so that she was unlit for the last few songs. She went overboard with rage about this which was mostly directed at me, even though I could have done nothing to prevent it. She then refused to speak to us anymore and we returned to the hotel in silence. She was sharing with Carole and the silence continued.

Next morning when I knocked at their room she opened the door and immediately demanded her flight ticket home. I tried to reason with her as we only had two more nights to play, but to no avail. She was adamant that she should leave immediately. I said it wasn't possible, that I would not give her the opportunity to walk out on a contract. At this she grabbed my bag, assuming that the tickets were within. Carole, who had joined us by then, made to grab it back, whereupon Sandy gave her a fast left hook to the mouth, splitting her upper lip. Carole retired bleeding to the bathroom and, brushing Sandy aside, I picked up the bedside phone and rang Don Jones who was the English agent for this tour. I explained the situation and asked if we could get out cleanly from the last shows. Ever the smooth talker, Don spoke to Sandy and somehow persuaded her to play the last two dates.

We got through those two nights and the journey back to Stansted Airport without a word being exchanged. She walked away from us at the airport and we never saw her again. Carole, meanwhile, nursed the two stitches in her lip, kindly supplied by the Norwegian A&E department.

Jellystone Park

Bruised by the experience I was feeling pretty low when Carole took a call from Geoff Davey who we had met at Lakenheath Air Base. He asked if we would be prepared to play the costume characters Yogi Bear and

Boo Boo in a children's daytime Christmas show on a tour of American military bases in Europe. We could then perform our own act every evening. She relayed this to me and I was dead set against it. I did not want to debase the act and embarrass myself by performing in an animal costume in a children's show – that's how I saw it – it was definitely not for me or for my act!

After an evening of heated argument during which Carole often repeated the mantra *"I have a good feeling about this"* I finally relented and reluctantly agreed to, at least, investigate it further. My change of heart would prove to have a profound effect on the next decade.

After the new third member walked away I no longer had an act to perform. The contract negotiations for the *'Yogi Bear Show'* were, therefore, carefully played out so that we were able to recruit four dancers who would play parts in the kids' show. We then also rehearsed them up to be part of a 'new look' show. *'Stephen Gold with Flame'* would now become a singing, dancing floorshow.

Our old partner Lynne was roped in to manage the choreography and also came on the tour with us to play the part of Boo Boo in the children's show. We met up with comedian JJ Stewart, who was to play the part of the Park Ranger, and we set off by Hovercraft from Ramsgate on the 11th December. We headed across France and Germany with the agency's road manager, John Bell, at the wheel of the Volkswagon tour bus.

At the end of that first day on the road we checked into a fabulous old hotel near the Great St Bernard Pass in the Alps. The Posthotel Bodenhaus had some specimens from its old hotel registers framed and displayed in the lobby and they showed the signatures of Napoleon Bonaparte and Queen Victoria who had both stayed there in the 1800s. It was snow covered and gorgeous. I sat up late drinking a large brandy with John Bell and JJ Stewart and all was well with the world.

We were on our way to play several days in Italy at The Flamingo Club on the NATO military base at Naples. It soon became clear that although the *'Yogi Bear Show'* was very roughly cobbled together, amazingly, it seemed to work well enough for the audiences. Many years later, in a different life, I would go out of my way to avoid any reference to these shows in case they incriminated me! They were really awful! However, the evening shows blossomed as the tour went on and this gave me ideas and hope for the future.

We returned from Naples via Pisa where I took full advantage of the photo opportunity – the Leaning Tower from all directions. We then played several dates in Germany before the final show at Greenham Common US Airbase. Geoff Davey sat in on the last evening show with his American partner Vince D'Amico. This turned out to be the first of many tours we would do for Vince D'Amico Enterprises. It was Christmas Eve 1979 and I returned home full of ideas and optimism. The coffee shops were now just a memory, I owned a house for the first time in my life, I had cash in the bank and there were some good offers of work for the five piece *'Stephen Gold with Flame'* line-up in the new year.

While I was casting off my old responsibilities and

wrestling with the matter of finding yet another new direction Bowie was casting off his ties to West Germany with the release of the third album of the Berlin trilogy called Lodger. He was also winding up his marriage which would officially end in the year to come.

New image and back to the wild west Summer 1973

Trilogy

Outfits for the first single - only worn for this photo

Dear Jimmy Edwards always found the champagne

Me and Carole about to go aloft at Salalah, Oman 1977

Just another pyramid Cairo 1975

With Lynne and Frank Ifield Sheffield 1978

Glad the show's over! Ronnie Corbett - Bahrain 1978

Herne Bay

The ever stressful coffee shops! Trilogy headquarters were above Margate A recording studio above Herne Bay

Margate

Bailey's Club - Watford

Fun days with Kenny Lynch and Jimmy Tarbuck

Cromer - on stage with Denny Willis and partying with the cast and BBC crew

Keeping my head!

First Yogi Bear tour on top of the world at the St Bernard Pass 1979

Chapter 7
A Smouldering Flame

There's a flame running through me
Setting fire to my soul
Look what's happening to me
I think it's out of control
Getting higher I'm on Fire
Gid Taylor (I'm On Fire)

The first task in 1980 was to recruit permanent members to the new act. The dancers on the December tour had been roped in at the last minute and were mostly amateurs, one among them being only 16 years old, so not up to the standard I now required. Auditions at The Dance Centre in London produced two great dancers with good singing voices, Elaine and Teresa. I installed them at the Margate house and began rehearsing with Carole and a local dancer making up the four. It was a hectic few weeks recording backing tracks for the exciting new numbers, creating outfits for the several planned costume changes and photographing the act for future publicity.

I had decided that the new show would have a pop and rock music feel. It would be an interesting combination of glamorous cabaret with hard hitting vocals and heavy backing tracks. It would open with *'Fire'*, the 70s hit by The Crazy World of Arthur Brown and include other hits like Cliff Richard's *'Devil Woman'* and McCartney's *'Live And Let Die'*. I also introduced a sprinkling of original songs including a Terry Bolton offering called *'The Runner'* which new girl Elaine choreographed and which I recorded as a single many years later. We used the interior of the medieval Chilham Castle near Canterbury for a racy photo-shoot with the girls in some of the revealing costumes that had been designed for the stage show. The whole package was beginning to take shape and I liked it.

Up And Running
(Bahrain)

The Gulf Mirror - March 1980
"If it feels good do it! is the message delivered by Stephen Gold with Flame, the new colourful London floorshow at Bahrain's Infinity Restaurant Club. Well, it feels good and it looks good too."

On the 28th February we flew to Bahrain for our debut at The Infinity Club on the top floor of The Grundy Hotel. The act, with all the new material and the backing tracks, worked supremely well and I was satisfied that it was the right direction to head in.

However, for me, Bahrain was not a very social experience. There were certain restrictions imposed on places of entertainment which meant that the girls had to be escorted out of the club each night by a member of the management. We could, however, socialise with the clients after the show but since the vast majority of clubbers were men - Bahraini or Saudi Arabs and visiting businessmen - time spent in the club after the show was particularly boring. There were never any unaccompanied women. After the hustle and bustle of rehearsals, travel arrangements and generally taking care of business life felt rather dull. I had not had any kind of relationship since my dalliance with the married dancer in Cromer but on one occasion, when we were all invited to a Bahraini house for a late night party, I found myself, after a few too many drinks, close dancing with one of our new recruits.

> *Let's get high, have us a time that we won't forget*
> *Let's get high, nobody knows here that we just met*
> *Give me one good reason why*
> *We shouldn't make it happen*
> *Let's get high*
> **Stephen Gold (Let's Get High)**

Elaine could only be described, in the terms of the era, as 'a gorgeous leggy blonde' and things seemed to be progressing nicely. Unfortunately I had misjudged my alcohol intake and by the time we got back to the hotel I was too pissed to do anything except let her help me to my room.

Next day, thinking that something interesting could develop, I pondered on the impact a coupling with Elaine would have on the rest of the team. This was quickly revealed when I made the mistake of asking Carole if she thought it would have an effect on things.

She was adamantly against it and I will never know if she had words with Elaine or if Elaine just decided, in the light of the day and when sober, that I wasn't such a good proposition. For whichever reason, she managed to avoid my attentions for long enough to make it clear that 'sex was out of the question'.

Over the last few days in Bahrain Elaine teamed up with a young American guy with very dodgy smoking habits, who would soon manage to give us all problems at our next port of call - Egypt. A new contract had arrived – I abandoned our return flights back to London and instead I was provided with tickets direct to Cairo. I was not really sorry to see the back of The Grundy Hotel and on the 1st April, with some considerable apprehension after my previous experience in the Egyptian capital, we boarded a morning flight.

Cairo

We were greeted at the airport by two men from the Egyptian Entertainment Agency (EEA) who had arranged the one month contract at a hotel on the main road between the city and the pyramids. One was short and rotund with a bushy moustache whilst his partner was tall and thin. I could never remember their names so I always referred to them as Laurel & Hardy. I wasted many frustrating hours waiting for them to turn up at the hotel with our money. *"Sterphane you must trust us - no problem"* was their regular mantra. *"I will trust you when you pay me on time." "Sterphane, no problem with money." "Then where is it?" "We bring tomorrow." "You said that yesterday."* And so it went on at the end of every week.

A Smouldering Flame

The show opened and was very well received. It all seemed fine except that only one proper hotel room was allotted to us and I took it. The girls were given a large studio flat, or rather hut, which had been built on the roof of the hotel and made out of very light wood and plaster. It let in bugs and wind and sand and noise in abundance. The only positive was that it had an unrestricted view of the pyramids. They were not happy and I sympathised from my comfortable room while I was trying to get things improved for them. Then one morning, before anything had been changed, a great sand storm erupted with such ferocity that you could not see a building twenty meters away. Up on the roof the sand got in everywhere and everything. The girls were in despair. They were still finding sand in their clothes and costumes weeks after we left Cairo.

The manager of the hotel fancied Elaine, which was understandable, and he demonstrated it by inviting us all out after showtime to nightclubs and to other hotels where he could take the opportunity to chat to her away from his working environment. I suspect he was married and was trying keep it low profile. She responded favourably and was invited on various trips and lunch outings. This was good for us in the hotel. We were in favour with the manager and seemed to get everything we requested for our comfort. We ate well in the coffee shop, the girls' shack was improved and cleaned daily, I was able to use his office to make some calls and his secretary assisted with photocopying and other useful functions.

Most days we either taxied into the city centre or up to the pyramids where we had arranged for horses to be available. I was able to gallop off, full tilt, into the desert. As an inexperienced rider it was the only time I've ever felt safe at full gallop knowing that there would be a soft landing if anything went wrong. So, apart from the constant battles to get money out of Laurel & Hardy everything seemed to be going swimmingly. Then it all changed.

Ten days before we were due to leave, and after a couple of weeks of Elaine dating the hotel manager, the dodgy American from Bahrain appeared in the hotel lobby asking for her. He had flown in hoping to find her and she was happy to be found. Unfortunately the hotel manager took it badly when he was sidelined – he had lost face. He obviously felt humiliated in front of us, being usurped by this young American, and from then on the period of international cooperation was definitely over. All privileges withdrawn.

It became clear to me that Elaine's guy had arrived from Bahrain carrying a reasonable quantity of puff (marijuana) and that they were indulging. Under the legal system in Egypt I was quite sure that if the hotel staff or manager got a 'sniff' of it and called the police then Elaine, and maybe the rest of us, could disappear into an Egyptian nightmare. It was time for a word in her ear, which was never going to go well. She reluctantly agreed to see the American only off hotel premises and not to have any incriminating substances in the hotel or in the show dressing room. Fingers crossed, just a few days to go and we would be clear. What else could happen? It was Laurel and Hardy that happened.

We were due to fly out the day after our last show

with tickets to be supplied by the two agents. They had agreed in the contract to provide tickets for flights from Bahrain to Cairo and then Cairo to London. Three days before the homeward flight they came to the hotel with a proposition for us to move on to another hotel in Egypt for a further two weeks. We were already booked to go straight on to Norway and I explained this to them.

They tried to persuade me to cancel Norway and take this new booking. After a long and bitter wrangle their final throw of the dice was to say that they wouldn't give us the return flight tickets unless we stayed the extra two weeks. To play for time I said I would think about it overnight, but only if they paid our fees immediately up to the last show day. They agreed and the money was brought to the hotel.

In the meantime I considered my options. I realised that I still held the unused return tickets from Bahrain direct to London which were provided for the previous contract. I quickly contacted Middle East Airlines and, thankfully, they agreed to amend those tickets to a flight from Cairo to London. Next day, to their great surprise, I told Laurel & Hardy where they could stuff their tickets.

There was one more crisis before we departed. After our last show I went to my room while the girls packed up the costumes and props ready for the flight. Then a message came from the hotel manager that he wanted us to do a late show in the hotel disco. This was something we had done, extra to the contract, a couple of times before. Naturally the girls were furious and Carole tore a strip off the poor messenger and sent him packing.

When the news reached the manager that we would not be doing the extra show he decided to throw us out of the hotel immediately. Porters were sent to collect our luggage and place it in the street outside the hotel lobby. When I got wind of this I went to find him and eventually managed to get him to see reason. I guess by then he felt he could mellow about the embarrassment over Elaine because we would be gone the next day. I shook his hand and we slept in the hotel for the last time. In the morning we took taxis to the airport, thankful to be leaving. History repeated itself in Egypt, no-one came to see us off!

We quickly transferred to Norway where we played two cities, Stavanger and Tananger, with great success. It was good to be back in a cool climate after the heat and dust of Cairo and to be able to throw off bad memories of the last time I'd been in this beautiful Scandinavian country when Carole had received an unwelcome punch in the mouth!

The Italian Job – Vince D'Amico

In June we embarked on a second tour of American bases in Europe but this time without the burden of the *'Yogi Bear Show'*. We were now dealing solely with the American partner, Vince D'Amico, who was the dynamism behind the organisation.

Vince was a dark haired Italian/American around 50 years old, small in stature but with a larger than life personality. His only *raison d'etre* was to sell live entertainment around the world, mainly to the hundreds of American military clubs. He constantly flew from America to Japan then on to The Phillipines,

A Smouldering Flame

Korea and back to Europe. In fact anywhere he could set up tours for well known American stars of the era. He also booked house bands for military club residencies and less well known but highly entertaining acts like ours to fill in between the tour dates of the stars. Vince did, however, seem to have one major fault. He could not resist a sale, even if fulfilling it was a near impossibility, and over the following few years I was to benefit from this fault by stepping in to organise tours that on paper seemed unlikely to work out.

Overall Vince was a prolific raconteur and great company. No matter what disasters were unfolding around him he always remained upbeat and positive. If the cast of a show was unhappy about travel or hotels or dressing rooms they would be ready to attack him as soon as he appeared. But he was always able to quickly diffuse any such situation with his disarming humour and his readiness to please. His enthusiasm for selling impossible tours would eventually, and sadly, lead to his downfall. Some years later his company collapsed and Vince skedaddled back to America leaving a trail of unpaid bills and a partner ruined.

But back in 1980 he became a great promoter of *'Stephen Gold with Flame'* and we hitched up again with his roadie John Bell and set off for the German dates in the tour bus with a box trailer carrying the sound equipment and costumes. A few days later we crossed into Italy to play a show at the US base in Vicenza near Venice.

After a day off taking in the sights of the famous waterlogged city it was quickly on to Naples once more, where we stayed for three days, giving us the time to enjoy a visit to the ruins of Pompeii. *'Stephen Gold with Flame'* had headlined successfully every night of this European tour and it led directly to my first circumnavigation of the globe - the *'Flame World Tour'* was soon to come!

In the meantime the high summer of 1980 was spent in Portugal, on the wonderful Algarve coast, where we played three casino night clubs at Villamoura, Alvor and Monte Gordo appearing weekly in rotation. The stay was notable not only for the great weather and the sardine beach BBQs but for the vast amounts of currency I accumulated and guarded. It was way before the arrival of the Euro and we were paid Escudos in cash at each casino. It wasn't possible to open a bank account in Portugal so the money had to be constantly in my possession. By the end of the contract I was performing with wads of Escudos stuffed into the pockets of my stage costumes because it wasn't safe to leave the money unattended. There was an English guitarist, who we came across from time to time, who had ingeniously remodelled his stage shoes to accommodate his piles of bank notes.

As the season drew to a close two of the team decided to move on to other things so it was time to recruit again because we were going directly on to Dubai and then to South Korea. There was no time to set up auditions so I put in a call to Carol Hungerford, a superb dancer who had worked with us on the first *'Yogi Bear Show'* and who was then in the summer show at The Winter Gardens' Queens Hall in Margate. Carol accepted my offer of a place in *'Flame'* and she recommended another dancer, Penny Hogan, who was in the same show. I agreed to meet Penny on our return and she was signed up for the coming tour. This combination formed the happiest and most dynamic line-up for the *'Stephen Gold with Flame'* stage show.

We had one more date to fulfil with the old line-up. It was for a rather bizarre TV show called 'Up For The Cup' which was recorded at ATV studios in Birmingham. Hosted by DJ David Hamilton it pitched premier division football clubs against each other, not with football games but with live entertainment. We were in a team playing for Southampton Football Club and performed *'Fire'*. I can't recall which other football club we were supposed to be playing against but our team didn't win. This was not a big disappointment as we were well paid and the series dropped off the schedules pretty soon after our appearance. By the time our show was broadcast we had already left the country and didn't get to see how fantastic we were until some months later!

With such experienced new dancers we quickly put the show back together and strengthened it with everybody stepping up on strong backing vocals for the first time. The next few months would eventually become known as the *'Flame World Tour 1980'* but at that moment I still didn't know for sure if all the suggested dates would be confirmed.

Unparallel Careers!

World Tour

Bowie's single, *Ashes To Ashes, hit the number one spot in the UK charts as I prepared for what would become my biggest and most successful tour. The show was just as I wanted it – I was singing the songs I loved and the audiences were loving it too.*

We flew to Dubai on the 9th September 1980 stopping over in Damascus. Our arrival, sometime after midnight, was marked by a spectacular but inauspicious happening. We were appearing in the nightclub of The Dubai Marine Hotel and they sent two cars to collect us from the airport. One was a nice air conditioned Mercedes taxi which took the four girls. I was left with all the luggage and stage gear in a pick-up type vehicle that had seen better times. The girls were already downing a welcome drink in the hotel lobby by the time my vehicle rounded the last bend and suddenly lurched to the left in a shower of sparks and a deafening screech. We quickly came to a complete stop and I saw that one of the wheels was heading into the desert waste ground adjacent to the hotel. The driver seemed unperturbed and started off-loading the luggage and heading for the hotel on foot. No-one else came to our aid so I grabbed what I could and hurried after him.

It made me wonder about the standard of the health and safety regulations in Dubai, a thought that was reinforced one morning later in the stay when the hotel fire alarms sounded. I emerged from my room in time to see the hotel manager dashing down the stairs dragging a mattress emitting smoke and flames in all directions. He dragged the offending article out through the hotel lobby, to the astonishment of a number of guests checking in, and threw it onto the adjacent waste ground where it could join the wheel from my airport transport. The fire fighters arrived shortly after this and were delighted to see that there was nothing left for them to do except, I suspect, advise the management on how better to deal with a blazing mattress.

The show played very successfully to full houses every night and I soon fell into a social routine. For a Middle East country, in 1980, Dubai was surprisingly liberal with its alcohol laws. So liberal that there was an English style pub attached to the hotel called Wilkie's Wine Bar where we soon built up a rapport with expats Brian Wilks and his bar manager Chalky.

For me it was a relief to have a social life alongside the shows after the past months of celibacy. I was soon attracted to the pretty new girl Penny and, after a few days, managed to invite her for a late night drink in my room without our colleagues noticing. These secret assignations would continue well beyond the stay in Dubai.

It soon became a little complicated when a dance group called 'Blonde Feeling' arrived on the scene to perform in another hotel. One of the members, an attractive blonde called Pauline, had been in the Charlie Drake Show at Margate Lido Theatre in 1977 and had frequented our flat above the El Ranchero coffee shop. It was obvious that she fancied me and she told me that she had 'been in awe' of me in Margate – how's that for an ego boost - and I was too flattered not to respond. There were a couple of times when we were all together for a trip to the beach or for drinks after the show and this required all my latent diplomatic skills so as not to piss off one or both of the girls.

For a while Penny was enduring an attack of dysentery, which got me off the hook for late night room visits, so I was surreptitiously popping over to the other hotel. Eventually Pauline also went down with some tropical bug and shortly after I last visited her, in her sick bed, Blonde Feeling were shipped out to another venue and our paths did not cross again. After a few dodgy tablets from the hotel's doctor, which caused hallucinations and therefore some unconventional stage performances, Penny recovered and we resumed the late night trysts.

Shortly after our arrival in Dubai I had taken a call from Vince D'Amico to say that the following contract, for South Korea, had been brought forward by a week in order to play some dates in Japan. This meant the tour began a week before the end of the Dubai run and he pleaded with me to try to get an early release. I spoke with the general manager, a German called Rolfe, who said he would agree so long as I arranged a replacement show to take over for our missing week and the following month.

Frantic phone calls followed and I made contact with JJ Stewart who had been with us on the *'Yogi Bear Show'* tour. He agreed to take over from us together with his four new girl dancers. Rolfe was happy, JJ Stewart was very happy and I was heading for Japan – so I was the happiest! Until, a few days before we were due to travel, I received a call to say that the Japan dates had been 'postponed'. Panic!

A Smouldering Flame

We were now stuck in Dubai for a week with no work and no accommodation because JJ Stewart and his team would be taking over our rooms in the hotel. Luckily Rolfe came to our rescue by arranging for us to spend the week at The Marbella Club in Sharjah, the neighbouring emirate, in return for three performances. This was particularly fortunate because Iraq had invaded Iran on the 22nd September which caused many gulf states to close down clubs and live entertainment fearing that the war could spread.

In the event we had an idyllic week in a luxury resort, and the only battle we had was with the elements. The shows were staged outside around the pool long after the very heavy nightfall condensation had settled on everything. The equipment, costumes and stage surface were saturated and we slipped and slithered our way through the shows.

Vince D'Amico arrived towards the end of our week at The Marbella Club. He planned to check out any future show opportunities in Dubai and then travel on with us to South Korea. He was our next meal ticket and had arrived with a fist full of air tickets and news that the tour had been extended to take in three stop-overs in America – California, Colorado and Kentucky. We would indeed circumnavigate the globe!

The last night in Sharjah was party night. The friends we had made in Dubai came to give us a good send off and early the next morning, the 9th October 1980, with tired eyes and sore heads we met Vince at Dubai Airport. He checked us in for the journey which included a short hop to Bahrain in order to pick up a Korean Airlines flight to Seoul. As the flight was called for boarding Vince dashed off to make a call, to his office in Los Angeles, while we settled on board – there were no mobiles in 1980 so he was using an airport public phone.

As was the custom with airline protocol of that era the cabin crew started a head count to ensure that all checked-in passengers were on board. I heard the doors being closed and quickly informed a stewardess that one of our party was still not on board. She insisted that the head count was correct and that he must be sitting elsewhere in the plane. He wasn't – he was still in the terminal with all of our ongoing flight tickets in his briefcase.

On arrival in Bahrain we should have been in transit but could not produce any onward flight tickets. We were locked in an immigration department interview room while they checked out our 'missing passenger' story. We were still there three hours later when Vince arrived to rescue us. *"Hi guys, how yer doin' – call took a bit longer than expected – had to get the next flight. Let's get some beers."* As usual our anger quickly dissipated.

Seoul

We got to Seoul after a long overnight flight via Bangkok and checked into the Sheraton Walker Hill Hotel, which was the ritziest in the city. I agreed to meet Vince early evening for a drink and to talk through the tour schedule. When I arrived in the bar he was sitting with a beautiful young Korean girl who was poured into a tight local style dress with the thigh high split. He immediately asked if he should arrange for a girl to spend the night with me. *"She can call a friend"* he said. By this time I was seeing Penny most nights after the show, but didn't yet want it to come out, so I made some weak excuse about being too tired after the flight, which must have made him think I wasn't up to it – and he was probably right.

Later that night we watched a most spectacular production in the hotel's showroom and met some of the mainly Australian performers afterwards for a nightcap. Our stay at this five star resort lasted only one night. Next day we were moved to The Crown Hotel which was conveniently close to the main US Army base and near to the heart of the city – and probably cheaper!

The military base in Seoul, The Yongsan Army Garrison, housed the headquarters of the US Army in South Korea and was typical of many of the American bases that we visited. On passing through the gates of these massive areas you were immediately struck by the feeling that you had just arrived at any town, anywhere in America. The streets, side-walks, buildings, road signs, bars and shops were all there to make the US Military feel that they had created a bit of the home country wherever they were in the world. This base was home to around 7000 service men and women and several thousand family members. It had numerous clubs and we staged the show in seven different establishments over ten days on this one base. The Frontier Club, The Broken Heart Club, The Lucky Y Club and The Crossroads Club were just four of the many dedicated to the different ranks and to the numerous local civilian workers. The locals were the backbone of the club system taking up vital roles such as

Unparallel Careers!

club managers, chefs, bar tenders and waiters.

The Crown Hotel was a brisk walk away from the well known shopping area known as Itaewon where all manner of valuable items could be acquired for meagre sums. We threw away our old and battered suitcases and purchased new and better ones for a fraction of the cost at home. I took the opportunity to acquire some terrific silk shirts and before we left we were all sporting tailor made bomber jackets with our names embroidered on the front and, as Vince had by then confirmed all the ongoing dates, *"Flame World Tour 1980"* emblazoned across the back. Vanity knew no bounds!

In 1980 South Korea was not the manufacturing powerhouse that it has become today (2019) and was not nearly so westernised. There was still a nightly curfew in Seoul, a hang over from the American occupation after the Korean War, and we had to time the shows so that the Korean road manager could get us back to the hotel and get home himself by 11pm.

The hotel was very good but it did have some drawbacks, not least of which were the rats that frequented the restaurant after it had stopped serving for the night. We saw them several times while we were taking a late coffee and I once tried to complain to the hotel reception. Unfortunately a complete failure of linguistic communication led to me retiring hurt after fifteen minutes of shouting and waving my arms about. I said *"There are rats running about in the restaurant"* with the reply being something like *"Ras you want ras. We no have ras."* Then me, getting ever more desperate *"No, I don't want them but you do have them in the restaurant."*

"Aah yea ras, in lestaurant, ha ha ras. You like?" "No no no – oh never mind!"

Most days we wrapped ourselves up in scarves and woolly hats and wandered, in the -10°C morning air, to a warm coffee shop that we had discovered. It was here that we encountered an even more amusing take on the language mismatches. The waitress, a charming and polite young lady, had obviously learnt a few good phrases which were useful for serving English speaking customers. She always approached the table and addressed each of us in turn with what should have been *"Are you for coffee?"* but, when spoken with her strong oriental accent, it came out as *"You fuckofee?"* Though she didn't know it she was asking us to leave!

Before we did 'fuckofee' from Seoul we appeared in a major Korean TV show as guest artistes. It was a kind of oriental take on the Eurovision Song Contest. We didn't realise it was such a major TV show until we took a taxi into the city centre the next day. The driver recognised us and proceeded to radio his colleagues with the news that he had the foreign stars in his cab. It had been broadcast to several million viewers. Big fish in a small pool again!

Gateway To The USA

Appearing in the US Army club system on alternate days to us was the singer Billy Paul of *'Me And Mrs Jones'* fame. Vince contacted me to say that Billy was going on to Hawaii for some extra dates and, because we had a few free days before we opened in California, would we agree to travel with him? We could stop over in Honolulu where there might also be a show for us. Would we agree? What a silly question. We hopped over to Japan where I met Vince's travel representative in Tokyo. I eagerly grabbed the flight tickets and we were off for a blissful three days at Waikiki Beach.

On arrival we met Frenchie, Vince's representative in Hawaii, who drove us to the Waikiki Marine Hotel. On the way he told us he hadn't been able to set up a show for us so we should just 'hang loose' until the onward flight to California. Vince had, in effect, given us a free holiday in paradise and we appreciated every minute of it before the next leg of the tour. I guess it was in Hawaii that my relationship with Penny blossomed. The other girls had clocked it by then which made it more relaxed for the rest of the tour.

> *So when I build a castle it's for you*
> *With golden sunlight shining on it too*
> *And it will be a place for us to go*
> *To learn about each other as we grow*
> **Stephen Gold (Growing Together)**

We entered mainland USA via Los Angeles on the 30th October and checked into a motel near the airport where we met up with some relatives of Carole. They were somewhat dismayed at the location which apparently was a hang out for prostitutes and pimps. Happily the night passed without incident and I did not receive any decent, or indecent, offers for the girls!

The next day we flew to Monterey, around 100 miles south of San Francisco, and checked into The Magic Carpet Lodge. It was just outside a massive army base called Fort Ord where we were to perform over several nights. We were allotted a driver for the stay who owned a real passion wagon. It was a large customised transit type vehicle with fur covered seats, a bar and high quality hi-fi system.

Ted picked us up each day and showed us the sights as though we were paying tourists. Monterey itself boasted the famous Cannery Row which featured in the book of the same name by John Steinbeck. It had been restored as a characterful upmarket waterside shopping centre, as had Old Fisherman's Wharf in Monterey Harbour. Our willing driver took us on The Seven Mile Drive around the Monterey Peninsular and we stopped off at the small historic town of Carmel where Clint Eastwood was mayor at that time. He also owned a local restaurant called 'The Hog's Breath'. It was a wonderful opportunity to be able to visit these places while on a working tour. The shows continued to work superbly in front of the American military and it all bode well for the future.

From California we flew to Colorado, arriving in Denver on the 9th November with warm and pleasant weather which, within three days, turned into a freeze up with two feet of snow falling overnight. This time we had no driver so I hired a car and we just managed to visit the museum around Buffalo Bill's grave before the weather closed in. We played several shows at Lowry US Airforce Base and on the last night found ourselves supporting the American hit band Air Supply who had just enjoyed a smash with their single *'I'm All Out Of Love'*, a song I still hear often on smooth or relaxing radio shows.

After Denver it was Louisville, Kentucky where

Unparallel Careers!

we played the Fort Knox Army Base and visited the enormous General George Patten Tank Museum. Within the surrounds of the base sits the US Bullion Depository where the American gold reserves are kept. The base was the principal training ground for armoured vehicle operations and covered an astonishing 170 sq miles (441sq km).

It was in Louisville, while dwelling over a monster American breakfast, that I decided it would be great to visit New York again. We were due to pass through there in transit on the way home so it was easy to rearrange the flight tickets. Penny and Carole decided to stick with me while the other two girls took their London bound flight.

We had a glorious time seeing the sights and taking in some shows. Although I had spent many days in New York during the QE2 years I had never visited the city solely as a tourist and it was time to do the top of the Empire State Building and enjoy the Radio City Music Hall show again. Three days later, after a night witnessing Mickey Rooney in a clever comedy on Broadway, we followed the others home.

At exactly the same time Bowie was also starring on Broadway as John Merrick in 'The Elephant Man'. We democratically chose to see Mickey Rooney but not before I had reminded my companions about my Elephant Man connection. It was fifteen years since we both sang with 'The Lower Third' and now we were both 'on Broadway' but in slightly different circumstances!

To wind up a fabulous year we travelled to Germany for another combined *'Yogi Bear and Flame'* tour and it was difficult to make the change back to a children's show mindset after such a fantastic world experience. This time we travelled in a converted coach which had a kitchen, bar and sleeping area at the back. It was owned by a German called Reiner Schaefer who had converted it himself in order to tour shows. It was certainly a much more relaxing way to travel.

To play the extra characters in the *'Yogi Bear Show'* we added some additional bodies including Carol Hungerford's fiance Derry James, a talented trumpet playing comedy entertainer. For some reason Derry, who was normally the life and soul of any party, managed to wind up the girls about the conditions in some of the clubs, the travel schedule and whatever else he could find to gripe about. Their complaints boiled over into a bit of an attack on Vince when he turned up at one of the clubs with his usual jovial *"Hi guys, how's it going?"* It was necessary to remind everybody that he had recently given us three glorious days in Hawaii and covered all the hotel bills. Swings and roundabouts! The rough with the smooth!

Vince had provided a road manager for this tour who was a 'resting' musician. He was a member of a popular rock band from the Isle of Wight. There was an instant attraction between him and Elaine that would soon lead to her exit from the act.

Managing Expectations

At the beginning of 1981 I made a decision that would take me in an entirely different direction. I set up a new company, *Solid Gold Promotions*, in partnership with Carole. The idea was to build on the contacts that had been nurtured over the past few years and to produce new and exciting shows as well as continue to promote *'Flame'*. The headquarters of the new enterprise were some quickly converted rooms in my house at Hatfeild Road, Margate. I soon had an office, a store and a rehearsal room. We would go on to promote shows by some well known American come-back artistes like The Floaters (*'Float On'* 1977) and Danny And The Juniors (*'At The Hop'* 1957). Meanwhile I accepted contracts for *'Stephen Gold with Flame'* to appear in Germany and Spain.

Cologne

The first booking was to headline in a prestigious nightclub in Cologne, West Germany. We were accommodated in a strange apartment above the club. Strange because everything was black – doors, ceilings, walls, carpets and even the toilet equipment. The main bedroom that I shared with Penny had a large mirror on the ceiling and a black fur lined headboard. It took me back nearly two decades to La Discotheque Club and its black mattresses!

The reason for the strange decor became clear one evening when there was a knock at the door. I was confronted by a middle aged man and my limited knowledge of the German language was, together with some pointing and gesticulating, just enough to realise he was asking to book a girl for the night. Tempting as it was to make some extra money I decided that pimping wasn't for me. The flat had obviously once been a knocking shop and still had a few regular customers!

The sojourn in Cologne was hardly memorable except for our departure which turned out to be somewhat more dramatic than the show. We had travelled to Germany in a rented VW mini-bus which I had deposited in a nearby long term car park for the duration of the contract. The night before we were due to return to England I moved the van to a parking spot in the street outside the club to allow for a quick getaway early on the Sunday morning. Unfortunately I had not noticed the temporary signs that had been fixed to the lamp posts.

Early in the morning I was awoken by loud vehicle noises and voices barking orders in German. Swinging open the curtains I was just able to watch our mini-bus disappearing round the corner mounted on a tow-away truck. There was a carnival scheduled to pass through the street later that day and the temporary signs banned parking from midnight onwards. There were a few fraught hours while I tried to locate the police vehicle compound and summon up the 150 German marks in cash to pay for the van's release. Having retrieved our transport I then had to find a way to get back to the apartment without falling foul of the carnival again. It was eventually achieved but there was no possibility of getting to the French coast in time to catch our booked ferry. Altogether 'one of those days'.

It was during this stay in Cologne that Elaine announced her intention to leave the act and join her new boyfriend on the Isle of Wight. I was sad to see her go because I thought she had great potential - an ever improving singing voice and the looks and dance ability to be a successful pop recording artiste. I had written and recorded a song called *'Giving In'* which featured her on lead vocals and it had to be shelved. The chance to promote it had been lost.

> *Principals can get embarrassing*
> *Stop you gettin' a lot of things*
> *You write a song with a stolen line*
> *It can put you in the big time*
> *All the years I had integrity*
> *Tried to keep my identity*
> *Spent my life in mediocrity*
> *And that aint good enough for me*
> *I'm givin' in, I'm givin' in*
> **Stephen Gold (Givin' In)**

Barcelona

I was able to replace Elaine before we travelled by coach across France to Barcelona where we checked in to a hotel near the Ramblas. The act was booked into a city centre nightclub and we took the opportunity to have a look at the club and its entertainment on the night before we were due to start.

I was aware that Spain had cast off its inhibitions, after President Franco had died, and that there had been great social reforms, but I wasn't prepared for how far reaching they had become. The entertainment included strippers, which was not shocking for a late night club, but it seemed to be a requirement that other acts throw in a bit of sex too. We were astonished to see the main artiste that night, an excellent singer, present her penultimate number while stripping and then her finale completely topless. I immediately had forebodings about our rehearsals the next day which turned out to be justified. When we arrived to go through the sound checks the club manager informed me that we would be required to do a number between each of the other acts. It seemed that we were being scheduled as 'dressing' for the show programme rather than a featured act. This was not as per our contract which was to perform one or two thirty minute show sets – our normal show schedule. There was no way that I could agree to this so I told the girls to pack up the costumes and equipment and we left the premises.

I immediately contacted the Spanish agent who had dealt with the contract and who was based in Barcelona. I complained bitterly that the club was in breach of the contract they had signed. He told me to 'hang loose' and enjoy Barcelona for two days and he would place us at another venue where we could do our established show.

We explored Barcelona, enjoyed the tapas, sampled the wine, and waited for news. It did not come. I visited the agent's office several times but he was never there. I came to accept the fact that there would be no replacement booking and that we were stranded.

After several days filling in time the girls were, understandably, getting restless and demanding to know what was happening. There was no alternative but to head back to England as soon as possible. Unfortunately I had no return tickets and very little cash left.

In 1981 I could not pay overseas bills with my UK credit cards and there was a limit to how much cash you could draw on a credit card at any one time so, using

Unparallel Careers!

mine and Penny's cards, we wandered about Barcelona from one bank to another withdrawing the maximum twenty five pounds in pesetas at each cash machine until we had enough to pay for the coach tickets and to settle the hotel bill. Thus we returned home with tails firmly between our legs!

Before we left I made contact with a Spanish lawyer to get advice on claiming damages from the agent for breach of contract. Unfortunately, subsequent efforts to sue through our union, Equity, soon fizzled out and, after paying the girls, I had to take the financial hit, which was considerable.

The only really good memory that remains of the stay in Barcelona, apart from sampling some good wine and tapas, was that on one frustrating day wandering the city we suddenly spotted the Greek ship SS Navarino docked at the cruise terminal. Penny had worked on the ship with the 'Black And White Minstrels' before joining *'Flame'* so we went to see if any of her old friends were still on board. Bingo, we were invited for drinks with the Commodore and other officers who she knew well. It was a ray of sunshine in an otherwise overcast period.

***As I was suffering** this dip in fortunes a song went to number one in the UK charts called 'Under Pressure'. It was from Freddie Mercury and Queen with David Bowie. He was exploring new associations and about to enter his most successful period of hit making.*

A Dark Cloud

The summer of '81 was spent mostly on The Isle of Wight, the holiday island lying a short hop across The Solent channel from Portsmouth on the English south coast. *'Stephen Gold with Flame'* successfully toured a number of major holiday centres.

It was during that season that I recorded an album of the most popular songs from the stage show and promoted it at each performance. Although there exists several video clips of the act these were the only sound recordings made of *'Stephen Gold with Flame'*.

We rented a flat in East Cowes which was shared by the whole team. Once in a while we escaped from the island for a day or so to do shows on the mainland. It was a happy summer until August when my father fell ill and was hospitalised again. I got the news shortly after that he had died.

It was a deeply sad time but I continued to do all the scheduled shows, even on the day of his funeral when I drove to Margate to attend the crematorium and drove straight back immediately afterwards. It's something I regret to this day. I didn't spare the time to see him in hospital or spend time with my family on such an emotional occasion. My grandmother, Nan, was already in a care home and she died a few weeks later. For several days after my Dad's funeral I went to a hall where I had access to a piano and I wrote some words and music and cried for him.

What I should have said, what I never learnt
On my own instead, all my bridges burnt

Unparallel Careers!

It was a year when I should have reflected on the priorities in life, but I didn't. I just crashed on regardless leaving behind family and friends. I took my obsession with 'the show must go on' to ridiculous lengths which, later in life, I would come to realise was a sign that I was a chronic perfectionist – I was never fully satisfied with any performance and fell out with numerous people during my performing years over what must have seemed to them insignificant details.

Still Growing

At the end of 1981 *Solid Gold Promotions* had secured several contracts for the Christmas and New Year period. The *'Yogi Bear Show'* for US bases in Germany, a version of the *'Flame'* show in Portugal, and *'Stephen Gold with Flame'* in Bombay (now Mumbai) and Delhi. It was a frantic few weeks recruiting and rehearsing new teams for Portugal and Germany as well as polishing up my own act and introducing two new members for India.

I remember a particular language breakdown in the confusion of organising the various teams. I phoned the French rail company to book train tickets from Paris to Lisbon and asked the very nice lady in my best schoolboy French for *"deux cochons pour Lisbon."* She sounded a little confused because I should have said *"deux couchettes pour Lisbon."* After a quick consultation with my handy French-English dictionary I realised I had asked for two pigs for Lisbon - when I really wanted two sleepers!

To complicate logistics still further I got a call from

A Smouldering Flame

Vince D'Amico just before the German tour was due to start. He had overbooked the *'Yogi Bear Show'* tour so he asked me to take a second team out to Germany for four days to stand in on the doubled up dates. I agreed to help by taking my *'Flame'* team, which was scheduled for India, on the condition that Vince himself played Yogi Bear because we didn't have enough people to play all the parts.

We hired a 'man with a van' and set off for the first date at Hahn US Air Base in Southern Germany. As we neared Germany snow began to fall and quickly thickened on the ground. The going was slow but we arrived in the town of Hahn in early evening and checked into a hotel. After a relaxed meal in the hotel restaurant I decided to prepare for the morning and asked the hotel receptionist for directions to the American base. There was no American base at Hahn, or rather, not at this Hahn! She confirmed that there were several different towns called Hahn in Germany but only one could boast the Hahn US Air Base. The right town was some considerable distance further south.

Next morning we thundered down the autobahn as quickly as the snow would allow and arrived at the correct base a few minutes before the show was due to start. We immediately leapt into action unloading costumes and props. Vince was there already and quickly donned his Yogi Bear outfit but, unfortunately, he was pre-occupied with selling shows for the future and missed several important cues. Yogi would be speaking on stage while Vince, with his bear head off, was negotiating in the adjacent bar. Typically, he treated it all quite casually and we muddled through a few shows in much the same sloppy manner. Years later, taking a Ryanair flight to Frankfurt, I realised that I had landed at what had been Hahn US Airbase, many kilometres from the city!

India

We zipped back to England and immediately picked up our flight to Bombay where we played two nights in a sumptuous 5 star hotel. On Christmas Eve we flew on to New Delhi to open at The Sheraton Hotel and on Christmas morning I found myself sharing eggnog with the hotel's managers around the swimming pool while Penny recovered from a bout of 'Delhi Belly' and the other girls slept in.

What I found most striking about Bombay and New Delhi was the contrast between the sumptuous hotels with their wealthy guests and the poverty right outside their doors where there were people spending the nights sleeping in cardboard boxes. In spite of the poverty Delhi was a colourful, fascinating and exciting city full of history, both colonial and Indian.

On a rare day off we took the opportunity to board a bus for a hair raising three hour journey, through pouring rain, to Agra and the Taj Mahal. As we passed through towns and villages, scattering people and animals in our wake, I prayed that the driver could see more than me through his rain soaked windscreen which was without functioning wipers. The hazardous journey was compensated by my first glimpse of the mystical building through the clearing haze – unforgettable.

A Smouldering Flame

We celebrated the New Year with a final show in the hotel's vast banqueting suite and flew home early on New Year's Day.

The War Year

After a brief break I was summoned to a meeting on The Isle of Man. The manager of The Villa Marina, an entertainment complex on Douglas seafront, had received and was impressed with our publicity for *'Stephen Gold with Flame'*. It was agreed that I would produce a full length summer production based on the regular *'Flame'* show. By 1982 I had already inserted into the show several arrangements based on film themes. We had successfully used the Star Wars and the Bond movie music as the basis for routines and I was able to adapt and extend them for the summer show. I incorporated fairly basic slide projection and added some audience participation to extend the show to two full hours.

We opened in June and played for twelve weeks during which time the Falklands War was drawing to its end. This was significant because after the Argentinians surrendered we got a call in our Margate office from Derek Agutter at CSE who was putting together a show to go immediately to The Falklands.

I still had some weeks to go on the Isle of Man so Carole St. James cobbled together an act with two of our previous dancers, called it *'Dream'*, and offered it to CSE. They were flown down to the South Atlantic and performed, with other acts, on the principal warships and at Port Stanley. The resulting press interest was intense after pictures of the girls socialising with Prince

Andrew on HMS Invincible were splashed over the red top front pages - 'The Prince and The Showgirls'. I wrote to the palace on behalf of Carole and the girls in *'Dream'* to apologise for the photographs escaping to the tabloid press and received a reply from the Queen's press secretary reminding me that Prince Andrew was quite used to suffering that sort of publicity.

When the excitement of the Falklands adventure died down, and the Isle of Man season came to a close, I returned to Margate with Penny to ponder on the next move. We didn't have to ponder for long because, on the journey back from the Isle of Man, we had stopped off to talk to the owners of Blackpool Pleasure Beach about our, just completed, summer show.

A few days later they called to ask me to present an adapted version of the show for a Christmas season in their Horseshoe Showbar. I called up some of our favourite previous *'Flame'* members who all jumped at the chance of a few weeks back in the show. I added some Christmas music and Penny choreographed some fun routines which played well with the audiences all through December. We played the last show on New Year's Day 1983. The first day of a year that was to bring another major change of direction and the start of yet another exciting and rewarding adventure.

That Christmas *a recording, first heard on an American TV show some years before, was released in the UK and was a hit for Bing Crosby and David Bowie – 'Peace on Earth/Little Drummer Boy'. That performance was much nearer to what I had been doing for many years and out of character for Bowie. I didn't lose the opportunity to point that out to anyone prepared to listen!*

A Smouldering Flame

During the year to come *one member of the group 'David Bowie and The Lower Third' was to come back into my life in a significant way and was a constant reminder of the 'old days'. Denis 'Teacup' Taylor had given up professional music not long after the demise of the group and he had become a talented photographer. I was able to take advantage of these new talents to produce show publicity photos for the next few years.*

*First photos in the dungeon
at Chilham Castle, Kent*

*The Flame dream team 1980
Carole, Elaine, Penny, Carol*

*Carmel, California - seeking Clint Eastwood!
Flame World Tour 1980*

Denver, Colorado in the snow and the passion wagon in Monteray, California

Flame - Hot Stuff!

Getting dramatic with Elaine World Tour 1980

On stage at Margate Winter Gardens circa 1984

Jumeirah Beach - Dubai

Chapter 8
Island Hopping

I was not an island
Love kept me connected
Hope remained eternal
But the dreams were all rejected

Early in the new year I spotted an advert in The Stage newspaper asking for proposals for the operation of Ryde Pavilion on the Isle of Wight for the forthcoming season. Based on the success in the Isle of Man and Blackpool, with the full length *'Flame'* production, I decided to offer my services.

After a visit to the venue it was clear to me that it did not lend itself to a glamorous show. It was an old multi purpose building with a large auditorium featuring a stage and dressing rooms at one end plus a licensed bar and a snack counter. Its early 1900s interior seemed to make it an ideal setting for a night out in a wild west saloon. Absolutely perfect for *'Way Out West'* which I had last produced for the Pontins Holiday Camp season ten years earlier. My proposal was accepted and I duly took over the Pavilion, its bar and catering for a one year contract. I was now a theatre manager and producer!

At around the same time I discussed with Penny the possibility of her staging and managing the *'Flame'* show for another season and, relying on my somewhat outdated memories, I thought Jersey would be a great place to look for an available venue. We were then offered some extra financial backing for the project from a family member and that enabled us to look around. Some initial enquiries found that The Watersplash at St Ouens Bay, the most well known show venue in Jersey when I was working there thirteen years before, was available for that summer of 1983.

I flew to Jersey and met Harry Swanson, who was the doyen of the well known Swanson family. They owned a number of venues and properties on the island including The Watersplash. I agreed a shared profit deal with Mr Swanson who was delighted to have a show in the venue which had been closed the previous season. There was a good reason why it had been closed. The tourist season in Jersey had declined enormously in length and visitor numbers since my glory days at The Caribbean Bar and I was setting us up to suffer the consequences of this later in the summer.

On the Isle Of Wight I discovered the services of a brilliant scenic artist, Jim Harrop, and he designed and built the decor needed to create the illusion of a wild west saloon inside the Pavilion, which we renamed The Pavilion Showbar. Jim would come to be a loyal friend and would be involved in many more projects through the following two decades.

The cast was auditioned and contracted and

included the guitar duo Campbell & Reid who would evolve into the musical mainstay of the show. They also provided much of the comedy with their superb way of improvising around my script while playing the two hapless deputies. As with the earlier versions of the show there was a town sheriff, a saloon hostess and a piano player. I set up bar and catering systems and recruited front of house and box office staff. Having found a house to rent for the season I sublet part of it to Tony Campbell and Brian Reid who were planning to stay overnight for part of the week, when they could 'mix' with their fans, and return to their wives in Portsmouth for the rest.

The Pavilion Showbar was not set to open until June but the *'Flame'* show in Jersey was to get underway earlier. In May I travelled, with Penny, to The Watersplash to prepare for rehearsals. It was to be a complicated production using projected film and slides as well as much more complex choreography than in earlier incarnations of *'Flame'*.

The three hour show featured a new line-up of girls who, like Penny, were all singer-dancers. To complete the cast there was a Portuguese male singer, Fernando, and the impressionist Adam Daye, who would take over the linking of the production - my job in its previous life! I struggled, together with the sound and lighting engineer Alan Frayne, to perfect the timing of the film sequences. At that time, well before digital video, they had to be run from a film projector. Inevitably we had some serious teething troubles when the show opened but it was positively reviewed by the Jersey press and I felt I could leave the island feeling it was a job well done.

Unfortunately the perpetual Jersey problem of seasonal accommodation for the artistes reared its ugly head and couldn't be resolved before I departed. This led to a rift between me and Penny which was not mended by the time I took the flight back to England. Was I abandoning a sinking ship? The matter was eventually resolved by the positive reaction to a write-up that Penny managed to get in The Jersey Evening Post about the plight of the showgirls with 'no fixed abode'.

Wight Nights

Back on The Isle of Wight The Pavilion Showbar opened to the public at the beginning of June and was immediately successful. The show, *'Way Out West'*, ran every evening from Monday to Friday and bookings were good for a new enterprise.

It was free to enter on Saturday and Sunday evenings when Campbell & Reid held the stage with their own repertoire of country music, pop songs and comedy. I relied on bar and catering takings to cover the costs and, fortunately, the weekends were always packed and the bar takings exceptional.

To anyone observing the operation from the outside it looked like I was making my fortune and this would come back to bite me when the contract came up for renewal for the 1984 season. The running costs were considerable, the contract payments to Ryde Council, alterations to the venue, the cast wages, the staff wages, publicity, my living costs and a whole lot of other irritating little expenses meant that until August the project was only just breaking even. It was therefore timely that I was asked if I could provide a show for a few nights each week at The Ventnor Winter Gardens which would bring in an additional income.

I persuaded Carole St.James to come to The Isle of Wight. She was still looking after the *Solid Gold Promotions* office in Margate and had acquired a fiance earlier in the year. Carole was to front up a show which featured a new version of her three girl group *'Dream'* so that we could use the mantra *'First act to the Falklands after the war'* for publicity. That proved to be the last period that Carole was involved with my adventures – she left showbiz and celebrated her wedding later that year when she became Carole Jardine – surname number four!

In August The Pavilion Showbar came good and I worked hard dealing with the many full houses for the main show and the knackering weekend nights. I had to do my bit behind the bar to cope with the ever increasing numbers.

During this period *I heard about a book that had recently been published called The Pitt Report. It was written by Bowie's one time manager Kenneth Pitt and was one of the first books to emerge detailing the early days of Bowie's career. I was quick to point out to new friends and acquaintances that I had been a member of the group 'The Lower Third' that was described in the book. Never missed a chance!*

Business Affairs

Meanwhile, in the English Channel things were not going too well. I had left Jersey in mid May and my contact with Penny was by regular, but not frequent, phone calls which were difficult to coordinate. There were no mobile phones and no internet. So when it became clear that the income from The Watersplash was not covering costs, the calls became increasingly strained. I was absorbed with the day to day running of Ryde Pavilion and found it a distraction to have to listen to Penny's woes. I didn't want to hear about how she was having to deal with the Jersey bank and the many other minor things that inevitably become major when the money runs out. We had been together for three years but, with the stress of the season, there was now a distance between us. The situation was not helped by the fact that I had started an on-off affair with a married member of the Pavilion staff and Penny was in a similar situation with a Watersplash manager. This only came to light during difficult conversations after the season ended and it took a while to mend.

> *In the blinking of a wandering eye*
> *It seemed so easy to deceive*
> *I still don't know the crazy reason why*
> *Cos I don't wanna see you leave*
> **Stephen Gold (On A Train)**

By August I knew the Jersey show could not survive without some further financial support and realised I was going to have to go 'cap in hand' to Harry Swanson and ask for his support. I banked on the fact that it would not look good for his company's reputation if the show closed early. He agreed to make up any shortfall by paying some of the cast fees until the end of the advertised season. This was a good example of an artistic success turning into a financial disaster. Unfortunately it would not be the last! When the Jersey show closed in September Penny came to The Isle of Wight. It was a sticky few nights when we kind of confessed, anguished and accepted. By then my dalliance had long since ended. Soon after that Penny took a new show, that we called *'Mystique'*, to The Algarve and we were apart again for a month.

Immediately following the summer I had meetings with the Ryde council representatives about an extension of the contract for 1984 and 1985. There was some opposition to an extension on the same financial terms because several of the councillors had witnessed the packed houses on summer weekends and expected that I would agree to a much higher fee. Luckily I had a champion among the councillors called Jeff Manners who was chairman of the leisure committee. He took a more realistic view and held sway with his colleagues. A new agreement was signed and I was now able to plan for the next two years. I hoped the project would eventually reap the benefits I had expected at the start. Before taking a break from the island I managed to secure the tenancy of a flat that was in the process of being renovated and that I would be able to move into when I returned in the new year.

Around The World Again

In December 1983 *'Stephen Gold with Flame'* flew off on another of Vince D'Amico's magical mystery tours which started when we emerged from Manila International Airport in The Philippines. We were whisked away to Clarke US Airforce Base, the principal

Unparallel Careers!

USAF facility in the Far East at that time.

The tour started less than perfectly when one important costume suitcase was lost somewhere between London and Manila. Tony, my stage manager from Ryde Pavilion who was on the tour with us as road manager, had to make a mad dash back to Manila Airport when it had been located. The case, and a frazzled roadie, arrived at the base just before the first show.

Clarke was, like many of the US bases I had seen before, enormous – an American city in a tropical paradise. It had spurned a massive local economy with several small towns having sprung up right outside the perimeter fences.

We were roundly welcomed by our hosts who invited us to join them for a night out in one of the local nightclubs outside the base. A sergeant who was driving us that night explained that most of the clubs outside the base were very seedy but, seeing that we had young girls in the show, we were heading for the classiest. The club was in the open air with a beautiful tropical setting and we enjoyed some good food and listened to the excellent house band until the cabaret was announced.

Five girls entered to the punchy recorded sounds of The Rolling Stones' *'Satisfaction'*. Three girls had guitars slung around them, one was behind drums and the last girl did all manner of things with a microphone and its stand. Their tribute to the Rolling Stones differed from the real thing in several important ways but the most striking was that they were all completely naked.

We were seated at the edge of the stage and at the climax of the act the girl emulating Mick Jagger slid towards us on her knees with her legs apart. Our hosts were beside themselves with embarrassment and profuse in their apologies to the girls but I could only reflect on what the entertainment must have been like in the seedy clubs.

While in The Philippines we were scheduled to do the only *'Yogi Bear Show'* of the tour and had the honour of performing in the heavy character costumes at midday in full sunlight with a temperature well over 40°C. We all lost some weight that day and were pleased to see the back of Yogi and Boo Boo – hopefully forever! After three nights at Clarke Airbase and another night at Subic Bay US Navy Base we left The Philippines and headed for Japan.

Japan

***Our arrival in Japan** had been preceded by Bowie's 'Serious Moonlight Tour' which was still being lauded. Our Japanese driver and several Americans told me about the tour and I took the chance to mention 'David Bowie and The Lower Third'! Of course I did!*

The first dates were over the Christmas holiday on the Japanese island of Okinawa where the Americans had a US Marines base. On Christmas Eve we staged the show in the enlisted men's club and were advised on arrival that we would be escorted in and out of the club by the military police because the guys would get very drunk. They feared that the girls would be mobbed after the show because it was an unattended posting for the marines, meaning no women on the base.

As we left the dressing room heading for the stage I could see that there were a number of MPs with their batons in hand positioned around the room and in front of the stage. They were surrounding a sea of teenage crew cuts all trained to kill. Needless to say when they saw the girls there was an immediate uproar and I was truly thankful that our opening number was very loud and punchy.

The crowd gradually realised that there was more to us than just scantily clad dancers and began to get in the groove. When I sang our Christmas number, *'When A Child Is Born'*, including my cheesy patter *"We are all thousands of miles from our homes and families on this special evening etc...."*, and the girls appeared in red cloaks lined with white fur, to my great satisfaction the whole room fell silent. They flicked on their lighters and started to sway, holding them above their heads. It was a spectacular sight and a moving moment to see these young skin-head killing machines brought to such emotion. When we left the stage we were told to remain in the dressing room until they brought a police vehicle to escort us away. A fight had erupted in the club - just a normal Friday night out with the US Marine Corps.

On Christmas Day, surrounded by spectacular traditional Japanese ice sculptures, we enjoyed a meal in the hotel restaurant before we congregated in one of the bedrooms to celebrate Christmas with our stock of booze. Tony and I had bought a litre bottle of very cheap Japanese whisky while the girls had found some drinkable wine. By three in the morning the whisky bottle was dry, the girls had got into bed and Penny was asleep in a chair. Tony staggered off, fumbling for his room key, while I woke Penny and we crept out, mindful that we had a flight booked later that morning.

Island Hopping

I awoke four hours later with practically no ill effects and we assembled in the hotel lobby to await our transport. Everybody was there except Tony and only my continued banging on his door got him awake and moving. He was not well – he had the mother of all hangovers which lasted most of the day. At the airport we decided it would be appropriate to present him with an award. I had kept a large Filipino coin which was a one Piso, so he was photographed being presented with the 'Piso of the week' award.

We flew to mainland Japan for shows at another US base in Hiroshima. It was a weird feeling visiting the city that was destroyed by the world's first atomic bomb attack in 1945. I'd grown up with the image of that destruction from newsreels and books and it was sobering to be standing there at ground zero.

South Korea

Next stop was South Korea where I started a serious cough that left me gasping each time I came off stage. After one show I coughed so much I pulled muscles in my rib cage making it even worse. But sympathy from the team was short-lived, especially after Tony took a tumble.

We had just arrived on the US base at the demilitarized zone between North Korea and South Korea and the snow was heavy on the ground. I had hurt myself laughing at the large thermometer-like sign at the entrance which was called *'The Clapometer'* and indicated the number of venereal disease cases treated by the medics that week and in which clubs they had been contracted.

Unparallel Careers!

I had told Tony the sound equipment had to be guarded with his life. Our backing tracks were played on our Revox tape recorder which was absolutely vital to the show. This night, while disembarking from our transport with the said machine in hand, he was still laughing about the entrance sign. Then he suddenly slipped on the ice and disappeared under the bus, while somehow managing to stop the Revox from hitting the ground. We hurried to his rescue, after first securing the tape recorder which was, we realised, more essential to the tour than Tony, only to discover he had cracked a rib. Thereafter the more we both laughed, and we laughed a lot on that tour, the more it hurt. Two weeks into the tour Tony, after one of several sudden changes of the tour schedule, came out with his unforgettable comment *"The only constant thing about this tour is that nothing ever stays the same."*

At the end of the run we were due to fly from Seoul via Tokyo and Chicago back to England. As had been the case in 1980 we were to pick up the main flight tickets from Vince's travel agent at the airport in Tokyo. The newest members of the show were missing home and eager to get back to see their friends and family – it had been a first time working abroad for two of the girls and the Far East had certainly been a baptism of fire. When we arrived in Tokyo and met the travel agent she asked if we would like a two day stopover in Hawaii before the final leg back home. Vince had done it again for us. I said yes yes yes! The new girls burst into tears knowing it would be another delay before they got home.

On entering Hawaii we were split up into different

immigration lines and I noticed that new girl Michelle, who was still disconsolate about the delayed journey home, had been taken off to an interview room. She had given the wrong answers to important questions. *"Do you have ongoing flights scheduled?"* and more importantly *"How much money do you have to sustain your visit to the USA."* She had told them that she didn't have tickets or money. I had to bluff my way through to the interview room in order to confirm that she was with my party and that I had loads of money and a fistful of tickets. At the end of the two days and three nights in Hawaii the 'desperate to get home' girls had tried the discos, swum from Waikiki beach and met some nice American boys. Now home seemed like the poor option and the tears flowed again.

European Tour

Returning to The Isle of Wight in 1984 I moved into the new flat and set about preparing for another summer season which was to be a repeat of *'Way Out West'* with almost the same cast.

But before the season was upon us I booked Campbell & Reid for another altogether different adventure. In April I organised and embarked on what would turn out to be the last European tour for Vince D'Amico's organisation. He had formed a partnership with Bournemouth agent Don Jones who, having a German wife, had agreed to move to Frankfurt to open a European office. I put together yet another line-up of *'Stephen Gold with Flame'* and then added Campbell & Reid who would open the evening as the support act.

The tour was extensive, taking in American bases

in Germany, Italy, Spain and Portugal. When I received the schedule I realised there was no margin for error with the travel arrangements. The show was rehearsed on the Isle of Wight and then we all travelled, with the 'man and van' that I'd hired, to my house in Margate. It was the evening before we were to cross the English Channel and I was anxious that everything was in order. The tour bus was loaded for the following morning because we were booked on an early ferry. When everybody was assembled to eat I decided to remind them to have their passports handy when we arrived at the port. As soon as I spoke it struck me like a bullet and my heart jumped a beat. My own passport was still in my desk drawer at Ryde Pavilion on the Isle of Wight.

I quickly withdrew from the room grabbing Penny on the way – this was not a good omen for the tour. *"What do we do?" "Don't tell the team!"* I put in a call to Tony, who was still my stage manager at The Pavilion, and begged him to help. *"Will you get my passport and drive it to Margate first thing in the morning?" "Yes!"* I now had to come up with a reasonable sounding excuse for the delayed departure – *"We unexpectedly need additional costumes that are being delivered from the theatre on the Isle of Wight"* – well, I couldn't think of anything better at the time.

Missing the morning ferry and taking one late in the day meant that we would have to travel through the night to keep to the very tight schedule. This inadvertently worked in my favour because, under the contract for the tour, I was responsible for all travel and accommodation costs. What was certainly a bad start redeemed itself by saving me a bundle on the first night.

We were behind schedule but already ahead in the budget! All I had to do now was make every date on time.

The first breakdown was on the autobahn in Germany. We were rescued by the ADAC, Germany's version of the AA, and the minibus, with us still inside, was loaded on to the back of a truck and carried for fifty kilometres to the nearest garage that was still open in early evening. I could not help but remark, as we sailed along at an elevated height, that this was a saving on petrol – yet another aid to the budget. I do not recall which of the minibus' technical failures was experienced that day but it would be the first of many. Our roadie, the owner and driver, was profuse in his attempts to persuade me that it was not normally prone to breakdowns – I received this with considerable scepticism.

We rested that night in Germany but our first date was in Italy and, because of the breakdown, the journey was once again behind schedule. The next day we crossed the Austrian border under a renewed head of steam aiming for the American base at Vicenza in the Veneto region not far from Venice. Studying a good old fashioned map, no satnavs in those days, I noticed what looked like a short cut to our destination, saving a long trek down the motorway, so I ordered a change of course. We started to ascend what became more and more like a mountain range as we gained kilometres. There were some very steep winding inclines and some vertiginous drops. Some of the team began to groan as they peered over the edges and I soon realised that the route might be short but it was definitely not fast. After an hour or more of this frustratingly slow progress we reached what seemed to be the snowy peak and came across a sign which said *Strada Chiusa* (Road Closed). While I pondered the next move several of the team took some air and two of them, the most nauseous, offloaded their lunch.

Just as I was deciding that we would have to turn back, and suffer the consequences of a late arrival, a car appeared from the opposite direction and we flagged them down. One of the girls spoke a little Italian and asked if the road was passable. There was a lot of snow, they said, but it was passable with care. We strapped ourselves in and set off down a tortuous icy mountain road. I was immediately fired as navigator and my map of short cuts was confiscated.

After a successful show at Vicenza we had two days to reach Brindisi, which was an easy 950 km drive south, in the heel of Italy. There was time for a casual stopover on the way and spirits were high again. We indulged in a few drinks in Campbell & Reid's hotel room and, to illustrate a joke, Brian Reid climbed inside the wardrobe, which was of the old fashioned high bottomed ornate wooden variety. After he closed the door we heard a crash and a yell and the door flew open again to expose Brian up to his thighs in wardrobe floor. He had fallen through and grazed his legs, completely ruining his joke but nevertheless leaving us all in fits of laughter. Unfortunately the noise alerted the hotel manager who feared an accident. He was not a happy bunny when he inspected his damaged wardrobe so I had the difficult task of persuading him not to throw the boys out. The budget was hit the following morning

Island Hopping

with a bill to recompense for the damage.

At Brindisi we played the San Vito des Normanni Air Base and then, after a short hop to Naples, two nights at the NATO Joint Forces Command HQ near Bagnoli. After that, three days off – oh joy, some leisure time. Until I studied the map. The next date was at Zaragoza Air Base in Spain which was almost two thousand kilometres away. We set off up the west coast of Italy breaking down twice on the way. I've no idea what went wrong but the driver always seemed to find a solution, once with the help of a passing police patrol of the Carabinieri who were attracted by the sight of several beautiful girls milling around a minibus with the bonnet open.

After dark that evening we checked into a hotel on the French Riviera and set off again early the next day. I wanted to cross into Spain so that we would have a reasonable last run to Zaragoza. We stopped overnight at Lloret de Mar and we all went on the town for some light relief. The girls had discovered a disco that was open mid-week out of season so we gave it a go, not knowing that it would be the last 'light relief' of the tour! We reached the Zaragoza base the next day in good time for the show but we were exhausted after three non-stop days on the road. I was encouraged that, after Zaragoza, the schedule showed two free days in which to drive to Lisbon where we were to connect with a flight to The Azores, out in the Atlantic Ocean, on the morning of the third day.

We started out a little later than usual to give everyone a lie in. We took it easy, stopping a couple of times for coffee or to admire the scenery and, after we had enjoyed a leisurely lunch in a roadside taverna, it was time for the daily call to the office in Frankfurt. I found a call box and set up a collect call. Don Jones was frantic. *"Stephen, thank God you've called. There's been a change of schedule for the Azores. It's been brought forward a day and your flight is now tomorrow morning at 8am." "Don, we're still in Spain and it's already after two o'clock – it's nearly 900 km away!" "Can you drive overnight?"* No choice, so I had to break it to the team that the leisure time was over again and that they should settle down for another night huddled in the bus. The only positive for me was the saving of the cost of several hotel rooms – good for the budget again.

As we trundled on that afternoon I could not help but reflect on the miracle that, in spite of everything thrown in our way, we had so far made it to all the dates. I was not going to let it beat me this time. However, there was one last Spanish brick thrown at us. As we reached a small town around six that evening the minibus decided to break down again. The clutch cable snapped.

We soon realised that everywhere was closing up, including garages, because the next day was Good Friday and the holiday weekend was starting. Our driver managed to find a motorbike shop still open and, in spite of severe language difficulties, somehow got the owner to convert a cable so that it worked with our vehicle. We crossed into Portugal some time after midnight and I finally felt we were going to make it as long as the pesky bus kept going.

About 2am we arrived at a closed railway crossing with no sign of life or of a train. There was a call button at the roadside which I pressed continually to no effect. As I was starting to despair someone drew my attention to a flickering light some way up the road and a little man on a bicycle emerged through the darkness. He said something in Portuguese, which I hoped was a greeting, and then proceded to operate the barriers. We drove through and watched him close the crossing and climb back on the bike as we sped away.

We reached the airport at Lisbon at 7am which was tight to collect the tickets and check in all the gear for the 8am flight. I sent the girls straight to the check-in desk to make sure it was not closed. Luck was on our side because at that precise moment Margaret Thatcher was passing through the airport to take a flight back to London and the security measures caused some flights to be delayed – including ours.

At the ticket desk I was astounded to discover that the tickets were booked but had not been pre-paid. There was no time to call Don in Frankfurt. They just had to be paid for. I didn't have enough cash and they would not accept payment by credit card so it was down to an embarrasing whip round of the team to raise the money. When I later spoke to Don about it he was honest enough to tell me that they did not have the money to pay for the flights when they were booked. Sadly the writing was on the wall for the failure of Vince D'Amico Enterprises.

Our two nights at Lajes Field US Airbase in the Azores passed without a hitch. I collected a large fee in cash and we took our flight back from Ponta Delgada to Lisbon. On arrival we discovered that one flight case was missing. Unfortunately it was the one containing all

Unparallel Careers!

the cables, microphones, and other items that connected to the sound equipment. I had agreed a price with Campbell & Reid for the use of their sound system on the tour and it was their responsibility to look after it and set it up at each venue.

After some hours of waiting around Lisbon airport the airline finally confirmed that this particular case had not been checked in. Where was it? The last place anyone could recall seeing it had been at the side of the stage in the club we had played the previous night. A furious row started between Brian Reid and Tony Campbell as to who had left it behind and why it hadn't been missed. In the meantime, using a call box in the airport, I managed to raise the club manager who found the case and agreed to get it on the first available flight to Lisbon which, unfortunately, was not until the following day.

Our next show was also the following day at Torrejon Air Base in Madrid. Would this be the first show we had to cancel? It was a dilemma and there was only one solution. I sent the tour bus and the team on ahead to Madrid. By now it was early evening and they would have to drive through the night again. I stayed in Lisbon with Penny and we collected the flight case from the airport the next day before taking a late afternoon flight to Madrid. Our driver collected us from the airport and drove straight to the show venue where we just had time to set up before the performance. Phew! And all without the aid of a mobile phone or the internet – however did we survive without them? Spectacularly well actually.

Now we had only two days to get from Madrid to

Frankfurt, some 1800 km, for the last date of the tour. We made it, played it, and headed for home. To this day I am still amazed that we did not drop one date on that tour.

Whitegold & The Big Idea

Back on the Isle of Wight an old acquaintance, from our time touring the island in 1981, approached me with the idea of setting up an entertainment agency to take advantage of the many opportunities that existed for placing musicians and artistes on the island, especially throughout the summer seasons. John Young was a manager at Whitecliff Bay Holiday Park. He was ready to quit his job in order to run the new agency with the blessing of Whitecliff Bay's owner, Martin Humphreys, who was prepared to invest in the new enterprise.

I agreed to support the new project and we set up *Whitegold Entertainments* with the directors being Martin, me and the holiday park's financial director. As part of the initial set-up it was agreed that all future acts and musicians employed at Ryde Pavilion and Whitecliff Bay would be booked through the agency.

At around the same time I came up with a new and ambitious scheme – with the benefit of my degree in hindsight I recognised later that it was an *over*ambitious scheme. I floated the idea of a major international song festival that would attract entries from around the world. Song writers and performers would enter a competition in several musical categories which would each carry a large cash prize for the winner. Travel and accommodation costs would be provided for all the finalists. The final would be held on the Isle of Wight with star guest artistes attracting large paying audiences. The considerable costs would be covered from ticket sales and sponsorship and it would attract valuable publicity for the island's tourism. It all sounded so good that it was certain to be a hit!

After several meetings with the great and good of the island I persuaded them that the IOW Tourist Board should be the principal event promoter whilst I devised and managed the whole event as Festival Director. It was officially launched in the autumn with sponsorship by Sealink Ferries. It was *'The Sealink Isle Of Wight International Song Festival 1985'* - known more simply as *'Song 85'*. There was a lot of work to do.

The Waltons

Meanwhile I decided to dabble in the island's music scene which was always rich with talent. I followed several established bands, one of which, Kite, featured a bass player who I had known from the QE2 and another, The Garage Band, whose singer later recorded with my old *'Lower Third'* partner, songwriter Terry Bolton. But my main interest settled on one very original outfit.

It was back in November 1983 that Tony, our stage manager, had first taken me to see this local band that he had been raving about. The Waltons played regularly at a music venue, The Prince Consort, in Ryde. Their outrageous stage presence was mainly carried by the antics of front man Tony Walton (Tony Gregson) who would, amongst other things, pour gunge down the ladies' tights he was wearing until they ballooned and oozed. All done while singing such gems as *'We Eat Shit'*, *'Hail Mary'* or *'Fall Out Waltz'*. They drew large crowds and, in spite of the dodgy sounding titles, many of Tony's songs had strong left leaning messages.

In 1984 they still had a weekly residency at the same popular music venue which was owned by a sometime professional actor-producer called Brian McDermott, erstwhile founder of London's Bush Theatre. The BBC decided to shoot a major series on the island and, when they were seeking a venue for the night time scenes, they gravitated towards Brian's music bar at The Prince Consort. When the scenes were shot The Waltons were featured heavily as the night club's live band. The series was called *'Annika'* and was broadcast on the BBC network that autumn. I saw an opportunity to show off the band to some of the contacts I'd been nurturing for the benefit of the planned song festival. My efforts succeded with the offer of a record deal by Red Bus Music. They recorded their first single, *'Brown Rice'*, in November 1984 and it was scheduled for release the following year. I had high hopes for a profitable liaison with them because it was a great record reminiscent in style to the Madness singles.

During the summer of '84 Penny got to know our new leading lady at the Pavilion, Ali Hawkins, and they formed a singing duo called *'Poppy'*. They started to get some bookings for the winter and in December they flew to Sanaa in Yemen to appear for a month at the Taj Sheba Hotel. This was to be a big mistake that got me involved in daily anxious calls to Yemen and angry calls to the

London agent responsible for the booking.

Yemen was not quite in the twentieth century and the powers that ran the hotel and local politics expected to treat any visiting western women as they liked. The hotel director had tried to hit on Penny and her refusal to play ball had, as usual in this part of the world, encouraged bad treatment and various 'punishments'. It came to a head one night when Penny, on returning from a visit in town, was locked out of the hotel by order of the director. This had to be resolved and after some heated haggling I insisted the London agent cancel the contract and move the girls to somewhere safe or bring them home. They flew to Bahrain to appear at another hotel for the rest of the Christmas period. Many years later, in a completely different set of circumstances, I crossed swords again with this agent who was still as bullying and unreasonable as I had found him in 1984.

Another Japanese Christmas

In mid December, while Penny was in Yemen, Vince called to ask if I could help him out by filling in some Christmas dates with the *'Flame'* show. I said I was without my partner and choreographer but I would try to put something together. I expected another quick dash over to Germany but the dates turned out to be in Japan. I recruited two amateur dancers from Margate and two of our old hands and between us we quickly cobbled together enough elements of the show to get by.

This was to be the third time I would circumnavigate the globe – this time east to west! We flew to Tokyo via America with a night stopover in

Island Hopping

Chicago where Vince had booked us into a hotel near the airport. The flight was delayed by several hours and landed a little after midnight. I called the hotel for a pick-up to be told that they had let our rooms as we hadn't shown up.

Chicago Airport was closing down for the night and I was stranded outside at one in the morning with four attractive young girls being eyed up by the druggies, drunks and pimps. Some frantic and panicky phone calls from a public call box eventually found some rooms and a hotel proprietor willing to come to my rescue. That was my one and only experience of the great city of Chicago – not *'my kinda town'* that night.

We were in Japan from the 23rd December and played the first date on Okinawa island. We were lodged at the same hotel as last year, IHA Hotel at Ishakawa, but without the boozy nights. We flew to the mainland the next morning and spent Christmas Day at Yokota US Air Force Base on the western outskirts of Tokyo, another massive base with 14000 personnel. We also played the vast naval base at Yokusuka on mainland Japan and the more modest outpost of Misawa Air Force Base on the northern island of Honshu.

At the naval base a young rating invited me to tour his ship and I had the great experience of walking on the flight deck of the enormous aircraft carrier Dwight D Eisenhower. This lowly sailor even introduced me to the captain in his bridge cabin who chatted about his holidays spent in Scotland. This emphasised the stark difference between the informality of the American military and the complete opposite of the British. I could not envisage being introduced to the captain of a large

Unparallel Careers!

British warship by a rank and file sailor.

The last night in the Hotel at Yokusuka was marked by a severe earth tremor which set all the bottles and glasses in the bar rattling. It alarmed me but didn't seem to faze the locals who lived their lives with the constant threat from earthquakes.

While the girls flew back to England I took a leisurely detour by stopping over in Hong Kong and then flying back via Singapore. I hoped to make some useful contacts and to make a pilgrimage to the Shangri-La Hotel where I would carefully avoid the Reuben sandwich in the coffee shop!

Chapter 9
The Shipwreck

When you're heading for the rocks
And the weather's stormy
Hold on tight and believe you're right
To try and try again

With plans for *'Song 85'* gathering pace and a new format to devise for the summer at Ryde Pavilion the start of the year was hectic. Sealink Ferries were on board for the big event with a donation of £10,000 and it had finally been scheduled to take place from September 26th to October 2nd. At the end of January, with publicity material and entry forms in hand, I travelled with Penny to Cannes in the South of France to promote our festival at Midem, the annual global music industry event. We took a small stand and passed out flyers to the visiting music executives, songwriters and artistes. We attended various functions and music presentations and generally enjoyed the unique atmosphere of this prestigious event. We were fortunate to be able to attend an award presentation to Prince for his hit song of that era, *'Purple Rain'*, which he performed together with other songs from his latest album.

On my return to the island *'Song 85'* took over much of my working day which was to the detriment of the new Ryde Pavilion season. I had moved from the office at the Pavilion into a room at the *Whitegold Entertainments'* offices at Provincial House in Ryde High Street. It was from these offices, still working under the banner of my own company, *Solid Gold Promotions Ltd.*, that I put together all the detailed arrangements for the song festival.

For the Pavilion season I decided on a tropical theme and I scheduled a seven day programme of shows and features to run from June to September under a new name – Ryde Pavilion would now be The Tropicana. It was not an ambitious plan because all my time and thoughts centred on the song festival. With my head and heart elsewhere it was inevitable that the Pavilion season would stumble. It proved to be far less popular than the previous years and, without my daily hands-on attention, its lack of popularity added to the financial problems I encountered later in the year.

In the midst of the summer melee The Waltons single, *'Brown Rice'*, was released on the Excaliber Records label and was a minor success, leading to *'Brown Rice - The Long Grain Version'* being released a little later. Unfortunately it was not successful enough for a follow up and I was too distracted to chase any new opportunities. I did stick with the band and much later, in 1987, produced an album with them at studios in Maidstone.

*'**Live Aid**', the massive benefit concert, took place in July at Wembley Stadium and I watched with the rest of the world while Mick Jagger and David Bowie girated to their duet of the old Martha and the Vandellas' hit 'Dancing In The Street'. For Bowie it was a high point of the 80s while I hoped my high point was to come later in the year with a successful 'Song 85'.*

Progress on the planning for *'Song 85'* sped up as the year seemed to fly by at an alarming rate. I had decided to stage the event in a circus 'big top' tent, to give it a true festival feel, and I had arranged to site the tent at Westridge Leisure Centre just outside Ryde. I could pitch the tent near to the leisure centre buildings and make use of several rooms as offices and dressing rooms for the artistes and musicians.

I hired the 'big top' from Robert Fosset of the famous Fosset's Circus family. He was contracted to deliver, install and maintain the tent. He turned out to be a difficult man to pin down and to deal with but I could not find an available alternative at a price that suited the budget. I had to remember that, while the sponsorship mostly covered the prize money, the operating budget was based almost entirely on ticket sales. The success or otherwise of the festival relied heavily on high attendances at all the shows and contests.

After the hire of the big top there were a multitude of other expensive things to organise. I arranged the hire of a big concert sound system and lighting rig. There was going to be a fifteen piece orchestra for the grand final under the direction of experienced band leader Paul Jury. Well known guest artistes were to be booked

Unparallel Careers!

to appear on the various special nights. In particular, the opening show needed a really big name to gain maximum publicity and I managed to book The Three Degrees who were still riding high after several chart hits in the 1970s. They were managed by an American called Richard Barrett who had a fierce reputation among club and theatre managers for his aggressive approach to achieving the best conditions for his act. Fortunately my old manager Bob James dealt with the contract on my behalf and I avoided crossing swords with Barrett until the festival was over – then I would feel the full force of his notorious business style.

On one night of the festival week I planned to stage a 'Sensational Sixties Show' headlined by Dozy, Beaky, Mick and Titch together with Pinkerton's Assorted Colours. As guest star on the night of the Country Music Finals I booked the American country music singer-songwriter Sonny Curtis. Sonny was an original member of Buddy Holly's Crickets and wrote many hit songs including the Everly Brother's smash hit *'Walk Right Back'*.

For the grand final night TV star Jan Francis was joining a music industry judging panel and the famous BBC Radio One and Top Of The Pops DJ Peter Powell was scheduled to present the finalists on stage. Guest star was to be the American singer-songwriter Gerard Kenny who would perform his hits *'I Made It Through The Rain'* and *'New York, New York'*. This was a special thrill for me because I had performed both these hit songs on several of the *'Flame'* tours.

By the beginning of July I had organised judging panels to sift through the many entries coming in from various parts of the world. They had to be whittled down to the festival finalists in each category – Country Music, Rock Band and Pop. The 63 finalists included song writers and singers from countries as far afield as Singapore, Canada, South Africa, USA , Eire and Belgium, together with a large contingent from Great Britain. They were invited to present their songs live and vie for a share of the prize fund of £7,500. All travel costs were covered as well as accommodation on the island which was supplied by Warner Holidays at one of their holiday centres. It was all beautifully set up – for a fall!

Teething Troubles?

It started with the late arrival of Robert Fosset and his 'big top' amidst copious non stop rainfall. The build up was seriously delayed and, when finally complete, it quickly became obvious that the tent was well past its sell-by date and leaked like a sieve. Sections of seating had to be moved to avoid the incoming deluge. This meant that there were major problems with the ticketing because the seat numbers did not comply with those on the tickets. The leaks were potentially disastrous for the sound and lighting equipment so sound and lighting engineer Alan Frayne, who was previously our technician with the *'Flame'* show in Jersey, had to practically sleep in the tent to make sure the rain did not get to the sensitive parts of the gear.

Mr Fosset had clearly sold me a pup and we were stuck with it. No amount of cajoling or threats seemed to get any action towards plugging the holes and solving our problems. Miraculously the whole site was just

Unparallel Careers!

about ready for the opening night of the big event.

The Three Degrees arrived on the island, with high ceremony, on the bridge of a Sealink Isle of Wight ferry and I was full of anticipation and excitement that *'Song 85'* had started at last. But that night I had the first big hint that all was not well with the festival – the big top held over 1400 people and for two performances The Three Degrees filled less than half the available seats.

In spite of the good press coverage for the opening show the attendances did not improve over the following days and by the last night the writing was surely on the wall. But I was determined that I would see it through with confidence and at least take due credit for organising and managing the mammoth event.

The Grand Final was a great night to have been part of and I was rightly proud of its success. The orchestra leader, Paul Jury, had been up all night scoring music arrangements for each song that had won through to the final. He did a magnificent job staying alert and directing the superb orchestra throughout an unpredictable night. Peter Powell, as we expected from an experienced radio and TV presenter, linked the show perfectly. I started the evening by introducing him on stage and spoke with some emotion at the end to congratulate the winners and to thank everybody involved. I left the festival site that night elated by the artistic success of the event and with the many congratulations ringing in my ears, but with a great foreboding about what horrors the next few days would reveal.

The Island Echo - 3rd October 1985
"The Island International Song Festival came to a glittering and spectacular end last night after a week in which ticket sales were often disappointing. Last night more than 900 people attended the Grand Finals inside the big top tent at Westridge Leisure Centre. The show was hosted by Radio 1 DJ Peter Powell."

The Final Breakdown

It did not take long to gather in all the bills and expenses and to set the total against the advance ticket sales and the on-site box office takings. My stomach knotted as I realised that the festival had lost over sixty thousand pounds – equivalent to one hundred and seventy thousand in today's money (2019). Over the next days and weeks I was fraught with worry. Fortunately, cheques for the prize money had been presented to the winners at the event and were guaranteed by the Sealink sponsorship, but many other bills remained to be settled. One afternoon I received an angry call from Richard Barrett, the Three Degrees' manager, who was chasing payment for the act. His aggressive approach more than bore out his reputation. He threatened to send his 'boys' over to the island if payment wasn't received within 48 hours. I managed to divert him to Ewan Brenchley, the head of the tourist board. Brenchley, he said, would end up in the Solent with concrete shoes if he didn't pay up that week. Thankfully the shoes weren't required as the bill was paid and I did not hear from Mr. Barrett again.

There were council meetings, tourist board meetings and other open meetings to determine what went wrong. Thankfully, due to the way the project was

Unparallel Careers!

set up, the Isle of Wight Tourist Board was ultimately responsible for settling the bills - but there was a final twist to come. It emerged that the tourist board, which was funded by the two main councils on the island, did not have enough money to clear the debts because it was, unbeknown to the councils, already running a large deficit from year to year. The tourist board was promptly closed down, Ewan Brenchley lost his job and I slunk away to lick my wounds with a couple of grands worth of my own overdue invoices for company. Under the circumstances I could not reasonably expect to be paid.

It was a dark time, a low point, a severe blow to my self-confidence, and it got to me badly. I started having what I guess would now be called panic attacks. I would feel dizzy in a supermarket queue or feel my heart racing when trying to board a train. I recall one time getting to London Victoria station, on the way to a meeting, and having to get back on the train for home - I couldn't get out of the station!

Back on the island I felt, probably wrongly, that I was almost persona non-grata. The Pavilion had not paid its way, mainly due to a lack of attention, and then my bank in Margate nearly pulled the rug completely from under my feet by bouncing the salary cheque of Marie, my assistant in the Whitegold Entertainments' office. They had mistakenly moved money to my personal account from the company's account leaving it overdrawn. Although they corrected the mistake by reversing the transaction the damage was already done. I withdrew all my remaining funds and have never used Barclays Bank since that day.

***In 1981** Bowie wrote and recorded the hit song 'Under Pressure' with the members of Queen. It then featured on Queen's next album in 1982. I identified fully with the lyrics of that song at the time of the demise of the 'Song 85' festival. It uses the old mantra 'it never rains but it pours' and that was exactly how it felt.*

At the end of the year my head remained in a bad place. I was still living in the Ryde flat because my house at Margate had been sold, following an unfortunate burglary, and I had moved all the contents of the house to the island. The council had loaned me a store at Puckpool Park but, with the Pavilion contract ending, I was under pressure to empty it. For various reasons Penny's partnership with Ali had come to an end but Penny had already secured a contract for *'Poppy'* at the Meridian Hotel in New Delhi. It was for one performance on New Year's Eve so she hitched up with our old partner Carole. I saw them onto an Aeroflot flight to India via Moscow before spending a lonely and depressing New Year's Eve by myself in the Ryde flat. It felt like the world was collapsing around me.

The Twilight Zone

At the start of 1986 I gave up the flat in Ryde and moved in with Penny. A few years earlier she had bought a park home near Maidstone, the county town of Kent, and some time spent in the peace and quiet of that little place at Harrietsham started to rekindle my optimism and zest for life. Now that I was no longer on the island the drama caused by the failure of the song festival had faded. It was time to take stock and decide

Unparallel Careers!

what to do next. We took a week out to, once again, visit the Midem music convention in Cannes. This time it was more of a holiday which gave me some time to think.

After the success of the *'Stephen Gold with Flame'* tours, and the equal success of the first two years at Ryde Pavilion with *'Way Out West'*, it proved difficult to pick myself up and start again from scratch. But it was necessary to earn money so Penny and I set ourselves up as a singing duo called *'Chance'* with me playing keyboards. Later that year Penny sold her charming little park home and we bought a property together in Maidstone which would become the base for our projects over the next three difficult years. 3 Littlecourt, Upper Fant Road.

During the summer we occasionally returned to the Isle of Wight to sing at Whitecliffe Bay Holiday Centre and it was during one of these visits that I learnt that our agency company, Whitegold Entertainments, was to be put into liquidation and John Young was to return to his old job at the holiday centre. I crossed to Portsmouth with the other directors and visited the company's accountants where we put the final nails in the coffin. That was the end of the often happy, frequently stressful, and sometimes ignominious Isle of Wight years.

I set about converting the ground floor of our townhouse at Little Court into an office and store. It was time to come up with new projects but in the meantime, to keep the wolf from the door, I flogged our duo around southern clubs and hotels. We also did a brief spell in the bar of a ferry sailing back and forth between Ramsgate and Dunkirk!

The Shipwreck

New Delhi

On December 24th 1986 I flew to New Delhi with Penny and Cheryl Mortimer, who had been one of the mainstays of our *'Flame'* team. We were booked to appear at the brand new Meridian Hotel where Penny had appeared the previous New Year's Eve. It had still not been completed so the only parts open were the coffee shop and the banqueting suite on the ground floor where we performed for the first few nights.

The hotel's twenty, as yet uncompleted, guest room floors were built around a spectacular atrium – you could gaze down in awe from the top floor to the lobby twenty storeys below. At the top, in the middle of the building, suspended from the roof, was the new nightclub which was uniquely accessed by crossing narrow walkways from the 20th floor. It was opening to the public on New Year's Eve with us appearing as the featured cabaret show and we were charged with seeing in the new year on stage.

During the day we attempted to set up and rehearse while an army of workers were laying carpet, setting up furniture, drilling, hammering and constantly shouting. If there were international awards for last minute work this would have taken first prize!

To get a feel for how the evening would go I asked the club manager how many people the room was licensed to hold. *"180 people,"* he said. *"And are you fully booked for tonight? How many will there be?" "About 250,"* he replied, with a perfectly serious face. It seemed we would be performing in a nightclub which was hanging over a void 20 floors up and which had never yet been tested with a full house, let alone a full house plus!

As midnight approached we took to the stage and completed our show just as the clock struck twelve. Everybody was on the dance floor and, as we welcomed in the new year, they all started singing and jumping around. I could feel the whole club bouncing beneath my feet and I shouted to the girls that we should scamper over the nearest walkway in case the whole lot plummeted into the lobby. It is a testament to the designers and architects that, as far as I know, the club remains hanging from the roof of the Meridian Hotel.

Rich Records

One day in early 1987 I was chatting to my long standing accountant, Richard Piper, who had been a childhood neighbour and grammar school classmate. To my amusement Richard had always waxed lyrical about his ambition to play the guitar and be in a rock band. I talked about my involvement with The Waltons and their Excalibur Records release as well as mentioning another act that I'd spotted called Hammy Haze and the Heroze, who were writing and performing some excellent new songs. Something about this conversation appealed to him – it was his chance to be involved with the music scene.

He offered to invest some money so that we could set up our own record label which I could run from our Maidstone base. I was excited by the prospect of a new venture and readily agreed. Richard went ahead and acquired a limited company called Graphicsound to cover the project. We decided that the record label would be called *Rich Records* and I immediately signed

The Shipwreck

up Portsmouth based Hammy Haze and started to listen carefully to all his songs, looking for a potential hit suitable for a first single release.

At the same time I had to remember that an income was required to pay the mortgage and generally stay afloat so it became a varied and sometimes confusing year. I agreed to stage several southern heats for the Miss England contest after being contacted by the Morley family who ran both the Miss England and Miss World contests. The sponsors were Townsend Thoresen Ferries and on March 6th 1987 we were presenting a heat in Kent when news arrived that a Townsend Thoresen ferry, The Herald Of Free Enterprise, had capsized while leaving the port of Zeebrugge in Belgium. It was quickly apparent that there had been a great loss of life and it was a very difficult night to handle. Needless to say the sponsors withdrew from the following heats and that was the end of the contract.

In spite of the Isle of Wight experience I bravely staged another song contest, this time at Dorking Halls in Surrey and *'Song 87'* produced some excellent songs restoring my faith in the concept. I also resurrected *'Stephen Gold with Flame'* by calling on Cheryl Mortimer to join us again on a cruise ferry between Stockholm and Helsinki.

By the end of 1987 I had recorded and released the Hammy Haze and the Heroze single called *'Lucky'* on *Rich Records*. I was pleased with the record but it failed to get major radio coverage. I had also put together an album of country music by artistes who had appeared in the song festivals – it was called *'Rich In Love'*. On one memorable Sunday at Picnic Studios, not far from our

Unparallel Careers!

base at Maidstone, I presided over the recording of a complete album by The Waltons – all songs played live and in one take. It was impressive. (The album, *'Out Of Control'*, was to be revived and re-released thirty years later.)

To top off the muddled year I took another hastily reconstituted *'Flame'* song and dance show to Abu Dhabi for the New Year celebrations.

Bowie, meanwhile, *had released an album called 'Never Let Me Down'. He later described it as his nadir and said it was "an awful album". His Glass Spider Tour the same year was maligned by the critics! 1987 was certainly a year for heart searching!*

The Little Man

One day in the spring of '88 I took a call from a guy who said he was looking for songs and a record deal for the young actress Letitia Dean who was starring in the hit British TV soap opera 'Eastenders'. I had a song signed to *Flame Music*, our newly formed publishing company, that had been successful in the *'Song 87'* event and I sent him the demo with the offer of other songs if this didn't appeal. He liked the song and came back to me with a rather convoluted story about his management of Letitia and of her brother, Stephen Dean, who was also an actor.

A meeting was arranged at his address in London and I went along with no particular optimism. When I arrived at the address it was clearly a private house and I discovered, to my surprise, that the guy I had been dealing with was Letitia Dean's father. He was a shifty little man who never seemed to be totally honest about anything we discussed. However, the chance to record a TV star and the possibility of getting major radio exposure was more than alluring so I dived in with both feet.

The first knockback was his insistence that the record had to be a duet with Letitia's brother, who was a young unknown actor with a just passable singing voice. This diluted the promotion possibilities for the record and I could see that he was setting it up to enhance the career of Stephen Dean by association with his sister.

The song that they had chosen to record was called *'You Taught Me Everything I Know'* by award winning songwriter Arthur Pelteret. I was to produce the record and the *little man* was confident he could obtain a release through a major record company. It all sounded like a perfect arrangement to me.

We recorded the track over several sessions at Picnic Studios with Letitia and Stephen attending one of the sessions to lay down the vocals. Everybody involved worked hard to produce a highly commercial single and the singers left the session proud of what they had performed. Then the bombshell dropped – according to the *little man* Letitia and Stephen weren't happy with the arrangement of the song so they'd been to the studio of a pianist friend and recorded an alternative version. It was a poor recording and way below standard for a commercial release.

Eventually they agreed that our version was king but the *little man* continually came up with excuses for delaying the release. In exasperation I set a release date on our own label, *Rich Records*, and attempted to promote the single as best I could without Letitia, who was always 'too busy filming' to attend any signings or radio interviews - it was an uphill struggle. Finally we did manage to have the record on sale in the two theatres where Letitia and Stephen were starring in Pantomime that year, but by then the advantage was lost and the record was a flop. I still do not understand what the whole sorry shambles was about and I never heard from the *little man* again.

With this loss and the cost of the Hammy Haze single Richard's investment had been wittled away and I was so sorry that all he had to show for it was a garage full of unsold records.

Last Chance – Time Running Out

Sometime early that same year I had, what I thought at the time, was the idea of the century. Themed parties were becoming popular and I planned to record music for a range of party themes and package them with a booklet giving advice and ideas on all aspects of running a themed party. Penny set about researching the book contents and illustrations whilst I started recording the music. The brand was called *Theme Schemes*. In order to finance the recordings, cassette duplication and special packaging we took advantage of the rise in our house price. It was to be a fateful decision – who could have anticipated the housing crash of 1989? The great *Theme Schemes* project did not take off as expected and cost a lot to set up. Therefore it was inevitable that the most serious matter for us, at the end of 1988, was the parlous state of our finances. We had paid £34,000 for the house in Maidstone in 1986 with a mortgage of

The Shipwreck

around £20,000 at a time of very high interest rates. The property was valued at the end of 1987 at £68,000 so we borrowed £30,000 against the house value. I also had an unsecured loan of £5,000 which was paid off monthly. Late in 1988 house prices began to fall and we were soon heading for negative equity. The cash from the loans had all been spent on the new projects and on keeping us alive. We needed a miracle to keep us afloat and it came in the form of an advert in The Stage newspaper. Entertainment Controller required for busy theme park.

Cast at Ryde Pavilion Showbar 1983

Campbell & Reid

Another breakdown - European Tour 1984

Piso of the week award presentation Okinawa, Japan 1983

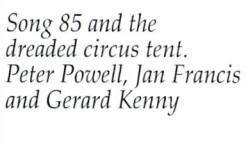

Song 85 and the dreaded circus tent. Peter Powell, Jan Francis and Gerard Kenny

Celebrating with Gerard Kenny

The Three Degrees open the Festival

*Photographing Penny
at the Taj Mahal*

*The three piece Flame
and on stage in the
hanging night club
Meridian Hotel New Delhi
1986*

*And then
there were
two
Chance 1987*

*Rich Records
1988*

Chapter 10
Sunlit Uplands
(The Theme Park Years)

One day in the park
One day full of great fun for everyone
One day in the park and I'm feelin' fine
Gid Taylor/Stephen Gold (One Day In The Park)

On the 9th January 1989 I attended the interview which landed me the seasonal position of Entertainment Controller at Thorpe Park in Chertsey, Surrey. Thorpe Park had been established ten years earlier as a family leisure park by the company Ready Mixed Concrete. The RMC Group owned the land on which the park was built and they had financed its creation to fulfil their obligation to restore the land after exhausting its usefulness as a quarry for aggregates – sand and gravel for building materials. The lakes on which the park sits are flooded quarry workings.

I set off from our house in Maidstone on the 13th February for the first of many commutes around London's orbital motorway, the M25. I wondered, with trepidation, what my first salaried job in 25 years had in store for me. I was paid the princely sum of £350 per week, which was a life saver at that moment in time.

Thorpe Park had invested in a spanking new 600 seat theatre, The Thorpe Park Palladium, to complement the many rides and attractions already in the park and they had contracted a production company to stage a show for the 1989 season. No person on the management team had any insight into dealing with singers, dancers, choreographers or stage directors so it was left to me to smooth the way. There was also an established children's show, a large format cinema, a pirate attraction and some costume character mascots for me to supervise.

One of my first tasks was to recruit performers for these costume character roles and among the various actors, singers and dancers who auditioned for that first season was a young Tony Lee who was studying drama at college in Guildford. He was to become a crucial part of the entertainment offering over the following couple of years, appearing in a multitude of roles and recording several character voices. At the time of writing (2019) Tony, under his stage name Antony Audenshaw, is a regular and long standing cast member of the popular UK TV series 'Emmerdale' in the role of Bob Hope.

The following months continued to be a daily routine of a minimum one hour M25 commute, then 8 hours at the park followed by another M25 struggle to get home to Maidstone at a reasonable hour. But I was enjoying the work and, later in the year, I was offered the permanent position of Entertainments Manager and my brief was to set up the infrastructure for a completely new entertainments department. I received a regular salary, a company car and a healthy budget to spend for the next year's entertainment.

Life felt good again. I still had an uphill journey ahead to relieve the financial pressures but money was flowing in and my self confidence had returned. Whilst the Thorpe Park job had staved off bankruptcy we still had a larger mortgage than the value of the house and the repayments and insurances were heavy. To alleviate the daily commute we moved to small flat in Twickenham and installed some tenants at Maidstone. This helped for a while, but I knew that any efforts to sell the property would just end in a large shortfall. Thus I ended 1989 celebrating the Christmas holiday while, at the same time, contemplating an uncertain year ahead. It would be an enormous challenge to impress the directors with my first season in charge at Thorpe Park while trying to find a way around the deteriorating debt problems.

While I was embracing a new beginning *that was to take me out of the dark valley and into the sunlit uplands again (to paraphrase Winston Churchill) Bowie was in the process of dumping his solo career and setting off in a new direction as part of the group Tin Machine. My new direction would continue upward for the next decade – Bowie's lasted barely a year. I must note that the album 'Tin Machine' did go gold in the UK charts and they completed a successful world tour - but I had a company car!*

In the spring of 1990 I was offered a flat at Beomonds Farm on the Thorpe Park estate. This was an isolated building with some garages and stores set around a courtyard and it housed, on the ground floor, a creche for employees' children. I borrowed the park's minibus and transferred what little we still wanted from the Maidstone house in two journeys. We moved into this spacious three bedroom flat where we would remain for several years.

One weekend, soon after, Penny and I took a weekend trip to one of our favourite getaways near Chelthenham. While there we made the monumental decision to give up chasing the debts and to send our house keys to the bank which held the mortgage. The next morning we posted an envelope containing the keys and a short note of explanation before having breakfast at a Little Chef on the way to a glorious day at Slimbridge Wildfowl Reserve.

I had an instant feeling of relief that day, even though I expected that there would still be a price to pay. At least I did not have to lay awake at night thinking about it anymore – the Maidstone era was finally over. It remains somewhat of a mystery to me that, for some unaccountable reason, we were never asked to pay the mortgage arrears and a year or so later actually received a substantial rebate on our mortgage insurance.

During the same period two aged aunts, my dad's sisters, died within weeks of each other. One of them, Aunt Connie, had been living on a meagre state pension for many years in a rented flat in Streatham, London. While clearing her things I was surprised to find a building society pass book showing she had over sixty thousand pounds deposited – my share was invaluable. My Dad had always told me to *"Keep in touch with your aunts because they've no children of their own to leave anything to."* His advise had finally paid off!

It was an exciting time. I had put together a budget for the 1990 season which had been approved and for the first time in my life I was able to set about creating and producing shows and other entertainment without being governed by ticket sales or sponsorship. I was playing with over half a million pounds and, after the financial stresses of The Isle of Wight and other ventures, I was determined to enjoy it to the full.

It was agreed that I could engage Penny as choreographer and director for the shows, which meant we could put some of our grandiose ideas into practice. We never mentioned our earlier flirtation with costume characters and prayed that nobody would ever unearth any pictures or other evidence of us playing Yogi Bear and Boo Boo. This time we would take it all very seriously.

At Thorpe Park I was officially reporting to the park operations manager but it was the managing director, Colin Dawson, who was more interested in entertainment and he was eager to upgrade the park's attractions. He had been promoted the previous year from the park's parent company, RMC Group, and was keen to set out his stall and make a success of this new challenge. Colin was always enthusiastic about the live entertainment and often joined me at auditions or showcase events. Over the years he eagerly supported my most ambitious plans.

I soon learnt *that, in his youth, Colin had been a member of 'The Who', before their rise to fame, and was still in touch with Roger Daltrey. In this we had a common interest with my similar, but often exaggerated, connection to Bowie.*

Unparallel Careers!

Those first years at the helm felt like I was in heaven. I teamed up with my old band mate from the sixties Terry Bolton (aka Gid Taylor) to create music – my first love! We wrote and recorded music for dramatic theatre productions, for children's shows, for stunt shows, for radio jingles and for television advertising. Everything we had both dreamed of being able to do for so many years. I wrote scripts for all the shows which Penny then directed superbly.

I had an assistant manager, Stephen Gallagher, who was a Thorpe Park 'veteran' as well as an enthusiastic musician and, with his help, I was able to install and operate a professional recording studio in the Palladium Theatre. I also set up a radio station, Thorpe Radio, and loved playing at being Mr DJ. It broadcast to the park with a mix of pop music and park information. On its opening day I shared the controls with well known radio and TV presenter Chris Tarrant. Over the next few years Thorpe Radio employed numerous DJs, some of whom went on to a full time career in broadcasting. Finally, I installed a video editing suite and this, together with the broadcasting and recording studios, provided excellent opportunities for the young people around me to gain valuable experience in these disciplines.

Stephen Gallagher (2019)
"I still do a lot of composing, arranging and recording as part of my job and all because of the amazing experience I got working in the studio. Also I work in school management and again got great experience at the park at such a young age.

The first major Palladium Theatre offering was *'Space Fantasy'* which borrowed music from Star Wars, The Carpenters (*'Calling Occupants Of Interplanetary Craft'*) and of course Bowie – his lyrics to *'Space Oddity'* rang out - I had to include it!

***I could now boast** at dinner parties that I was once with Bowie's first band and now produced shows at The Palladium!*

For the theatre and outside in the park I was able to employ some of the best Britsh talent as singers, dancers, musicians and guest artistes. I had a brilliant Charlie Chaplin impersonator called Adrian Kaye, a very successful ventriloquist Jimmy Tamley, the wonderful impressionist Adam Daye and many others. Penny handled all of these disparate talents expertly and I was extremely proud and happy with what we had created.

There were some minor blips along the way. The Space Fantasy show featured a robotic character which was played very well by a twenty something stage school student called Michael Blackledge who performed it in an uncomfortable metal costume. However, his timekeeping left a lot to be desired and I often had to warn him for missing his call time which was 30 minutes before the first show. One afternoon, five minutes before the show was due to start, he had not put in an appearance. Penny, naturally following the *'show must go on'* tradition, decided she would have to play the part of the robot. She struggled into the costume, covered her face and arms in heavy silver make-up and waited in the wings. Seconds before she was due to go on stage Michael appeared next to her saying *"Sorry - I was stuck in traffic in Chertsey"* to which Penny replied, uncharacteristically, *"Well Michael now you can fuck off back to Chertsey."* His career at Thorpe Park ended a week or two later when he feigned a collapse on the theatre stairs. It was part of his excuse for missing his call time again – he said he'd been to hospital with gall stones. That time I told him to 'fuck off' for good. The robots that followed him were never quite as talented but were always reliable, which was far less stressful.

The Guardian, August 30th 1990
"The dramatic ending complete with spectacular lighting effects and a spaceship makes the Space Fantasy Show a thrilling experience for the whole audience."

Jollies

In order to get a handle on this theme park industry I made several visits to established theme parks in Europe and America in order to learn from their successes and even from their mistakes. At EuroDisney in Paris, which was newly opened, I was able to witness the daily parade from 'backstage' and noted the disciplined regime that existed for their staff as well as the entertainers.

One autumn I flew with Penny to Los Angeles which brought back floods of memories of that *'Flame World Tour'* some twelve years before. We spent a few days visiting Disney World, Universal Studios and The Queen Mary which was docked as a visitor attraction at Palm Beach. We then drove across the Nevada Desert to Las Vegas.

Sunlit Uplands

We took in several shows and were overawed by the sheer scale of the productions. The pirate spectacular had just opened in front of the new Treasure Island Hotel and we were stunned by the technology used to recreate a sea battle and the sinking of a ship which had sailed into view from the rear of the hotel. The whole effect was breathtaking, especially when the sunken ship re-surfaced with the captain still standing in salute on the bridge. It made me realise that if I could emulate just a small part of this Las Vegas magic back in Europe I would be well ahead of the game. We left Vegas full of great ideas and flew on to Orlando where we completed the trip with visits to the Florida parks – Walt Disney World, Epcot, Sea World, Busch Gardens and the now long gone, but charming, Cypress Gardens. It was a fabulous tour and I returned full of enthusiasm for the future. These visits inspired me to do better and I quickly assimilated with the entirely unique world of theme park entertainment.

As the early 90s rolled on I continued to revel in the position I had found for myself. Apart from the sheer pleasure I took in the music and entertainment there were other exciting distractions, some good and some not so good.

There were two wonderful occasions when Diana Princess of Wales visited us with the young princes and I was able to join the party to take photographs for the park archives.

Then there was a frightening occasion when I was awoken at 2am to see smoke and sparks showering over the flat at Beomonds Farm. I shouted at Penny to wake up, thinking that the building was on fire. It transpired that the barns and storage around the courtyard were ablaze, making it impossible to leave by the front door. We grabbed some clothes and started down the stairs which were searingly hot by this time. I managed to open the door into the creche below us and then force open the outer door at the rear of the building. Hearing our names being called by the Thorpe Park security men we made our way to join them in the car park where we were stunned by the extent of the conflagration. The firefighters took several hours to extinguish the fire and make the area safe. When we were able to return we saw that parts of Penny's car, which was parked in the courtyard, had melted, as had the signage and window frames at the front of the building. Later that day we learnt that the fire had been deliberately set and the police were searching for two disgruntled Thorpe Park ex-employees. We spent the next night in the comfort of a nice hotel in Staines so that we could catch up on sleep and avoid the acrid smell of smoke that had pervaded the building and our flat.

The African Interlude

In 1991 Penny and I started a wonderful three year association with The Diani Reef Grand Hotel on the beautiful Indian Ocean coast just north of Mombasa in Kenya. My old agent/manager, Bob James from the *'Trilogy'* days in the 1970s, visited me at the park with his new wife. Wendy was the personal assistant to a London based businessman who owned this five star hotel. They were looking for someone to temporarily take charge of the entertainment because they were planning a programme to celebrate the hotel's tenth anniversary which was coming up in December that year. It was a no brainer for me. Our season at the park ended in October and I had several weeks of holiday so I offered our services.

We flew to Mombasa on the 16th December and were quickly immersed in organising the anniversary celebration which would take place on the 20th. The hotel general manager was a German called Ziggy Jogshat who, immediately, became 'Ziggy Stardust' to me. He ruled with a rod of iron and he didn't discriminate over who he was rude to. The guests often got the same gruff treatment as the staff. This made him very difficult to work with but we somehow managed to get an evenings programme agreed for the big day.

There would be five or six Kenyan groups performing who, between them, would present acrobatics, ethnic dance, local music and fire eating. An English singer, doing Frank Sinatra standards, was flying out to top the bill. He was well known to Bob James and Wendy but not to us and I can't recall his name. All this would take place on the tropical garden restaurant stage, which was surrounded by a moat and had the ocean as a backdrop. It was decided that the dynamic duo, Penny and me, would open the proceedings with our rendition of Lionel Richie's *'All Night Long'* and close out the show with *'Celebration'*, neither of which we had performed for several years.

The guest list included several government ministers, an assortment of local dignitaries and miscellaneous important business people. As they arrived at the entrance to the hotel they were greeted by a group of traditionally dressed Masai tribesmen whose speciality is jumping high on the spot in total unison supported by typical African harmony chanting. The tribesmen arrived early and had each imbibed several beers by the time the first guests started to appear. Penny had been designated to oversee the welcome in the lobby and started to panic when it was apparent that a number of the jumpers had gone walkabout. I wandered up to the lobby to see how things were going and I have an undying image of Penny waving her arms up and down trying to get the remaining Masai tribesmen, who by this time were anything but enthusiastic, jumping and singing.

Like most of the frantic one-off events that I have organised the whole evening passed in a blur. I was running about trying to make sure all the ethnic groups appeared on stage when announced. Their dressing room was the beach and in the dark it was difficult to locate each separate group and even more difficult to gather all the members together. We would soon learn that timekeeping does not feature high on the average Kenyan's list of priorities. Somehow, miraculously, the evening was proclaimed a great success and we gladly took the compliments even though, from our perspective, it had been a chaotic muddle. Sleep came very easily that night.

We stayed on at the hotel until the 13th January and helped with the Christmas and New Year entertainment. After seeing in the new year we took the time to explore Mombasa town and the local area. We treated it all as a free holiday, the highlight of which was a wonderful safari trip to Tsavo East National Park where we stayed overnight in the Sarova Salt Lick Game Lodge. It was made up of a series of bedrooms in typical African palm roofed huts. They were mounted on stilts and joined to each other and the main hotel reception by rope walkways. The lodge overlooked a waterhole where we could watch animals coming to feed while enjoying an ice cold gin and tonic. Heaven!

We returned to Mombasa in February 1993 – this time for an altogether different task. We had been to meet Benine, the hotel's owner, at his flat near Clarence House in London. In the opulence of this magnificent apartment he regaled us with his many criticisms of the way the hotel's guest relations was run and his regrets that he was not there more often to introduce changes. He said *"The hotel just functions by inertia."* He wanted us to retrain the entertainment staff, look at the guest activities on offer and make a general report on the hotel as seen through the eyes of a guest. *"Stephan, leave no stone unturned, no corner unregarded."* These are the words, in his heavily accented English, that were left ringing in my ears as we left.

On arrival at the hotel we soon realised that it was going to be a difficult task because 'Ziggy Stardust' was not really interested in guest relations. He seemed to treat the guests as unwelcome intruders into his world of German efficiency. It was best, it seemed to him, to leave the guests confused, or at least uninformed, so that their expectations were low. That way he could minimise the complaints. For example there were seven restaurants in this vast hotel but it could take at least the first three days of your stay to discover that they existed and even longer to find them. Signage was an anathema to Ziggy – if there were signs then people would find their way to parts of the hotel where they were not always welcome. If you found the charming French restaurant in your first week you were very fortunate. Some guests never found it, which suited 'Stardust' because it meant it was never too busy – less staff needed. He preferred that they ate at the enormous beachside restaurant where they would not be under his feet wandering about the hotel.

*It's **interesting to note** that Bowie had visited Kenya and in Mombasa he met a band of German pilots drinking in the bars. He said that these expatriates fascinated him as they seemed to be aliens in an alien environment. I had discovered a similar German expatriate also seemingly out of step with his environment!*

I decided that the hotel guests needed, at the very least, some basic information and he reluctantly went along with this ground breaking and innovative idea. Information sheets in each room – wow! The times of the various activities and the restaurant opening hours seemed to me the minimum of information that guests should have. The problem was that giving the guests times meant sticking to them and that was not normally a priority in this establishment. It was best to avoid being specific about restaurant opening times or the time of the keep fit class on the beach because guests might just turn up at the advertised time, whereas the staff never did.

There were three young men and two girls who made up the guest relations and entertainment staff. They all ran some daily activities like beach volley ball, water polo, snooker competitions and the aformentioned keep fit classes, but they were largely unsupervised.

When I had managed to get information into all the guest rooms eager participants began to arrive on time for the various activities and Penny had the unenviable task of trying to convince the team that they needed to be in place before the advertised time and not ten minutes after. It should be noted that as the team did not seem to possess qualifications in any of the activities they supervised it was perhaps a good thing that many guests avoided joining in. In spite of Penny's intervention and repeated training sessions the keep fit class, taken by the two girls, probably did more harm than good for those guests who were unlucky enough to take part.

Each evening the three men also had the task of introducing the bands and ethnic groups who appeared on the outside stage. They did this very badly. Although their main language was English their mumbled and rambling announcements were virtually incomprehensible to the majority of the English speaking guests. They all spoke perfectly well off-stage so we spent many hours getting them to announce clearly and correctly by scripting various versions of a typical evening's introductions - introducing the band, introducing the artistes, giving information on the next day's activities and handling the 'signing off' at the end of the evening. On our last night we had our farewell dinner at the outside restaurant and listened to them utter the same incomprehensible gibberish that we heard on day one.

Unparallel Careers!

I wondered if this was an omen and if I would ever get to return to find out if any of my report had filtered through or if any information was still arriving in the rooms. We were therefore chuffed, at the end of '93, to be asked once again to run the Christmas and New Year celebrations at the hotel and we flew out on December 20th. In the room allocated to us I found the same information sheet that I had distributed back in February, which was now tea stained and crumpled. The times of activities had been changed but the information sheets had not! The presentation of the shows was, predictably, just as unintelligible as it had been ten months before. I mentioned these observations to 'Ziggy Stardust' but, as expected, received a short sharp negative response as he marched away. Information for the guests - ba humbug!

Nevertheless we have some great and some amusing memories of that last trip. Great memories like the wonderful private bird safari we arranged in Tsavo National Park where we stayed overnight in a tented camp run by Hilton Hotels. At the end of a fabulous day of exotic bird watching Penny got the runs, so it was lucky that our tent had a luxury toilet and shower – we weren't slumming it, this was true glamping. Next day on the way back to the hotel, and while she was still suffering, we got stranded for the best part of an hour on a broken down, packed and stifling river ferry. The thing bobbed about and drifted downstream while Penny groaned *"Just get me back to the room."* Eventually it was taken under tow and the mass of humanity disembarked permitting our taxi to speed on to the air conditioned comfort of our hotel room.

Then there are amusing memories. One is the vision of 'Stardust', wearing a moth-eaten Santa's beard and a red coat of doubtful origin, disdainfully distributing gifts to the hotel guests on Christmas Eve with a less than enthusiastic 'Ho Ho Ho'. Another was witnessing his demeanour when he was unable to avoid a guest who complained that when she had opened her wardrobe a large rat jumped out at her. He couldn't bring himself to apologise but instead offered a strange explanation. He said it was obviously because the rooms on the ground floor were built into the rocks, as though she should have known, and therefore it was her fault for booking that room in the first place. He then marched away!

Thus we departed The Diani Reef Grand Hotel for the last time knowing that nothing would change. Everything would continue to be run by inertia, as Benine had explained to us that evening in London. I *'left no stone unturned'* as he had requested, but they had all been turned back! The hotel is now (2019) called The Diani Reef Beach Resort and I hope it is much better managed.

We flew home on January 3rd and we were lucky enough to get a magnificently clear view of the vast desert areas of Egypt, which brought back vivid memories of my time spent on the ground below us many years before.

Heroes, Fairytales and the BBC

As the 90s wore on I was able to create ever more complex shows for the theatre and at other locations in the park. I introduced the park's new costume characters, The Thorpe Park Rangers, and staged the first of two very successful shows in the newly converted Rangers Theatre.

A large grassed area was turned into a show arena and I was suddenly immersed in the world of high diving stunt shows. Taking advantage of Penny's, by then, prodigious talent for show directing and helped by a wonderful bunch of technicians and stage managers I created *'Tarzan's Jungle Adventure'*, a quite unique production that mixed teams of traditional American high divers with great young British actors. This was to be a combination that would feature in several future projects.

I produced a new show for the theatre called *'Legend of The Ring'* which ran for two years. It was loosely based on the Indiana Jones films and featured a battling dinosaur which was a large and unwieldy costume with very poor vision worn by one of our character performers. Not being used to the restrictions of the theatre stage the dinosaur often wandered dangerously close to the edge until at last, while fighting the handsome hero, he fell off. Well padded in the costume the performer was unhurt but, laying on his back, it proved impossible to get up until two stage hands went to his rescue. We vainly hoped the audience might think it was part of his defeat by our hero!

In 1993 I was able to secure the services of Bruno Brooks, then a leading BBC Radio One and TV presenter, to play a part in my first (and last) Christmas Pantomime. I adapted an existing script for the pantomime *'Babes In The Wood'* and wrote in a special part for Bruno which would not overly tax his non-existent acting skills. The park's various department managers got together to build a nativity scene at the theatre entrance which included animals brought down from Thorpe Farm – it was a magical time. The whole organisation was very well coordinated and the talented cast became adept at pushing Bruno about and prompting him in accordance with the script.

In the quieter periods I managed to record two albums by the park's mascots, The Thorpe Park Rangers, which featured all the songs we had written for their shows plus extra tracks that Terry Bolton and I knocked up specially for the purpose. I ordered cassettes from our own music publishing company, *Flame Music,* which gave us a small profit. The cassettes were on sale in the park shops and were given away to members of The Thorpe Park Rangers Club.

Several versions of my old Song Contest were staged in the theatre culminating with the most successful one on the 20th June 1993. That year BBC Radio had decided to cover the event and while I presented the contestants on stage Bob Holness, the well known and established BBC presenter, handled the radio commentary. The winner that day was a writer called Gerry Markey with an unforgettable song called *'Marvelous Marvin Gaye'*.

To recharge the batteries after the 1994 season I flew to Orlando with Penny for two weeks of relaxation. We discovered, for the first time, Sarasota, Sanibel Island and the wonderful Myakka River State Park where we encountered numerous species of water birds, saw our first bald eagle, and photographed alligators from a safe distance. We returned to Gatwick airport early on

Unparallel Careers!

Christmas Day and spent a relaxing Christmas languishing in a luxury hotel. Soon I would embark on my busiest year to date at Thorpe Park but it would be a year of great changes and challenges.

The New Venture

As a result of Penny's excellent work directing and choreographing the shows at Thorpe Park she had been engaged to direct a magic show for the 1995 season at Alton Towers, the most well known of the British theme parks. It occurred to us that, for prudent financial reasons, we should set up a company for her work to be channelled through. In the spring of '95 we rented a small office in Terminal House at Shepperton where the meeting room was a 1920s Pullman railway carriage still on the rails at the station – very theme park! And thus began *Parkshow Production Associates* (known thereafter as *Parkshows*). In a press release about the new entity I was listed as a consultant to the company which ruffled feathers at Thorpe Park where, understandably, it was seen as a possible conflict of interest. I was questioned as to my intentions and I confirmed my undying loyalty to Thorpe Park, which was not strictly honourable.

I had enjoyed an incredible six years doing what I loved but I was never happy to be part of a management team. I was an employee and had to abide by certain conventions which did not sit well with me. Luckily, because my work was a mystery to the other managers in the team, I was mostly left alone. However, there were certain duties and responsibilities that I could not avoid and I had to take my turn with these dreary tasks along with the catering, landscaping, retail and other managers. I was definitely feeling the adverse effects of several years of corporate submission and I was looking for a way out. I was no longer short of money – compared to earlier years I had been coining it in with a salary and music royalties, while paying very little to live, so now seemed the time to think about my freedom again.

Calling Time

A new project to build a Legoland in the UK had passed from the designers' drawing boards and was then in the early stages of construction at Windsor, just a few miles away from Thorpe. It was necessary to up our game for the new season in order to counteract the effect of another theme park opening in the same catchment area. For this reason I had secured my biggest budget yet for live entertainment and I set about planning an entirely new programme for 1995. I felt it was my last chance to bring a little of the Las Vegas magic to a British theme park!

I created a new theatre experience called *'Merlin's Magic Castle'* and The Thorpe Park Rangers were given a new show, *'Picnic By The Sea'*. The high diving stunt show in the arena was extended, I introduced a permanent street theatre team and staged a daily 'Disneyish' parade through the park.

For the theatre production I had discovered, just on the market, a new system whereby stage lighting changes could be controlled by a computer programme, which in turn took instructions from a code recorded onto the soundtrack tape. This was ground breaking technology and was still very much in its infancy but, in order to carry out all the lighting effects I had planned for the new show in the theatre, it seemed the perfect solution. Thus the lighting nightmare began. Programming this software proved nigh on impossible for my technicians. After they had struggled with it for several days, without success, I insisted that one of the software creation team came to the theatre to properly programme the lighting when the final rehearsals were over.

It was early evening when we started the process and we were still in the theatre at six the next morning. Each time the system appeared to be completely programmed we played it back and it crashed. I had obviously bought into an expensive product that was hardly ready for the open market. It did eventually come good but throughout the season it occasionally threw 'curved balls' which our technicians could never catch or understand. Although I vowed to avoid such technology in the future, until it was thoroughly proven, a version of this system would come back to haunt me sooner than I expected.

During the course of that summer the marketing department came up with their latest greatest idea! Thus Harley The Cat was born. He was meant to be a cool dude so, with Terry, I wrote a song for him called *'Cat Rap'*. I then spent an hour or two in a London studio recording Paul Whitehouse, from the hit BBC TV programme 'The Fast Show', as rapper Harley. Although we set the cat up with his own mini-show I never really felt that he added anything to the entertainment offering. In fact he stuck around for a few years after I had departed - so what did I know?

I was elated by the success of all the 1995 productions but towards the end of the season I received some disappointing news. In spite of the park's increased budgets the season had not proven a financial success and with Legoland due to open in 1996 Thorpe Park was anticipating a big drop in attendances. Therefore all budgets would be cut for the next year. As always when money is scarce entertainment is the easiest thing to attack so I took the biggest cut. My budget was halved and, as a result, I was subjected to some unwelcome internal reorganisation which led to being allocated reduced office space. After such an exciting and creative year my future at the park began to look bleak. The golden days were over! It was time for big thinking. I was now financially independent with all the old debts way back in the past so I decided that I would leave Thorpe Park and join Penny full time in the office at Shepperton.

My initial plan was to resign in early 1996, when arrangements and contracts for the surviving entertainment were well advanced. I was gambling on there being a good chance that I could win some contracts for *Parkshows.* We would be well placed to produce at least part of the remaining entertainment, in particular the arena high diving stunt show. I knew that there would be no other producers or directors in the UK with the required knowledge to stage it. However, as the season drew to a close, I got more and more restless and one day, without giving much thought to what would happen next, I knocked on the MD's door and resigned.

It was exactly like the time, almost thirty years

earlier, when I had resigned from my first office job. Freedom again – but what would the future hold? For the first time in six years I would have to pay rent and other household charges – it was an anxious time and vital that this new project worked.

> *Life in the fast lane*
> *Trying to make the grade*
> *Pushing for the final accolade*
> *Keeping spirits high*
> *No more wondering why*
> *Only one more trial to have it made*
> **Stephen Gold (The Colour Of Dreams)**

First among the immediate problems was where to live. We were still at Beomonds Farm and we needed to find somewhere close to the Shepperton office. We settled on a flat above an insurance company office in Shepperton High Street. This was to become our home and sometime office for the next few years.

Chapter 11
The Glory Days
(The Parkshows Years)

What day is it, certainly not yesterday
For that dissolved already into a sweet memory
A memory of a life that now can grow
Stephen Gold (Time)

So now I was 'flying by the seat of my pants' again. I settled into the office at Shepperton and then kept my fingers firmly crossed. Fortunately the gamble I had taken paid off when I was asked to submit a proposal for the 1996 Thorpe Park Arena show. I had been right in assuming that they would be forced to look for an American producer and director if they had decided not to use my services, and that it would have given them a big budget problem. I was, of course, perfectly placed to submit a proposal at an acceptable price because I had been party to the budget discussions and agreements while I was still employed. This was to be the first of many big contracts.

Over the winter months I had put together the first

brochures for the new company and they began to get responses. I travelled to Belgium early in 1996 to view a vast hangar like building in the Walibi theme park at Wavre, near to Brussels. The building had housed a sea lion show and had a large pool in front of an open stage area. The auditorium had banked seating for six hundred people. I immediately realised that we could use all our experience with divers, stunt performers, actors, full theatre lighting and special effects to create a truly spectacular show.

I submitted a set design of a jungle clearing with cliffs, rocky outcrops, native huts, rope bridges across the pool area and, of course, a smattering of palm trees. The storyline would follow a James Bond style adventure and include diving, stage fighting, and gun battles sprinkled with predictable ironic humour. They were suitably impressed and I signed a production contract for around four hundred and fifty thousand pounds.

We were now on the way up and I was thinking big. We took over a larger office at Terminal House and I brought in an old friend, musician Grahame Laurence, to look after the office on a daily basis while I was out canvassing for work and dealing with the productions.

Penny still had her contract with Alton Towers and we signed an additional contract with Lightwater Valley Park, near Ripon in Yorkshire, where we created some children's characters and staged a small show called *'Edgar Fox and Friends'*. It was always a delightful break from the more intense demands of the big shows to visit Lightwater and spend a couple of days in the Yorkshire countryside.

The Glory Days

It was at Lightwater Valley that the BBC decided to make a 'fly on the wall' documentary following one of our girls through rehearsals and up until the opening show. They approached our girl outside the park and tried to persuade her to cause an argument with Penny during rehearsals while they were filming. It was my first experience of the underhand methods used to get 'the dirt'. I had a face off with the programme director. If he didn't leave our girl to get on with her rehearsals without interference I would not give a copyright waver for our original music to be used in his programme, thus making any footage they had of our girl on stage unuseable. He agreed to back off but they got the last laugh by filming the dress rehearsal and then panning across the empty venue, giving the impression that it was the opening show to which nobody came!

Big Adventure In A Small Country

Plans for the Belgium show were complicated. I had written a storyline called *'Tropical Mission'* in which the hero – we called him 008 - would arrive by helicopter into a jungle village to search for a glamourous captured scientist. There was an existing apparatus in the building from which we could suspend the chopper. He would then board a small boat and cross the river – the existing pool. He would fight with the villains, encounter a witchdoctor, endure a violent storm, then release the scientist and escape with her under a hail of gunfire, blowing up a footbridge as he departed. The chopper would then fire on the village for an explosive finale. Phew! Was it all possible?

Unparallel Careers!

I visited Shepperton Film Studios to meet some special effects experts and eventually agreed for them to install all the required kit. This would include wind machines and a rain curtain for the storm, a collapsing hut and tree, an exploding ammunition dump, hanging creepers that would break on cue and the collapsing rope bridge.

The set was beautifully constructed with fibre glass to create the cliffs and the rocky outcrop above the river over which 008 and the glamorous girl would make their escape. It was built in England and assembled on site.

I recorded an opening video for the show which featured well known TV actress Julie Peasgood who is Penny's good friend from performing arts school days. It set the scene by showing a mission briefing for 008 by 'M', played wonderfully by Julie.

The special effects were installed in good time but this is where the first problems started to emerge. The highly experienced Shepperton Studios effects team had created everything that we asked for, but they were accustomed to setting up spectacular effects for a one off scene in a movie – not to be repeated several times each day and for many weeks. It took some adapting to ensure that the effects were durable and reliable. They had to be triggered remotely and this is when I encountered, for a second time, a system of control programmed from a code on a soundtrack tape. This time the computer system would have to control all the special effects as well as the lighting.

The beginning of the season soon turned into a technical nightmare but, looking back, there were some very amusing moments. We had built the underside of a helicopter onto the existing rail system that ran from the back of the building to the stage. There was a cable from which 008 would be lowered after passing over the heads of the audience. The chopper had two front pyrotechnic pods to simulate rockets that would be fired automatically by the computer software at the end of the show. On numerous occasions, the helicopter failed to move from the rear of the auditorium so 008 climbed off and made an undignified entrance on foot through the audience. Our technicians then had to make a mad scramble, between cues, to unplug the pyrotechnics. If not there would have been some badly singed hair in the auditorium!

On more than one occasion the storm sequence went wrong for no reason that we could identify. I was there to witness one such occasion when the storm erupted as usual with the wind machines blowing the palm trees and the rain curtain pouring down over the water area. The hut dramatically collapsed on cue but then it righted itself before collapsing again and rising again while the rain continued to pour until the end of the show. Our technician in the control box could do nothing except throw up his hands shouting *"The whole fucking thing's gone mad, it's all out of control. Sh** !! F***!!"*

During rehearsals, each time the ammunition dump exploded in a burst of flame and smoke the building's fire alarms went off, so we had to instruct the stage manager to turn off the alarms before each show – no risk assessment or *'elf and safety'* regime here. Unsurprisingly, the lack of fire alarms almost came back

Unparallel Careers!

to bite us one afternoon when, after a gunfire sequence, the palm fronds caught fire. The ever resourceful stage manager dashed up onto the cliff and doused them with a foam extinguisher. The foam settled on the stage and in the water and the actors slithered through the rest of the show getting unscripted laughs!

I waited each day in the office at Shepperton dreading the phone call from Belgium and what it might spring on me. When the time of the last show of the day had passed, and I had not received an emergency phone call, I let out a sigh of relief. I was, in spite of the initial setbacks, immensely proud of what we had all achieved – it was ahead of its time and, when it ran smoothly, it was highly impressive in its technical effects, stage fighting, diving stunts and brilliant original music once more inspired by Terry Bolton (aka Gid Taylor).

Dark and wild eyes that shine
Through the night into mine
No way out hard to breath
Fear is here underneath
Like an evil spell that threatens
Then you come to rescue me.
Gid Taylor/Stephen Gold (Voodoo Moon)

Unfortunately there was a dark cloud about to pass over the Belgian show. The general manager with whom I had negotiated the contract resigned to take up another post just before the season started. His replacement, who transferred from another Walibi park, was totally opposed to using foreign companies to produce their shows and he demonstrated this whenever I visited the park.

He and his assistant constantly criticised small elements of the show. I took it all with a smile and always promised to consider their points and make adjustments where possible. I kept my cool for some weeks until, on one routine visit, their criticism reached the limit of absurdity. They said that there was too much gunfire in the final scene - 008 could not possibly survive – he would be killed. I exploded – *"He's meant to be a James Bond character for heaven's sake. Have you never seen a Bond movie? He dodges bullets, knives, bombs, anything they throw at him, of course there's not too much gunfire, you're being ridiculous."* I walked away.

I was seriously pissed off because it was already two thirds of the way through the season and the show was brilliant – everything I hoped it would be. Bizarrely, after all the bitching, two weeks before the contract ended they contacted me to say they wanted to extend the season by four weeks. I told them we would only consider it if they paid all remaining fees, including for the extension, up front. They declined and we brought our actors, divers and crew home. It was a lucrative contract but I could not see any future in further contact with the miserable management. Fortunately, I left with a very positive impression of the season because I had learnt a great deal more about staging spectacular stunt shows and managing complex computer operated activities.

While the Belgian show was in rehearsal we had also prepared carefully for the new season at Thorpe Park. In order to keep the contract for the following years we needed to produce an excellent arena show. In the event we staged a superb version of *'Tarzan's Jungle*

Adventure' which cemented our future involvement with the park.

It had been a season of very hard work with precious little leisure time. *Parkshows'* first year had been highly satisfying, both artistically and financially, but by November I was feeling decidedly jaded and it was time for some fun.

New Orleans

I decided it would be a useful business move to attend the annual International Theme Parks Convention (IAAPA) that was being held in New Orleans. I flew out with Penny on November 18th 1996 and checked into a hotel near the historical centre from where we could explore a little of this fabled Deep South city, the home of traditional dixieland jazz. We quickly took in the 'old town' area which was, as I had always imagined it to be, full of southern tradition and lots of music.

When the convention was over we hired a car, found a seaside town called Biloxi on a map, booked a hotel and set off for a journey into unknown America. This popular resort, completely off the radar for Brits (unless they had read John Grisham's novel 'The Partner'), was stretched along a wide sandy bay washed by the warm waters of the Gulf of Mexico. We checked into the Holiday Inn Motel opposite a glorious sandy beach and settled into our room with a bottle of fizz to celebrate the holiday.

At around nine o'clock that evening a coach pulled into the hotel and disgorged forty or more adolescents on a school trip. They were shown to the rooms all around us and started to party hard. By ten we had endured enough. We packed our bags and headed for reception to check out. Well oiled from the bottle of fizz I drove unsteadily along the beachfront boulevard until we spotted the welcoming lights of the Beau Rivage Hotel & Casino.

The hotel was full but the receptionist called the Casino manager to ask if they would need their allocated rooms which were always reserved for any high rolling gamblers. Fortunately the high rollers were absent that night and they released a room for us which was charged at the standard hotel rate. When we opened the penthouse room door our desultory moods were swept away by what we found. A luxury king size bed, a balcony with a view over the bay, champagne on ice, a free mini bar, fruitbowl, and to top it off a magnificent jacuzzi into which we dived with champagne glasses in hand.

After two further days in this shangri-la we could bear it no longer! We hit the road back to New Orleans and the return flight to Blighty. Some years later I unexpectedly heard of the previously *'unknown Biloxi'* when, sadly, it was severely damaged by Hurricane Katrina, along with much of New Orleans.

Cairo Again

Although we had lost our clients in Belgium we had, by the beginning of 1997, a solid basis for a strong year. Lightwater Valley, Alton Towers and Thorpe Park all remained loyal and there were several other possible irons in the fire. For example, in response to our

Unparallel Careers!

brochure mail outs, I received a call from an Egyptian company, based in Cairo, who explained that they were involved in the development of a new theme park just outside the city. Would I visit the site and prepare some proposals for spectacular shows and look at suitable venues within the park?

I flew out at their expense and spent a tedious day hanging around their offices before being driven to the site. The route took me past the two hotels that I had worked in many years before and, on seeing The Cairo Sheraton, I was immediately reminded of the time, in 1975, when I had met a party of Americans who were there to discuss opening a Disney type park at the pyramids. At the time I had cast scorn on the crazy idea and it had come to nothing but, twenty years later, it seemed like I could be involved in making it actually happen! The site was only partly built but had the potential to be a big money spinner for us.

I prepared some plans and ideas for shows and general entertainment and a month or two later Penny and I were both flown out, once more at their expense, to discuss the proposals and look at the newly built arena. We returned to England in a positive mood never to hear from Cairo again!

The only upside to this Egyptian episode was that, due to a mix up over flights, I ended up receiving a large credit note from British Airways which enabled us to pay for our flights to Singapore two years later. I never knew how we managed to get the credit notes when the Cairo company had paid for the tickets. I didn't think it was wise to inquire too deeply!

Hello Sailor!

The same high diving stunt show had survived at Thorpe Park for three successful years and everybody agreed it was time for a change. At a leisure industry exhibition I met John McInnerny who was the UK representative for the New York based company King's Features. They owned the rights to the characters from the Popeye cartoons and it occured to me that Popeye The Sailorman would be a great asset to a show based on water and high diving. The idea was well received at Thorpe Park so I set about writing a draft script for the new show. I presented our proposal to New York and secured the UK rights to present Popeye, Olive and Bluto in theatre and arena shows.

I designed an extended water area in the Thorpe Park Arena so that Popeye could make his entrance in a boat. The show was called *'Popeye's Pirate Adventure – Making The Movie'*. There was now the not inconsiderable task of finding actors who could record the voices of the characters and I called Adam Daye, the impressionist who had appeared in our Jersey show years before. He tried a few lines and easily fell into the voice of Popeye. Having failed to come up with a good option for Olive I asked Penny to have a try – she was a natural. The partnership of Adam and Penny as the voices of the two characters lasted for several years through many different scripts.

Popeye, Olive and the high diving show was a very successful combination which generated a lot of publicity for the park. For example, they had pictures in the national papers of a match-up between Popeye and the famous English boxer Frank Bruno. But the ultimate scoop was a visit by a carefully protected Michael Jackson, surrounded by an extensive entourage and 'secretely' driven into the park to watch the arena show. A photograph of Michael with Popeye and Olive made all the front pages next day but it was then discovered that it was all a major hoax by a PR firm using a Michael Jackson look-alike. Highly embarrassing for the park management who had afforded him every facility and sent out copious photos and press releases before the ruse was uncovered.

The Sun - Friday July 11th 1997
"A cruel Michael Jackson impersonator left thousands of youngsters heartbroken yesterday after conning them into believing he was the superstar. Twelve hours earlier the real Jacko had finished a concert in Sheffield and was in Paris as the conman went through his elaborate scam."

Popeye and Olive became the mainstays of our show productions for the next few years. I subsequently wrote the script and music for a Popeye theatre show and when Drayton Manor Theme Park near Tamworth in Staffordshire decided, in 2000, to convert a storage building into a theatre we were able to provide a plan for the building and install Popeye, Olive and Bluto for the first of two summer and two Christmas seasons.

I was beginning to feel that we had the makings of a very stable and profitable company and I decided to expand by moving from our base at Terminal House and taking over a suite of offices in Shepperton High Street. Robert Harrison, who had spent one season of his leisure

The Glory Days

degree course working for me at Thorpe Park, had joined the company as my assistant and along with a secretary/receptionist we installed ourselves at the new offices. It was here that I welcomed a lovely lady called Ann Kerr from the Kellogg's marketing department and signed a contract to manage the promotional appearances of their celebrated *'Tony Tiger'* character. It was an agreement that lasted well into the new century. Naturally we wrote a couple of songs especially for *'Tony Tiger'* which featured on his live appearances. It was 'Grrreat'!!!

Early one Sunday morning, in the midst of this happy season, the news burst upon the world that Princess Diana had died in a car crash in Paris. It was the 31st August 1997. I was, like the rest of the British public, devastated by the news and could only think back and picture the days she had spent with us at Thorpe Park. I still cherish the photographs I took of Diana just a few years before her death.

While time seemed to stand still for the millions who mourned her passing, for me the year continued to race by. As well as the Thorpe Park Arena show we were managing the second season at Lightwater Valley. Penny was still directing the show at Alton Towers Magic Theatre and the *'Tony Tiger'* promotions began. I was also planning and promoting a *'Sylvanian Families'* theatre tour – I had secured the rights to the popular characters and this would be our first venture in traditional theatres. The show toured from October 1997 until April 1998 and thereafter spent the summer in Great Yarmouth. It was great fun when I occasionally manned the theatre stand myself selling the Sylvanian merchandise. It was always overrun by the kids and their parents in the interval and I've always loved taking proper cash money - especially lots of it!

By October 1998 we had started the first theatre tour of *'Popeye and Friends'* with a successful weekend debut in Staines, Middlesex. The bookings flowed in and we were encouraged that, after a mild success with *'Adventure in Sylvania'*, this could be our big breakthrough into theatres. The show endured for nearly three years.

The Stage and Television Today - December 10th 1998
"Technically this lively production is a striking success. Costumes, voices, tapes, tracks, music and mime are expertly blended and timed. Deception becomes magic for all ages and the kids clearly understand everything that Popeye mutters and grumbles."

I had joined an organisation in the UK called The Institute of Entertainments and Arts Managers (IEAM) and I had been elected onto the national executive committee. This involved regular visits to the venues run by other members and to major London theatres where we would enjoy lunch before an afternoon 'business' meeting. When we came to sell our *Parkshows* theatre tours these jollies turned out to be useful. The connection with the institute and its members was invaluable. The IEAM also presented the annual Waterford Crystal Award for services to entertainment and I had the pleasure of lunching with two winners on different award days – Dame Judy Dench and Eric Sykes. On hearing that I had worked with Jimmy

Edwards many years before Eric was happy to disclose his many hilarious memories of his time touring with Jimmy in the outrageously ad-libbed play *'Big Bad Mouse'*.

Dubai

On the 11th January 1999 I landed in Dubai for the first time since our *'Flame World Tour'* in 1980. It was for a meeting with the officials of the Dubai Municipality. I was accompanied by a slick businessman from Windsor who had visited the Thorpe Park Arena and seen our *'Popeye's Pirate Adventure'* show. He had sold the idea of bringing Popeye and the high divers to Dubai during their annual Dubai Shopping Festival, which commenced as Ramadan finished and the celebrations began. For me this was to be the start of a whole new adventure. We stayed only two days but had finalised a deal to bring the full arena production to Al Mamza Park for the festival starting on the 16th March. They agreed to build a full size pool and stage area to our design before we arrived so that we could install the high diving mast and the scenery behind it. An enormous task.

The scenery had to be specially constructed for the Dubai stage. It was shipped out by sea in a container together with a diving mast and all the other stage equipment and costumes. The show was to run for 12 days and we were paid £34,000 which adequately covered our costs and profit margin. We discovered later that the aformentioned Windsor businessman received in excess of £60,000 for the contract and, apart from our fee, paid only for a useless 'road manager' to represent him in Dubai. This information was useful in negotiating an agreement with Dubai for the following year.

On the 11th March I returned to Dubai to approve the stage and pool construction and to begin the scenery and diving equipment installation. By the time Penny arrived from England with the performers everything was ready for some intensive rehearsals. The show opened as scheduled to wide acclaim from the local papers and Dubai officials who had not seen anything like it previously.

Khaleej Times - April 3rd 1999
"More than 75,000 people have watched the spectacular Popeye The Sailor Man Show in Al Mamzar Park since the start of the Dubai Shopping Festival. It is great entertainment for all the family. If you haven't seen it yet then this weekend will be your last chance, or else you will miss out."

Penny and I had to head back to Europe before the run ended and on our last night in Dubai we watched with pride as seven thousand enthusiastic people crowded the venue to see our creation.

As we walked away I thought about one of Bowie's biggest hits which seemed so appropriate. We were the king and queen. Heroes - just for one day.

Moving On

Soon after returning to England I took care of upcoming show commitments and then Penny and I flew to Singapore for a well earned rest, taking advantage of the British Airways credit note I had somehow inherited after our Cairo escapade. I was able to show Penny the delights of Singapore as I remembered them and once again visit the Shangri-La Hotel and tell her about my exit in an ambulance over twenty years earlier.

Much had changed in Singapore but, to my mind, only some of it was for the better. The wonderful Bugie Street was gone and replaced by an over sanitised version of its old self. It was a pity that so few of the old shop houses still existed but I could see the need, in such a small island nation, for much better use of the available space to cope with the ever rising population. While in the area we took a short sea trip to the island of Bintan in Indonesia where we luxuriated at The Banyan Tree Resort. Its unique selling point and strapline was "A Sanctuary For The Senses". It certainly was!

In June we moved out of the flat in Shepperton and into a wonderful house called The Barn overlooking the River Thames at Laleham. The flat then became our office and we accommodated a Thorpe Park team of high divers there, which was much against the spirit of the lease. On one occasion the flat's managing agents sent someone down from London to get me to sign a lease extension and we spent all day before he arrived removing any trace of the office and restoring it to a normal dwelling. He stayed for five minutes and looked at nothing – by the next morning it was an office again.

The American divers who were housed in the flat were the last that I engaged because the summer of 1999 was to see the end of our shows in the Thorpe Park Arena. It was, though, the beginning of an involvement with Legoland at Windsor. Our first task was to create and manage a street theatre team called *'The Lego Fun*

Squad' who would perform pre-scripted sketches around the park.

And so, in the dying days of the twentieth century, I was feeling positive and thoroughly enjoying a creative life that had finally paid off big time. It was a great thrill to be able to write scripts that made people laugh or cry and enhance these scripts with music and lyrics that inspired them. In the theme park world I had discovered a niche that I could develop and, in spite of the paperwork and office duties that were inevitable, I was able to start over again with my passion for songwriting and music that had its roots so many years ago with the band that became *'David Bowie and the Lower Third'*!

The new century took us back to Dubai for the Shopping Festival with a production starring *'The Smurfs'*. Our offer to work directly with the Dubai Municipality, and thus dramatically reduce their outgoings, led to a contract for a two weeks run at the end of February. Our fee of around £30,000, rather than the exorbitant £60,000 overcharged for the Popeye show, was the deciding factor.

In the summer of 2000 I was managing the *'Popeye and Friends'* show at Drayton Manor Theme Park staged in their newly completed theatre conversion. I also oversaw *'The Fun Squad'* at Legoland and the various *'Tony Tiger'* presentations while Penny directed the ice show, *'Peter Rabbit And Friends'*, at Alton Towers.

During that season Legoland made the decision to open their gates in December for the Christmas period. In the event they created a large grotto with separate areas and thrones for three simultaneous Santas to operate at one time – a recipe for disaster! We were contracted to supply the Santas and the elves which led to some hilarious auditions. When we had our team in place Penny presided over several training days to ensure that all the Ho Ho Hos were well tuned. Robert Harrison had the dubious honour of managing the project while I was busy elsewhere.

The system was such that the kids entered a general area where they were greeted by the elves and then directed down a short tunnel which split into three with a Santa at the end of each. One can imagine the confusion trying to schedule each Santa with breaks and time off. Children going down a tunnel to an empty chair, two children in the same tunnel, one Santa thinking he's having a break without his beard and hat when an excited child turns up in his tunnel, and so it went on. Robert was called in every day to sort out some problem or other and I think the Legoland management realised in the end that the whole idea was far too complicated. One Santa, with access for all, was the way forward if they opened for Christmas again.

To see out the year I created a new show to run in December at Drayton Manor Park. It was to be *'Popeye's Christmas Party'*. I loved everything about that show - it was quintessential Christmas fayre with all the seasonal elements included. The songs and background music were taken from an earlier attempt by me and Terry Bolton to write a Christmas extravaganza called *'Santa Claus The Musical'*. An attempt which ground to a halt when another production was launched with the same title!

On the penultimate day of December 2000 I received a letter of resignation from Robert Harrison. He was leaving us to go travelling with his girlfriend, a kind of belated gap year. I was to feel his absence because he had always dealt meticulously with the employment contracts and wages leaving me to concentrate on more artistic matters. I brought in one of our ex-performers, Vikki Sparkes, as administrator in the office. Vikki had been around since my first days at Thorpe Park when she was driving one of the lake boats. Then she was cast in several of our shows including the stunt show *'Tropical Mission'* in Belgium. She worked with us in many guises over the years and her work ethic was marvellous, which made her good to be around when things got pressured.

Alice & Holly

About this time I agreed on a joint project with lighting designer and theatre manager Bob Bustance to stage a new musical based on Alice In Wonderland. It was to be launched as *'Alice The Musical'* in his theatre at Stevenage in July. I was excited by the prospect of writing and staging a full length musical but at that point there was no script and no music. However, the idea of a resident run, followed by our own promotion of a theatre tour, was a great incentive to get to work. I thoroughly enjoyed re-reading the book and working on a script that brought the wonderland story partly into modern times. Alice was now Ali and she would fall asleep in the park and dream the story. I wrote the music and lyrics with Terry in record time and the show opened at The Gordon Craig Theatre on July 31st. The cast we had assembled was superb in every character part and it was a great success. Following the tour I recorded a version of *'Alice The Musical'* for radio and it still sells on CD and as a digital download.

Adam Daye (2019)
"Stephen was still being creative, and I was lucky enough to be summoned to his home to record some character voices for his new project: Alice The Musical. I think this is my all-time favourite piece of work for Stephen, playing several characters, obviously using different voices, and recording the dialogue and songs line by line, all written by the indefatigable Stephen. A very fulfilling experience."

It was a hectic few months. I had also signed a contract with Holiday Park in Germany which really put the pressure on. I had to create and stage a show featuring their park mascot and I had to come up with a script and songs translated into German. It was a pleasure to be able to drive out to Holiday Park every now and then and spend a few days in Germany, a country that Penny and I had come to love during our various 'fact finding' jollies for Thorpe Park and our earlier adventures on US military bases.

Holiday Park was in southern Germany 120 kilometres south of Frankfurt, near to the towns of Hassloch and Neustadt. A beautiful part of the country near to the French border. Once again I was able to call upon my old music buddy from *'The Lower Third'* to come up with some musical ideas which I completed with translated lyrics. While it was difficult to manage the show at such a distance it proved to be a success for the park and established their mascot character, *'Holly'* (a parrot), who we continued to supply with new feathers, I mean costumes, for several years!

Unparallel Careers!

The phone rang one morning in September and the caller simply said *"Turn on your television now."* I was working at home and immediately switched on to see smoke pouring out of one of the twin towers of The World Trade Centre in New York. I watched in awe as the cameras focused on another aircraft as it struck the second tower. I had passed by these enormous buildings many times while they were being built. Even in 1970, while still under construction, they were becoming a prominent landmark for us on board the QE2 as it sailed up the Hudson River to its berth at Pier 92. I watched incredulously as they tumbled to the ground in a massive cloud of dust and smoke. The 11th September 2001 was a very sad day.

The Lampies

Back in December I had met two budding writers, Dave Bonner and James Caldwell, who had invented some children's cartoon characters called *'The Lampies'*. We were now generally accepted as the leading UK company for the training and presentation of costume characters and they knew of our work with *'Popeye'*, *'Tony Tiger'*, *'The Smurfs'* et al. Would I be interested in creating live versions of their characters? They had secured a contract with the BBC to make a first cartoon series which began its run in the autumn and was proving very popular. So much so that the BBC had commissioned a second series and were already talking about a third. I thought this was manna from heaven. To have the rights to a set of characters that were currently on TV and set to remain a successful kid's TV series for some years ahead.

The Glory Days

For the two writers, one an actor and the other an ex-police officer, it was also the chance of a life time. They had raised several million pounds and ploughed a lot of their own money into making the animated series. I signed a contract with their company, Lampies Ltd, and set about having the costumes designed and made. They had also signed an agreement with Please!Ltd., a company who were to release records and videos of *'The Lampies'* and a Christmas single was recorded.

We started to sell a theatre tour for early 2002 and in November I was asked to make the characters available to record a promotion video for the Christmas record. We also agreed to manage personal appearances set up by Please!Ltd to promote the single. With the costumes newly completed we took a team to a number of prestigious events where *'The Lampies'* switched on the Christmas lights. It was an expensive operation because the venues were all over the country – Edinburgh, Bournemouth, Newcastle, Portsmouth, Manchester and finally Oxford Street and Covent Garden in London.

At the end of December we learnt that Lampies Ltd. had gone bust! They had been unable to raise the money to complete the second series and the BBC pulled the plug. Shortly after that, having not paid any of our invoices for the Christmas promotions, Please!Ltd. also folded. It was a huge disappointment – we were committed to the theatre dates already booked in but we were unlikely to make our fortune with *'The Lampies'*.

Unparallel Careers!

The End Begins
(Butlin's)

While I was preparing for the second Christmas show at Drayton Manor and charging all over the country with *'The Lampies'*, I had taken a call from the Butlin's director of entertainment, Mike Godolphin.

Butlin's was and is the most famous holiday camp brand in the UK founded after the second world war by Billy Butlin, later Sir Billy Butlin. He successfully brought cheap holidays to the masses by setting up a series of chalet based sites with the entertainment and sports activities included in the holiday price.

Mike was looking for something new for the Butlin's Skyline venues and was interested in using Popeye in some daytime shows. They firstly needed three different shows repeated in each of the three Skyline venues – Bognor, Minehead and Skegness. In addition to this they wanted a one hour feature in the main evening showroom, again featuring Popeye. At the time I felt that this was not for us and Penny agreed – we were now just a two man band and we were both feeling the strain after six years of battling away trying to keep *Parkshows* expanding and, more importantly, profitable. This project seemed like another back breaker.

Naturally, when confronted with the Butlin's directors, I went into performance mode and presented some good ideas well – I expected no less of myself. They asked me to put together a full proposal with costs and I decided to prepare a good presentation, but with a highly inflated price which we did not expect to achieve.

That would kick the project off the field.

On New Year's Eve 2001, with a glass of champagne in hand, I asked Penny to marry me – twenty one years after we first met. She said yes. We decided to do it on mid-summers day the 21st June 2002. It had not been a path I had considered before but something told me that big changes were about to happen yet again. There was no doubting the deep love and respect we had for each other after all the years of highs and lows that we had sailed through, always together. It just seemed like the right time!

> *Somewhere there's a rainbow*
> *That will take us to paradise days*
> *Way out in that somewhere*
> *We will capture our hopes*
> *And keep them always*
> **Gid Taylor/Stephen Gold (Dreams Can Come True)**

Two days later, as we celebrated this big decision, I received a contract from Butlins – they'd agreed to everything, including the price. It then became an offer we couldn't refuse!

The task was enormous. The Skyline venues were gargantuan domed buildings with an array of shops and eateries around the edges and a performance stage in the middle. In addition to the Skyline shows we would use our cast of acrobatic stunt artistes one evening each week in a full length production in the main showroom, which would also feature the Butlin's eight strong resident team of professional dancers and singers. We had to extend the Skyline stages to cope safely with the

Unparallel Careers!

acrobatics and install new stage scenery in each venue. The final crunch was that they all had to open during the same week in May.

I set to work creating a script for each show so that the scenery could be designed and original music written. The main evening production was to be on a pirate theme. Choreographing it was too big a task for Penny, because she would be directing each of the four shows, so I engaged an experienced choreographer and an acro-stunt coordinator. I also employed a production manager to oversee the installations in each venue. We designed and ordered costumes, assembled props, auditioned for the actors and acrobats and finally recorded the soundtracks for each show. Without Robert Harrison in the office I was now dealing with the artistes' contracts and accomodation while also attending regular progress meetings at each Butlin's site.

The holiday centres were at the three corners of a very big triangle – Bognor on the south coast, Minehead on the west coast, and Skegness in the east, with not a straight motorway between them. By the beginning of April the strain was starting to show. I was feeling extremely stressed as we tried to keep all the balls in the air. Just as the rehearsals were about to start and the stage equipment and scenery were being installed our production manager called from Minehead. He'd snapped, had enough, couldn't cope anymore, was leaving immediately and going home. I was now production manager as well!

As the rehearsals got underway the deadlines seemed unachievable and those of us left standing, that was Penny, Vikki Sparkes and me, were running around like the proverbial blue arsed flies. I was feeling unwell, I had a heavy cold and the old Isle of Wight panic attacks had returned, but I kept up appearances. I found relief in a heavy dose of alcohol at the end of each day. I still cannot say how we did it, it was a complete blur, but all shows opened on their target dates.

That opening week was the inevitable week from hell. Skegness to Minehead, back to Skegness then down to Bognor and back to......! When the dust settled I knew that this was not what I wanted to do anymore. It was not yet the end of an era but it was certainly the beginning of the end. Luckily, once the shows were all settled the money rolled in regularly and a calm settled over us at last.

Celebrate Good Times, C'mon!

The day has dawned the sun is shining bright
A sense of magic's in the air
A feeling we can set the world alight
I know that love is in this new born day
No one can take this feeling away
Stephen Gold (Today)

Our wedding on Friday June 21st was a glorious affair. We were married at the Registry Office at Weybridge, Surrey where Penny became Mrs Penelope Wyatt-Gold, taking on my birth and adopted names which I had officially registered by deed poll. Then, as Mr & Mrs Wyatt-Gold, we embarked on a river cruiser with a dozen close friends and relatives. We travelled slowly along the Thames in warm summer sunshine, passing Walton-on-Thames and Chertsey, while indulging in a sumptuous buffet, until we reached a spot facing our house, which we had never before seen from the river. We raised a glass or two of champagne. That evening we dined with the same party in a private room at The Shepperton Moat House Hotel.

The next day we invited the rest of our family members and lots of others besides to a garden party that we described as a celebration of our marriage and a reunion of old friends and colleagues. In keeping with our reputation we had the badger policeman character from *'The Sylvanian Families'* directing our guests from the roadside. Friends came from *'The Lower Third'* era, from my Jersey years, from Penny's theatre and cruising days, from the *'Yogi Bear Show'* adventures and the *'Flame World Tour 1980'*. What a gathering! This surely had to be the first day of a new beginning.

We had moved, in 1999, to this beautiful riverside house where the old 1920s games room had served as a sometime rehearsal space. It was rented by *Parkshows* at around £1450 per month and it was big enough to house, on the first floor, a costume store and a make-shift recording studio. Living there, within touching distance of the River Thames, was absolute bliss. Unfortunately, we were notified after the wedding that our house, The Barn, was to be offered for sale and that the lease would not be renewed when it expired at the end of the year. We would have loved to have been able to buy it but the asking price was a shade under a million pounds. As tempting as this idea was, we did not have that sort of cash and I had a vision of myself slaving on for years to come.

I had recovered from the Butlin's stress but had no

enthusiasm to face even one more year like that. Penny had become disenchanted with directing and choreographing for the same reasons. We started talking about bailing out big time. In September we travelled to France to view some properties and realised that we could buy a substantial French property outright and the idea was too attractive to dismiss.

Some weeks before Christmas Robert Harrison conveniently returned from his belated gap year. He had no immediate plans or job prospects so I suggested, over a beer or two, that he could come back to *Parkshow Production Associates* and head up any future projects, allowing Penny and I to drift serenely away into the sunset. He readily agreed and immediately after our meeting I secured a new contract to provide two shows at The American Adventure theme park in Derbyshire. Having given him a great start it was time to step away.

And so it was that, in January 2003, we left behind The Barn, at Laleham, with its unforgettable view over the river and set off for Charente Maritime in South West France where we began a brand new chapter in our lives. I met new people, both French and English, who could be regaled with anecdotes from my showbiz career and, even though it was nearly 40 years since I had left the band, it was *'The Lower Third'* and my usual exaggerated Bowie connection that interested people the most.

Looking back it is easy to remember all the highs and lows of a long career but less easy to remember the small details that made up every part of it. There are important people who passed through my orbit over the years and had a profound effect on my direction of travel both professionally and in my private life. I have recalled most of them in this missive but there are many others who passed through briefly and brought a little happiness or a little sadness or incited anger or confusion. Although I cannot remember many of them in detail, researching this book has helped me to recall snippets of conversations, vaguely familiar faces and words on old posters that almost bring them into focus. They all contributed in some small way to what has been a wonderfully exciting musical journey which still continues well into the 21st century with the output of my tiny recording studio in rural France.

When I heard, on that January evening, that David Bowie had died it revived sharp memories of those early days. I thought about the half century that had passed since we had both played with *'The Lower Third'* and how varied and sometimes precarious life had been for both of us in such remarkably different ways. It led to what has been, for me, a mighty and cathartic undertaking and I will be for ever grateful to David Robert Jones for finally inspiring Robin Stephen Wyatt and causing it to happen.

Bowie seems to tell us in words
from his last album that he is in heaven
and that he is free - I hope so

END

With Thanks

This book would not have been started and certainly not finished without the help, dedication and, for the later years, the superior memory of my beautiful wife Penny. This press article from 1997 pays tribute to her many talents first as a dancer and singer and then as a director and choreographer from which I profited greatly through the 1980s and 1990s. I could not be more grateful.

Priceless Penny

To many theme parks and their show spectaculars, choreographer and director Penny Hogan is a key figure

Directing with a diference – Penny Hogan

Penny Hogan is the only director/choreographer in the UK working exclusively in the theme and leisure park sector, entering it in 1990 with the direction of the Thorpe Park Rangers, developing a high-quality stage show featuring the five animal characters and working on their 'meet and greet' appearances throughout the day.

At Thorpe Park's Palladium Theatre she has produced dance-based shows, Space Fantasy being followed by Legend and Merlin's Magic Castle. In 1994, she took a major step forward by directing the Konica Splashtàcular, which involved working with actors and stunt performers on a vast arena stage. The following year she was called in by Alton Towers to take over the direction of the Magic Theatre Show, working with actors, directing them through a storyline and performing five major illusions. Last year she had the enormous task of staging a large-scale stunt and special effects production at the Walibi Theme Park near Brussels. This had spectacular fire effects, a rainstorm, a technical illusion and, to make direction more difficult, a 20ft river running in front of the set. Actors and stunt performers were directed in abseiling, fist fighting and diving in a James Bond-style production, the leading actor making his entrance dangling from a helicopter.

This year, in addition to directing the Thorpe Park Rangers for the eighth time, she has direction of Edgar Fox and Friends at Lightwater Valley, near Ripon, the Sylvanian Families Show, which tours nationally from October, and devising a show for Thorpe Park's newest character Harley the Cat. She is also running two-day training workshops called Creating the Magic, aimed at performers working in themed environments, which can be run in theme parks or other locations.

Peter Hepple

THE STAGE JUNE 5 1997

The impact of David Bowie's untimely death spread its influence to France and caught up with me soon after 10th January 2016

Vidici — Couple Insolite

Stephen & Penny Wyatt-Gold

Un destin en or

Un musicien hors pair, une danseuse talentueuse, ces deux êtres étaient faits pour se rencontrer, mais pas sans un parcours hors norme. Visez un peu...

Stephen est originaire de Margate, une ville du district du Thanet dans le Kent en Angleterre. Il est désormais en France depuis 13 ans, tout d'abord près de Gémozac où il a continué de travailler sa musique en studio, tandis que son épouse Penny s'adonnait à la réflexologie. « Nous avons quitté Londres et le stress fin 2002 pour trouver un endroit plus calme, plus à l'écart », précise le couple.

La musique

C'est vers l'âge de 11 ans que Stephen se découvre une passion pour les instruments, notamment pour la guitare. Dès ses 15 ans, il intègre un groupe en tant que guitariste-chanteur. Les jeunes gens écument les bars et les boîtes de nuit londoniennes durant cinq années, Stephen utilisant alors son nom de naissance, Robb Wyatt.

La fin du groupe

Après ces multiples concerts, Stephen décide de quitter le groupe "Lower Third", ce qui pousse la formation à auditionner de nouveaux chanteurs. « L'un d'entre eux s'est présenté avec un saxophone, c'était David Bowie », nous raconte Stephen. C'est ainsi que les musiciens restants tombent sous le charme du jeune androgyne et que Mister Bowie (qui avait le même âge que Stephen) débute sa carrière comme saxophoniste-chanteur, sans pour autant sortir de grands tubes à l'époque. On connaît la suite le concernant...

L'après Lower Third

Pendant 2/3 ans, le jeune Stephen se produit en solo avec sa guitare, jouant du folk. Puis, il part sur l'île de Jersey et, de nouveau seul avec son instrument, s'essaie au showroom. Ensuite, il embarque durant 3 ans sur un paquebot avec un autre groupe, "Big Woods". Bref, il ne passe jamais longtemps sans jouer.

La rencontre

Après la musique en mer, il monte un groupe formé de quatre chanteuses et danseuses qui se produira pendant 10 ans. L'une des danseuses n'est autre que Miss Penny. Ensemble, ils parcourent le monde entier : le Japon, les États-Unis, le Proche-Orient, etc.

La créativité

Ils montent de nombreux spectacles pour lesquels Stephen s'attelle à la création de mélodies, de textes, s'avère extrêmement productif, tandis que Penny crée les chorégraphies, prend le rôle de metteuse en scène. L'entente est parfaite. Ils créent

Contact : 06 52 84 47 22

Space Fantasy

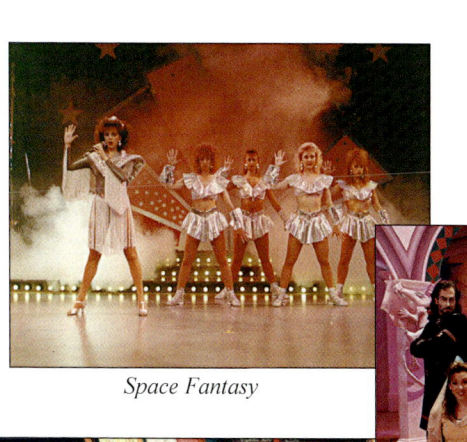

The Big Shows

Merlin's Magic castle

The Thorpe Park Rangers

Duty Manager with collar and tie!

The first arena cast

Jacko with Popeye. Maybe not!

Great fun with Diana and the Princes

The fabulous set in Belgium 1996

*Photographed with superstars
The mice were honoured!*

Popeye's theatre tour 1998

*Seven thousand watch our spectacular show
Dubai 1999*

The Lampies

The Smurfs Dubai 2000

Great character performance by Richard Esdale in Alice the Musical

The great team of '99 celebrate at our lovely house on the Thames

We finally tie the knot 2002

VILLA MARINA GARDEN ROOM
SUMMER SEASON 1982
From Monday to Friday
JUNE 28th-AUGUST 20th
ADULTS ONLY
Stephen Gold
presents his
INTERNATIONAL FLOORSHOW & CABARET
'FLAME'
Direct from The Marine Hotel, Hawaii
LICENSED BAR • TABLE SERVICE • PUB PRICES
TICKETS NOW ON SALE
(LIMITED NUMBERS)
The Famous
WATERSPLASH
Five Mile Road, St.Ouen's, Jersey
STEPHEN GOLD
presents his
International Cabaret Sensation
"FLAME"
and friends
FERNANDO
Exciting
International
Hearthrob
ADAM DAYE
Starbursts
Favourite
Impressionist
Spectacular
Costumes
Direct from the Waikiki Hotel Hawaii
An Evening of Glamour, Fun and Fantasy
COMMENCING MAY 25th
The Hottest Show on the Island
FLAME
All seats bookable
Box Office 82884
Flame
HORSESHOE SHOWBAR
POOL PLEASURE
DECEMBER TO 31ST DEC
LIVE ON STAGE
POPEYE
in an
HILARIOUS ADVENTURE
The show is supported by
SAFEWAY
GREAT PRIZES to be won!
also starring
OLIVE OYL
and
BRUTUS
cartoon characters in a show for all ages from 0 - 90 years!!!
Family Pantomime
Babes in the Wood
18th December - 9th January
Starring
Bruno Brookes
Thorpe Park
Palladium
Theatre
SPECIAL FEATURE
CAROUSEL KINGDOM
FOOD
featuring
FREE RIDES ON THE FA
SWEET PALACE
The Gordon Craig Theatre
in association with PARKSHOWS presents
ALICE
THE MUSICAL
ADVENTURES IN WONDERLAND
Gordon Craig Theatre
DUBAI MUNICIPALITY
PRESENTS
THE SMURFS
Come to
AL MAMZAR PARK
to meet the naughty Gargamel chasing Smurfs in an exciting and scintillating display that will offer the children a lot of fun
MARCH 3-24
Except 13th & Tuesdays
LET'S SMURF!
First show: 5pm
Second show: 6pm
Third show: 7pm
Fourth show: 8pm
For enquiries call:
090 400 99
Ahlan Dubai
Tickets are available at
Al Mamzar Park
DUBAI MUNICIPALITY

Appendix I
Out Takes
Other bits that didn't get in the book!

Growing Up In Margate

Margate is a seaside town situated at the far eastern tip of the county of Kent in the South East of England. It forms part of the Isle of Thanet which includes two further towns – Ramsgate and Broadstairs – as well as a number of villages. The summers of my childhood were magical times because Margate transformed itself into a major holiday resort, mainly for Londoners. The seafront beach, known as Margate sands, would be packed everyday from June to September, even when the weather was chilly and blustery, and it was fringed by ice cream parlours, restaurants, bars (pubs) and amusement arcades. Right across the road from the beach the entrance to Dreamland beckoned. For me it was a paradise – like a toy shop on a grand scale. Its roller coaster, The Scenic Railway, snaked around one end of the amusement park and was dwarfed in height by The Big Wheel. There were bumper cars, carousels, a miniature steam railway, a ghost train and all manner of other attractions including freak shows where you could witness a mermaid in her tank or a woman with two heads – all trickery of course. Margate was essentially a day trippers' paradise but its 'posh' area, Cliftonville, was full of hotels and guest houses where holidaymakers from all over the country spent their summer breaks. So many people headed for the town in July and August that they overspilled the hotels and many locals opened their family homes to accommodate the hoards. My own grandmother took in holidaying couples even though she lived some way from the seafront and other attractions. In the 1950s it was a great place to be growing up.

La Discotheque Club
More views of those who hung out there.

"I used to visit the club around 1963/4. I remember the bouncer being shot in the knee, I was about 18 at the time and my parents started to worry about me as this made national news. I remember mostly live music being played - 'What I'd Say' was the house favourite. Always hot, packed, dark and sweaty! Excellent club."

"First went there in 1962ish.... an ill lit hanger upstairs full of old mattresses on the floor. To the left was the small dance floor packed with Mod couples dancing the Twist. I sat beside a small blonde and observed the dancing which was surprisingly good. As the music started up again I approached a girl sitting by the dance floor and asked her for a dance. She looked at me in astonishment and told me to "fuck off". I was an innocent but I loved the ambience, the music and the dancing but was too wary so I passed on the purple hearts."

Trilogy – Cairo 1974

Al Heath had stayed on our case and arranged a month at The Sheraton Hotel, Cairo through an agent

Appendix I - Out Takes

called Oscar Tewtel who was based in Beirut, Lebanon, where there was still a very lively entertainment scene in the early seventies. Beirut was known as the playground (or Paris) of the Middle East due to its myriad of different hotels, casinos and cabaret nightclubs and it was via Frankfurt and Beirut that we travelled to Cairo on February 1st with the Lebanese flag carrier Middle East Airlines. Sadly, after years of war and political upheaval, Beirut is no longer (2019) the playground that it was.

Trilogy 1974

New Year's Eve 1974 found us in Bristol at the Yew Tree Country Club. After the usual late and well lubricated celebrations it was a relief that we weren't appearing on the evening of 1st January. We went to the Bristol Hippodrome to see the pantomime Jack and the Beanstalk which starred the 'old timers' Dora Bryan and Norman Vaughan. Also on the bill were Little and Large who we had worked with in Liverpool earlier in the year. At that time they were well known in the northern clubs but had yet to find national fame. Lynne had a friend among the panto dancers and we hung out with her and Eddie Large for the few days we had left in Bristol before taking to the road and heading north again for a week in Morecambe at the Inn On The Bay. During that week and the one that followed in Liverpool (Knowsley Cabaret Club) we were able to rehearse new material and put in, among other things, a medley from West Side Story which gave Lynne the opportunity to shine at what she did best. This was to be the emerging style that sustained us over the following years.

Unparallel Careers!

Trilogy - Record Deal 1975

Bill Crompton wanted us to change our image for the record release publicity and he introduced us to Colin Wild who, with his partner Danny Benjamin, ran Carnaby Cavern in Ganton Street, London. They had become well known for making stage clothes for many pop stars of the 60s and 70s.

Colin sketched something out for us that Bill Crompton liked and he immediately offered a deposit to get things going. Bill would eventually pay for the costumes which we duly used in a pre-release photo session and never wore again.

Isle Of Man
Why I Fell Out With The Producer – The Full Story!

With the re-recording of *'Summer Song'* in the bag we embarked for the Isle of Man by ferry from Liverpool. We had rented a bungalow at Onchan, just outside Douglas, where we arrived on 22nd May. The following morning we met the rest of the artistes at The Palace Hotel. We would be appearing nightly in the showroom attached to the Palace Casino. There would be two shows each night at 9pm and midnight and we could be scheduled for either. Over the summer we found ourselves on the midnight show most of the time. But on this first day we had no idea what was to come or how the season would turn out.

We learnt that there would be a finale to the show which merely consisted of a bunch of sing-along songs. It quickly became clear that we were expected to be the mainstay of this medley since nobody else sang! There was a choreographer who would put together some

Appendix I - Out Takes

movements and we had to learn the lyrics and steps by Sunday night's grand opening, which gave us just two days to perfect it and run up our own act with the band. The show finale would continue to be a highly contentious issue for some days and weeks to come. Firstly, the songs we were expected to perform were way outside of our style and very 'end of the pier' old fashioned. Secondly, I was adamant that we could not perform the routine without proper rehearsals.

The rehearsals finally got underway on Saturday and were a shambles. There were no musical arrangements for the band, no lyric sheets, and the choreographer started with no routine in mind. This had the ability to make us look really stupid on stage. The girls and I worked on the routine back at the bungalow by making our own changes in order to get to something we thought was workable. However, on Sunday morning we were at loggerheads with the choreographer who was trying to overcomplicate the routine. In hindsight I can see that she was only trying to justify her engagement on the show but I didn't appreciate that at the time and I was dead set on avoiding an on-stage embarrassment for Trilogy.

We did perform the routine that night and it was as shambolic as I had anticipated. I set about trying to get it eliminated from the show. This now put me in conflict with the agent Billy Forrest who was also demanding that we shorten our own act to 25 minutes. The next night we did 29 minutes and he was irate. I tried to explain that to cut 4 minutes would spoil the balance of our act, but to no avail. Under pressure from him and the venue management we gave in. Looking back I can see that I must have appeared quite unreasonable, a pain in the arse, and, as a consequence, I did not endear myself to those in charge of the show or the venue. I was so focused on perfecting the act, and so used to keeping everything under my control, that I didn't see the inevitable downsides.

I did eventually get the awful finale routine scrapped and replaced it with a song suited to us – *'That's When The Music Takes Me'* (Neil Sedaka) – which we had used similarly at the Sheraton Hotel in Cairo. Billy Forrest never booked us again after that season!

Scotland (1977)
The Details!

On our return from Northern Ireland there followed a disastrous tour in Scotland. It should have taken in The Orkneys and I was excited at the prospect of visiting the islands. We first travelled to Perth for a band rehearsal at The Wheel Inn Motor Lodge.

The promoter was called Drew Taylor and the musicians he had booked for the tour included an amateur drummer who did not read music but who insisted that he would remember all the arrangements. The show went ahead that night but was a predictable cock-up. I was livid and demanded a competent replacement drummer for the rest of the tour. I also demanded payment for that first night before setting off for the next location and the promoter supplied a bank cashable cheque for £100.

Next morning we embarked on what seemed like an epic journey across the Scottish wilderness. On the way I phoned the promoter's office from a call box (no mobiles in 1977) and heard that a replacement drummer had been booked. Feeling reassured we carried on for several hours over many single track roads to the on-shore oil establishment at Loch Kishorn on the far north west Scottish coast.

The band didn't catch us up until 10.15pm so there was no time for rehearsals. We went on stage in front of a frightening crowd of drunk, noisy and abusive oil workers fresh in from the off-shore rigs. Enough was enough! We were scheduled to do another show the following morning at 10am when the night workers came ashore. I decided that wasn't going to happen. We hid in the dressing room until the venue was cleared, packed up our equipment and left for the hotel.

Early next morning we drove hard to reach the promoter's bank in Biggar, near Glasgow, so that I could cash the cheque before he had time to stop it. Thus we never got to see The Orkney Islands.

Trilogy 1978

In February we flew to RAF Guttersloh in Germany for a series of CSE shows for troops in Osnabrook and Munster. Following that we had a week at The Dolce Vita Club in Birmingham memorable only for a major fight that broke out on the last night with around 20 guys bashing hell out of each other, and the club, while we gamely carried on with the act.

Next day, having recovered from the trauma, I did an interview at Pebble Mill for Radio Birmingham to promote the act and they played *'Summer Song'*. I was delighted to meet Dave Clark who was there to promote an album of revivals. The Dave Clarke Five had recorded some monster hits in the sixties.

Norway 1978

On 5th April we flew to Stavanger in Norway for a dreadful two weeks in a newly converted night club called The Red Seahouses. When we arrived there was no stage, no sound system, no lights and no musicians. All was promised to be in place for our opening show the next night. To top off a bad day they had booked us into a hotel where we were all in one room. The Swiss band arrived who weren't used to playing for artistes and although they tried hard it was never going to be good enough.

The opening show was a complete disaster. The sound system was far too small for this large converted warehouse, the band struggled to play our music and the small audience were indifferent throughout the performance, probably due to the fact that they couldn't hear us.

The sound system was replaced with something better but at the weekend the place was packed with unruly, loud and ill mannered louts. It seemed that the normal Norway night out was marked by ferocious drinking immediately on arrival. In later years it would be called binge drinking. Five bouncers tried unsuccessfully to keep the morons off the stage and at one point Carole had to slap a drunk in the face to stop him from completely disrupting the show. This was not our finest hour – at least we were eventually allotted two rooms in a nice hotel for the duration.

Appendix I - Out Takes

Ted and Lil Cox
Stephen Gold with Flame 1980

Back in Margate Elaine, Carole and I met up with Penny Hogan and Carol Hungerford, who would henceforth be called Little Carol, at the showbiz hang out known affectionately as 'Ted & Lil's'. The Claremont, directly opposite the Winter Gardens, was a small hotel where artistes appearing in summer seasons or doing one night concerts gathered in the basement bar to relax or party after their shows. Over the years we spent many great nights at 'Ted & Lil's', often with the stars of the 1980s who were appearing across the road. One memorable time we boogied on down with American soul band The Floaters (smash hit *'Float On'*) who we had promoted at the Winter Gardens for a one night concert. They then insisted on staying at Ted & Lil's rather than the upmarket hotel that had been booked for them.

Dubai – World Tour 1980

We had some interesting outings during our stay including one to Jumeirah Beach, which is now (2019) the site of an immense tourist hotel and entertainment centre. In 1980 there was nothing but a deserted beach where we set up a picnic and enjoyed a splash about in the warm waters of the Persian Gulf. I was not a swimmer in those days but some of our party dived into the surf and swam. Penny had ventured out some way for a decent swim when we noticed some rather alarming fins gliding through the water near to her. We shouted and waved and she waved back and carried on swimming, blissfully unaware of the potential danger.

Needless to say no-one was brave enough to swim out. Thankfully she wandered back unscathed and was rather unmoved by it until I admitted that I'd been calculating how she could do the show on one leg!

From the book 'Not Quite Famous' about Hawaii 1980
"On our last evening Carol, Elaine and I were sitting on the beach at sundown when a couple holding hands came into view on the horizon silhouetted against the sunset and we realised it was Stephen and Penny. Romance had blossomed on that tour."
© *Carole Jardine 2015 (Not Quite Famous)*

The Last CSE Tour 1984

During the year I embarked on my last CSE Tour. It was to Northern Ireland and I had Penny and Cheryl Mortimer for company again. The management and technicians had all changed by this time - Derek Agutter and Johnny Harris had long since retired. The new team were young and very correct with a well planned itinerary, safe travel arrangements and definitely no more fiddle sheets! The tour was memorable only for some fun we all had at the expense of a group of three young and inexperienced girl dancers. The sound technician started to tell them, after each show, that their costumes were in some way interfering with the sound system and causing 'static'. By the third day, with the serious help of us all, he had convinced them that it was their metallic silver wigs causing the problem and, as a solution, they should wear the hotel shower caps under the wigs for the last shows. We watched with great amusement in the dressing room as they carefully placed the shower caps and managed to get the wigs on

Appendix I - Out Takes

top. After the joke was revealed to them they responded by gaining access to the sound technician's hotel room, 'rearranging' his luggage and making up an 'apple pie bed'!

On the last day of the tour we were flown by helicopter to South Armagh, known in army circles as 'bandit country'. The chopper could not stay at the base for more than a few seconds without running the risk of a mortar attack so when it returned to collect us after the show we ran to it and were dragged in by the crew. It immediately took off and rapidly gained height. The tour manager was the last on board and had one foot in the doorway as it soared upwards. He turned white when he looked down and realised he was already two hundred feet in the air and only halfway into the aircraft!

Berlin 1988

To help promote the recordings by Hammy Haze, The Waltons and Letitia Dean I joined an organisation for independent record companies called The Umbrella Group. In the autumn I travelled with Penny, by a specially chartered Umbrella Group coach, to a music industry exhibition and conference in Berlin. We took the opportunity to cross the Berlin Wall into East Berlin via the famous Checkpoint Charlie which was a sobering experience. Humourless border guards checked every detail of our identification and insisted that West German currency was changed before we were allowed to enter. We walked through the abandoned streets just beyond the checkpoint and emerged into the celebrated main street, Unter den Linden, where we could view the Brandenburg Gate from the eastern side. The street and its old buildings seemed to have been lovingly restored. It was shortly after this visit that the wall came down and I was pleased that we had taken the opportunity to experience East Berlin before the reconciliation.

Diving Consultants 1994 - 2000

The agent in Los Angeles who was contracted to supply the divers for the first season did not visit the UK or see the show but instead he sent a Canadian dive show promoter as his representative. We got on well with Tom Bertrand and before the end of the 1994 season Penny flew to Toronto to view his own show that was running at Canada's Wonderland theme park. We asked Tom to recruit the divers for the second year and we expected that he would work with us to source the divers for our first show as the new independent company. However, the entertainments manager at the soon to open Legoland, in Windsor, was a Canadian who had held the same position at Canada's Wonderland and was a long time colleague of our dive man. Tom was offered the contract to supply a diving show at Legoland and the contract conditions would not allow him to work with any other park in the UK. We therefore had to find a new contact for supplying the divers and Bruce Cant, an experienced American dive show organiser, was brought in to fill the void. Bruce stayed with us for several years and sourced talented divers from various parts of the world – not just America but Russia, Ukraine, Australia and France.

Appendix I - Out Takes

Old Friendship Pays Off 2001

As the winter approached it was a time for reflection. Since Robert Harrison had departed I was tasked with organising the weekly wages and fees as well as dealing with auditions, artistes contracts and all manner of other petty nuisances. At that time we were employing around 35 people and I was thankful that I had made contact with an old friend from my days in Jersey – a lifetime ago. June Gee had become a freelance bookkeeper and accountant and took over our payroll which was faxed back and forth each week. June stayed with us for several years and we occasionally reminisced about the Jersey days.

Appendix II
The Complete Thorpe Park Years
1989/1995

On the 9th January 1989 I attended the first of two interviews which landed me the seasonal position of Entertainment Controller at Thorpe Park in Chertsey, Surrey. Thorpe Park had been established ten years earlier as a family leisure park by the company Ready Mixed Concrete. The RMC Group owned the land on which the park was built and they had financed its creation to fulfil their obligation to restore the land after exhausting its usefulness as a quarry for aggregates – sand and gravel for building materials. The lakes on which the park sits are flooded quarry workings.

I set off from our house in Maidstone on the 13th February for the first of many commutes around London's orbital motorway, the M25. I wondered, with trepidation, what my first salaried job in 25 years had in store for me. I was paid the princely sum of £350 per week, which was a life saver at that moment in time. I reported to a young Rides and Attractions Manager called John Houston who was suitably impressed with my obviously superior knowledge of the entertainment industry.

Thorpe Park had invested in a spanking new 600 seat theatre, The Thorpe Park Palladium, and had contracted a production company to stage a show for the

Unparallel Careers!

1989 season. No person on the management team had any insight into dealing with singers, dancers or directors so it was left to me to smooth the way. There was also a children's show, based on large puppets, that had been running for several years and I quickly learnt the mechanical systems of this *'Mr Rabbit Show'*.

In addition I was charged with overseeing the park's costume characters out and about in the park for their 'meet & greet' sessions – that was Mr. Rabbit and his friends! One of my first tasks was to recruit performers for these costume character roles and among the various actors, singers and dancers who auditioned for that first season was a young Tony Lee who was studying drama at college in Guildford. He was to become a crucial part of the entertainment offering over the following couple of years, appearing in a multitude of roles and recording several character voices. At the time of writing (2019) Tony, under his stage name Antony 'Tony' Audenshaw, is a regular and long standing cast member of the popular UK TV series 'Emmerdale' in the role of Bob Hope.

Preparations quickly gathered pace as Easter drew near and, having never before entered any kind of theme park, the early months of 1989 turned into a very steep learning curve. The park opened to the public in April and I got my first real taste of theme park pressure on Easter Monday when over 20,000 people came through the gates.

The following months continued to be a daily routine of a minimum one hour M25 commute, then 8 hours at the park followed by another M25 struggle to get home to Maidstone at a reasonable hour. But I was

Appendix II - The Complete Thorpe Park Years

enjoying the work and, in July, was delighted to get some excellent news. John Houston had resigned to take up another job and the decision had been made to create a separate entertainments department. I was offered the permanent position of Entertainments Manager and my brief was to set up the infrastructure of the new department. I received a regular salary, a company car and a healthy budget to spend for the next year's entertainment.

Two permanent employees were assigned to me. Stephen Gallagher, as my assistant manager and Kevin Townsend as technical supervisor. Stephen was a musician as well as an experienced Thorpe Park ride supervisor and his expertise in both areas would come to be invaluable over the coming months and years.

The theatre show that summer of 1989 was a professionally staged pop music based song and dance show. It had no specific theme and I had thought from the start that any show staged in a theme park naturally should have a strong theme. I therefore made that my priority for the next season along with creating some activities around the new characters that had been designed for the 1990 TV promotion – The Thorpe Park Rangers had arrived!

I also took charge of two ageing attractions, *'The Captain Andy Show'*, which was a life-size automated puppet show on a hillbilly country theme, and *'Cinema 180'*, a wrap around film experience, the films for which were well past their sell by date in content and quality.

To complete the remit there was an attraction called *'Treasure Island'* which, bizarrely, was based on a narrow guage railway which ran a circuit around a promontory on the largest of the lakes. Halfway round the passengers were confronted by several swarthy pirates who emerged from the 'Admiral Benbow Inn' and enacted a swashbuckling scene with trusty cutlasses and plenty of *"aha me hearties"*. It fell to me to manage this attraction because the pirates and train drivers were all actors. But managing them was far from straightforward because they disappeared up to the 'island' each morning and it was not possible to approach their location without being seen. Time for them to clear away any incriminating evidence. On one occasion cannabis plants were discovered growing behind the inn!

That summer of '89 was frenetic. At the end of the season I was still commuting around the M25, which was becoming more and more stressful, so we decided to move into a small flatlet in nearby Twickenham and rent out the Maidstone property. Thus I ended 1989 celebrating the Christmas holiday while contemplating an uncertain year ahead. It would be an enormous challenge to impress the directors with my first season in charge at Thorpe Park.

1990/91

In the spring of 1990 I was offered a flat at Beomonds Farm on the Thorpe Park estate. This was an isolated building with some garages and stores around a courtyard and it housed, on the ground floor, a creche for employees' children. I borrowed the park's minibus and moved what little we still wanted from the Maidstone house in two journeys. We moved into this spacious three bedroom flat where we would remain for

Appendix II - The Complete Thorpe Park Years

several years.

At Thorpe Park, respecting the management system, I was officially reporting to the park operations manager, Chris Edge. However, it was the managing director, Colin Dawson, who was more interested in entertainment and he was eager to upgrade the park's attractions. He had been transferred the previous year from the park's parent company, RMC Group, and was keen to set out his stall and make a success of this new challenge.

My dealings with Chris Edge were somewhat strained at times. He had no empathy with entertainers or the demands of the '*show must go on*' ethos. Colin Dawson, on the other hand, was always interested and got directly involved in auditions, when he was free, and even attended several showcase events organised through The Stage newspaper. I learnt later that he had been an original member of The Who, before their rise to fame, and was still in touch with Roger Daltrey. In this we had a common interest with my similar connection to David Bowie.

It was an exciting time. I had put together a budget for the 1990 season which had been approved and for the first time in my life I was able to set about creating and producing shows and other entertainment without being governed by ticket sales or sponsorship. I was playing with over half a million pounds and, after the financial stresses of The Isle of Wight and other ventures, I was determined to enjoy it to the full. It was agreed that I could engage Penny as choreographer and director for the shows, which meant we could put some of our grandiose ideas into practice. We never

Unparallel Careers!

mentioned our earlier flirtation with costume characters and prayed that nobody would ever unearth any pictures or other evidence of us playing Yogi Bear and Boo Boo. This time we would take it all very seriously.

That first year at the helm I put together an early season show in the theatre called *'Spring Fever'* which was cast with entertainers who could also play various other roles in the park. This was followed by a main season show with a dedicated cast which played several performances each day, seven days per week. This was *'Space Fantasy'* which borrowed music from Star Wars, The Carpenters (*'Calling Occupants'*) and of course David Bowie – his lyrics rang out *"This is ground control to Major Tom...."*. I had to include it!

We recorded the soundtracks in the newly established 16 track recording studio that I had shoe-horned into an unused dressing room in the theatre. Chris Chapman, who had produced the Hammy Haze demos a few years earlier, came to the park and set up the studio for me. Stephen Gallagher, with his musical background, was an enthusiastic studio engineer in those early days.

Later that first season, as a spin off from the studio, we also set up Thorpe Radio which broadcast to the park throughout the high season with a mix of pop music and park information. On its opening day I shared the controls with well known radio and TV presenter Chris Tarrant. Over the next few years Thorpe Radio employed numerous DJs, some of whom went on to a full time career in broadcasting.

In the midst of preparing the season Colin Dawson announced that there would be a special induction day

Appendix II - The Complete Thorpe Park Years

for seasonal staff which would culminate in a presentation in the theatre for which he wanted an acted scene and a musical opening number. This caught me on the hop and, early in my first season as producer, it was a complete distraction from the rehearsals that we were doing for the theatre show and other park attractions. I gritted my teeth and got on with it but on the eve of the induction day we had to work through most of the night to get the stage set up and some sort of induction show ready. In the years that followed I was always prepared for this nuisance at the start of the season.

When the park opened to the public a week before Easter I was just about ready. *'Spring Fever'* in the Park Palladium featured four dancers and a singer and included a 1920s routine with a brilliant Charlie Chaplin impersonator called Adrian Kaye, who also entertained as Charlie outside in the park. The show cast was complimented by a guest artiste. Our first very successful guest was ventriloquist Jimmy Tamley with his excellent characters Grandad and Rufus. Penny handled all of these disparate talents extremely well and I was roundly congratulated for the first season's offerings.

There were some minor blips in the season. *'Space Fantasy'*, which starred Kevin Austin and Debbie Robbins in the leading roles, featured a robotic character played very well by a twenty something stage school student called Michael Blackledge, who performed in an uncomfortable metal costume. However, his timekeeping left a lot to be desired and I often had to warn him for missing his call time, which was 30 minutes before the first show.

Unparallel Careers!

One afternoon, five minutes before the show was due to start, he had not put in an appearance. Penny, naturally following the *'show must go on'* tradition, decided she would have to play the part of the robot. She struggled into the costume, covered her face and arms in heavy silver make-up and waited in the wings. Seconds before she was due to go on stage Michael appeared next to her saying *"Sorry - I was stuck in traffic in Chertsey"* to which Penny replied, uncharacteristically, *"Well Michael now you can fuck off back to Chertsey"*. His career at Thorpe Park ended a week or two later when he feigned a collapse on the theatre stairs. It was part of his excuse for missing his call time again – he said he'd been to hospital with gall stones. That time I told him to 'fuck off' for good. The robots that followed him were never quite as talented but were always reliable, which was far less stressful.

That first full season demonstrated how difficult it was for these young entertainers to maintain a constant performance discipline throughout the day when they were repeating their performances numerous times. No matter how many times they performed a show it was always the first time for the audience whether they numbered six or six hundred. I like to think that the disciplined regime they encountered benefited them throughout their careers.

During the first two years at Thorpe Park I made several trips to Europe with Penny to visit established theme parks to learn from their successes and even from their mistakes. I was surprised at how advanced some of them were in their approach to the value of live entertainment. For example, many of the two million

Appendix II - The Complete Thorpe Park Years

visitors they welcomed each year at Europa Park in Germany came only for the shows and to enjoy lunch in one of the many restaurants. At EuroDisney in Paris, which was newly opened, I was able to witness the daily parade from 'backstage' and noted the disciplined regime that existed for their staff as well as the entertainers. These visits inspired us to do better and I quickly assimilated with the entirely unique world of theme park entertainment.

Apart from me there were six other front line managers during my time at Thorpe Park. They covered activities such as rides, landscaping, maintenance, catering, retail and recruitment. There was also a farm manager, Ian Minshull, who mostly managed to avoid the bustle of the main park and remain in his little fiefdom at the opposite end of the main lake. The first time I met Ian he was wandering along the main office corridor followed by a sheep. Now living in Devon he remains as passionate about his sheep to this day!

The least enjoyable part of a manager's duties was to take turns in the role of duty manager several times each month. This meant being the person who visitors could confront with complaints, which could be harrowing at times. The unfortunate manager also had to attend to any other problems that occurred which could be arguments about queue jumping, minor accidents or illnesses, theft from the shops and a whole manner of other oddball incidents.

I was once called when a father had tried to follow his young son around the children's adventure area and had descended through a range of car tyres, only to get stuck with his hands trapped by his sides, unable to move up or down. Having assessed the situation I sent for the maintenance department who would have to cut him free. I could not stifle a smile, while others laughed, at the poor bloke's predicament. His wife and son left the area in embarrassment and he was stuck there in full view of the passing public for a good forty minutes. I hope he learnt a lesson that day and that his son got over the trauma and forgave him!

On another occasion when I was duty manager Colin Dawson, the managing director, asked me to arrange a mocked up accident so that he could assess the efficiency of the staff in dealing with a serious incident. It was decided that we would stage an accident with the train on Treasure Island. The story would be that one of our actors had fallen under the train during their performance. No one was to know except Colin, the actors and me.

At the agreed time I was at Treasure Island and I called in the incident over the radio communication system. This alerted our radio control centre who were responsible for calling the emergency services and dispatching the park's first aid nurses to the scene. Colin was quickly on hand at the control room to stop them calling out a genuine ambulance. The actor played his unconscious part extremely well and the duty nurse carried out all the right procedures, got him into the recovery position and then covered him with a thermal blanket.

About this time Colin radioed me to instruct everyone to stand down, the exercise was over. I winked at the 'unconscious' actor and, taking the hint, he suddenly leapt up and startled the nurse and others around him who had begun to think he was a gonner. It may well have been the highlight in his acting career.

It was quickly announced that no such fake incident would ever be staged again. If a call came in future it would be genuine. Sadly, not long after this there was a serious accident involving a disabled man in one of the interior rides and, thankfully, the emergency call systems worked perfectly.

1992

After returning from our exciting first Christmas visit to Kenya I devised the first *'Thorpe Park Rangers Show'* and roped in Terry Bolton, from *'The Lower Third'* days, to work with me on the original music. The theme of the show was The Rangers' battle with The Litter Lout who wanted to spread litter around the park. It was an early environmental lesson for the kids. Terry came up with some great ideas and I worked hard on the scripting and lyrics. The eventual show, for which a nasty looking Litter Lout puppet was created, was a great hit with kids and their parents.

There was one other important development that year. I was asked to take over the running of the special events and other activities that were outside of the normal park operations. My title had changed to Entertainments and Events Manager and I took on another assistant manager who would deal exclusively with the many and lucrative corporate functions, exhibitions and other hirings that the park was highly suited for.

In the main the year drifted along happily. There was a wonderful occasion when Diana Princess of Wales visited with the young princes and I was able to join the party to take photographs for the park archives.

There was also a frightening occasion when I was awoken at 2am to see smoke and sparks showering over the flat at Beomonds Farm. I shouted at Penny to wake up, thinking that the building was on fire. It transpired that the barns and storage around the courtyard were ablaze, making it impossible to leave by the front door. We grabbed some clothes and started down the stairs which were searingly hot by this time. I managed to open the door into the creche below us and then force open the outer door at the rear of the building. Hearing our names being called by the Thorpe Park security men we made our way to join them in the car park where we were stunned by the extent of the conflagration.

The firefighters took several hours to extinguish the fire and make the area safe. When we were able to return we saw that parts of Penny's car, which was parked in the courtyard, had melted, as had the signage and window frames at the front of the building. Later that day we learnt that the fire had been deliberately set and the police were searching for two disgruntled ex-employees. We spent the next night in the comfort of a nice hotel in Staines so that we could catch up on sleep and avoid the acrid smell of smoke that had pervaded the building and our flat.

1993

After three years of the *'Space Fantasy'* show in the Park Palladium Theatre it was time for some new ideas and in 1993 I created a new show called *'Legend of The Ring'* starring Max Hutton and Michelle Musty. This

Appendix II - The Complete Thorpe Park Years

was loosely based on the Indiana Jones films where the hero enters a forgotten world, sees off the villain, finds the magic ring and gets the girl. This was the first theatre show featuring some original music, written with Terry Bolton, plus a smattering of new technology. It opened with a giant projected face of the villain telling the audience to beware of entering the forgotten kingdom. It also featured a battling dinosaur which was a large and unwieldy costume with very poor vision worn by one of our character performers. Not being used to the restrictions of the theatre stage the dinosaur often wandered dangerously close to the edge during some shows until at last, while fighting our handsome hero, he fell off. Well padded in the costume the performer was unhurt, but laying on his back it proved impossible to get back on his feet until two stage hands went to his rescue. We vainly hoped the audience might think it was part of his defeat by our hero!

1993 was also the year that I set up the Thorpe Park Rangers Club. Children, or more likely their parents, could pay a fee to join the club and in return would get a Rangers Passport and a goody bag containing various Rangers souvenir items including a copy of a Rangers cassette. I produced two albums which featured all the songs from their shows plus extra tracks that Terry and I knocked up specially for the purpose. I ordered the cassettes via Penny from our own music publishing company, Flame Music. This gave us a small profit. The cassettes were also on sale in the park shops.

Several versions of my old song contest were staged in the theatre culminating with the most successful on 20th June. That year BBC Radio had decided to cover the event and while I presented *'Song 93'* on stage Bob Holness, the well known and established BBC presenter, handled the radio commentary. The winner that day was a writer called Gerry Markey with an unforgettable song called *'Marvelous Marvin Gaye'*.

One important corporate event in 1993 was the annual get together of the Virgin Holidays Travel Club which was attended by Richard Branson and his family. I got to know the Travel Club's events coordinator during the lead up to this day and when, some months later, I was sent on a 'fact finding' trip to America, she was able to arrange upgraded travel with Virgin Atlantic and special rates and privileges at several hotels.

During the year I had floated the idea to the management team of opening part of the park over the Christmas season. I suggested it could prove successful if we had suitable live entertainment and the obvious candidate for the theatre was a traditional pantomime. Some of the managers were dead set against this prospect as they had been accustomed to an easy life over the mid-winter period. I was determined to take the idea forward and knew I had to come up with a winning formula. When I was able to secure the services of Bruno Brooks, then a leading BBC Radio One and TV presenter, the die was cast. Colin Dawson, our managing director, took up the idea and the other managers had to fall in behind it. I adapted an existing script for the pantomime *'Babes In The Wood'* and wrote in a special part for Bruno which would not overly tax

Appendix II - The Complete Thorpe Park Years

his non-existent acting skills. Part of the park which featured children's rides was opened during show times and a nativity scene was built which included animals brought down from Thorpe Farm. The whole organisation was very well coordinated and the talented cast became adept at pushing Bruno about and prompting him in accordance with the script. Unfortunately first year ticket sales were not good enough to confirm a 1994 Christmas season and I was confronted with the directors' decision to delay the planning of another Christmas event until the summer results were known. I made it clear that it would be too late by then to secure a good star and cast. At that point my pantomime adventure ended.

1994

In September of 1993 Colin Dawson, the park's managing director, attended an international theme park convention in Los Angeles. He returned to announce that he had agreed with an American agent to book a cast for an *'All American High Diving Show'* and that they would be the new main feature for 1994. Not knowing what an American high diving show was I asked, innocently, who was producing it. *"You are,"* he replied. I protested that I knew nothing about that type of show and he said *"Then you'd better get up to speed on it because it's going to happen – I've booked the divers."*

Europa Park in Germany had just such a show that year so I flew to Germany to learn a little about high diving. Six divers did a traditional American high diving display. They started with comedy dives (referred to as 'dillies') and then performed some clever dives from a higher board. The spectacular stunts came at the end of the 25 minutes when one of the divers set light to himself on the 10 metre board and dived with the flames and smoke streaming behind. The finale was the high dive from a 30 metre platform. It was unique and entertaining but lacked any themed production which, to me, seemed necessary in a theme park. I returned from Europa Park with the germ of an idea for a high diving spectacular.

Our Thorpe Park high diving show opened to great publicity in July of 1994 in a brand new 800 seat open air arena. I had created a strong theme for the show which also included several actors and acrobats. It was to be staged on a film set circa 1930 where the film *'Tarzan and the Jungle Adventure'* was being shot. We built a circular pool themed with jungle huts and linked to a dry stage area by a zip wire down which Tarzan would fly to rescue the captured girl. The high dive 'ladder' was made from a Heathrow Airport lighting mast fitted with suitable diving platforms and we converted an old electric buggie into a 1930s car. This would drive onto the set carrying the irascible director suitably dressed in plus fours and barking out his directions with the obligatory megaphone.

The divers, four boys and two girls, flew in from California ten days before the show opened expecting to stage their traditional sports diving show. I had some difficulty getting them to accept the Tarzan theme and the fact that they had to act a bit as well as dive. It was traditional with high divers, they told us, not to perform an actual high dive until the first show – they were superstitious. That was never going to work for us. Penny, who was directing, insisted that there must be a

Appendix II - The Complete Thorpe Park Years

full dress rehearsal including the high dive finale. The oldest and visibly the least fittest of the dive team volunteered to do the dive and, after successfully completing the dress rehearsal, he admitted that he had not performed a dive from that height for over three years! I was glad we didn't know this before the rehearsal. Over the season we encountered a few slight muscle sprains from the acrobatics, some light burns from the fire dive, and the occasional winding from a belly flopped dive, but the season passed without serious incident. The experience of using stunt divers, actors and acrobats in a spectacular arena show was soon to lead me in yet another new and exciting direction. Life was good and I was at last using all my hard learnt skills to create successful productions that were enjoyed by close to a million people every year.

1995

A new project to build a Legoland theme park in the UK had passed from the designers' drawing boards and was then in the early stages of construction at Windsor, just a few miles away from Thorpe. Our managing director felt we had to up our game for the new season in order to counteract the effect of another theme park opening in the same catchment area. For this reason I had secured my biggest budget yet for live entertainment and I set about planning an entirely new programme for 1995. At last it was my chance to bring a little of the Las Vegas magic to a British theme park!

I created a new theatre experience called *'Merlin's Magic Castle'* and The Thorpe Park Rangers were given a new show, *'Picnic By The Sea'*. In the arena *'Tarzan's*

Jungle Adventure' was extended to cover the whole season and I introduced a permanent street theatre team as well as staging a daily 'Disneyish' parade through the park. In the theatre an extension to the stage was built which featured a rock from which King Arthur withdrew the sword Excalibur. The medieval theme was carried to several parts of the auditorium where various actions took place. I also included a spectacular illusion.

Just on the market was a new system whereby all the lighting changes could be controlled by a computer programme, which in turn took instructions from a code recorded onto the soundtrack tape. This was ground breaking technology and was still very much in its infancy but, in order to carry out all the lighting effects I had planned for the new show, it seemed the perfect solution. Thus the lighting nightmare began. After they had struggled with it for several days, without success, I insisted that one of the software creation team came to the theatre to properly programme the lighting when the final rehearsals were over. It was early evening when we started the process and we were still in the theatre at six the next morning. Each time the system appeared to be completely programmed we played it back and it crashed. I had obviously bought into an expensive product that was hardly ready for the open market. It did eventually come good but throughout the season it occasionally threw 'curved balls' which our technicians could never catch or understand. Although I vowed to avoid such technology in the future, until it was thoroughly proven, a version of this system would come back to haunt me sooner than I expected.

I was elated by the success of all the 1995

Appendix II - The Complete Thorpe Park Years

productions but towards the end of the season I received some disappointing news. In spite of the park's increased budgets the season had not proven a financial success and with Legoland due to open in 1996 Thorpe Park was anticipating a big drop in attendances. Therefore all budgets would be cut for the next year. As always when money is scarce entertainment is the easiest thing to attack so I took the biggest cut. My budget was halved and, as a result, I was subjected to some unwelcome internal reorganisation which led to being allocated reduced office space. After such an exciting and creative year my future at the park began to look bleak. The golden days were over! It was time for big thinking.

In September another bombshell dropped. Colin Dawson handed in his resignation. Rumours had reached RMC Group headquarters that he had been negotiating to work on a new project with a fairground entrepreneur called Jimmy Godden. With this conflict of interest his position became untenable and he announced to us at his last management meeting that Chris Edge would be taking his position. I was in a dilemma – I had never got on well with Chris and now I had lost my main supporter. I could not envisage working on without Colin as the main decision maker. The following day, without giving much thought to what would happen next, I knocked on Chris's door and proffered my resignation. It felt just like the time, almost thirty years earlier, when I had resigned from my office job. Freedom again – but what would the future hold?

Appendix III
Important People

I must pay tribute to the talented artistes and musicians who have passed through my orbit over the last 50 plus years. Sadly many are missing from the list because, although I might have a picture of them in my head, their names have evaporated from my memory with the passage of time and I have no programme or press cutting or diary to remind me. But I thank them all for being part of the adventure.

The Lower Third (1962/1966)

Denis (Teacup) Taylor - Lead Guitar (1962/1966)
Robin Wyatt - Rhythm Guitar/Keyboard/Vocals
(1962/1965)
Glyn Jenkins -Vocals (1962)
Eric (Duke) – Drums (1962)
Graham Smith – Bass (1962/1963)
Terry Bolton (Gid Taylor) - Keyboards/Vocals
(1962/65)
Paul Pinder – Drums (1962/1963)
Les Mighall – Drums (1963/1965)
Graham Rivens – Bass (1964/1966)
David Jones (David Bowie) – Vocals and Saxophone
(1965/66)
Phil Lancaster – Drums (1966)

Unparallel Careers!

The Wilderness Years (1965/1969)

The Three Keys - 1966
Robb Wyatt, Terry Bolton, Gillian Mason
Mike Squirrel (replaced Terry Bolton)

The Golden Garter Saloon Show - 1967
Sheriff Danny Arnold, Jack Friedman (Pianist)
Robb Wyatt, Jimmy Grant (Singer)
Maureen Saunders (Saloon Hostess/Singer)
Billy 'Doc' McNicholl (Comedy and Fiddle)
Yvonne Eyles (Dancer), Jane Austin (Dancer)

The Golden Garter Saloon Show - 1968
Bob Blaine (Sheriff), Valerie Leon (Saloon Hostess)
Ronnie Winters (Yodelling Country Singer)
Robb Wyatt, Billy 'Doc' McNicholl
Jack Rodney (Pianist)
Jeanette and Janet Jay (Dancers)

The Golden Garter Saloon Show - 1969
Jimmy Rose and Phil Brooks - Jimmy Rose Duo
(Singer/Guitarists)
Diana Noble (Saloon Hostess)
Sheila and Gina Rossley – Sugar & Spice
(Singers/Ventriloquists)
Roger Graham – Sheriff (Actor/Singer)
Frank Horton (Pianist)
Gill Carter (Company Manager)
David Bellamy (Director)

A Big Fish (1969/1970)

Friends for Life
Philip Mallen, Wendy Mallen, John Gasston
Angela Mallen(now Gasston), June Gee

Appendix III - Important People

America (1970/1973)

The Bigwoods
Bobby Bigwood (Cordovox/Vocals)
Anne Bigwood (Drums)
Robb Wyatt (Guitar/Vocals)

Bandleaders and Musicians
Harry Bence, Jimmy Bence, Count Basie
Alan Dale, Ernie Mellor, Mike Neagel
Dougie Watson (Drums), Tim Marshall (Bass)
Miff Mole (Saxophone)

Cabaret Artistes
Victor Borge, Donald O'Connor, Bert Weedon
Roy & Jackie Toaduff, Sheila Holt & Ron Dylon
The Karlins, Monya Windsor (Violinist)
Roberto Cardinale, Nigel Hopkins
Kristine Holmes-Sparkle

Sue Carrel (Julianas' DJ), Woody Ismail (Sketch Artist)

Cunard
John Butt (Cruise Director)
Terry Conroy (Cunard Entertainment Director)

Way Out West – Summer 1973
Robb Wyatt (Sheriff)
The Circles - Bob and John (Guitar/Vocals/Comedy)
Cathy Cota (Singer/Actress), Sandie Scott (Pianist)
Tanya Dean (Singer)

Unparallel Careers!

Trilogy (1973/1978)

Trilogy
Lynda Turtle (Lacey – Christenson - Quinton-Jones)
Carole Wallwork (Seton – St.James – Jardine)
Robin Wyatt
(Robb Wyatt – Stephen Gold – Stephen Wyatt-Gold)

CSE - 1974/1977
Some of the artistes
Nigel Hopkins, Joe Longthorne, Jimmy Marshall
Geoff Taylor, Chris Cox, Dave Butler, Ron Martin
Ray Merrel, Terry Lightfoot and Band
Musicians
Barry Francis, Ian Arnott, Maurice Merry (Pianists)
Ted Simkins, John Richards (Bass Players)
Barry Patworth, Alan Savage, Eddie Sparrow (Drummers)
Management
Derek Agutter (Director), Johnny Harris (Deputy Director)
Gordon Clarke, Basil Elmes (Technicians)

Palace Hotel and Casino Isle of Man - 1975
Trilogy, Bal Moane (Comic), Diane Chandler (Singer)
Dave Oliver (Mime), Silvari & June (Illusionists)

Haifa Theatre Club – December 1975
Trilogy
Pierre & Galia (Illusionists), Mali (Israeli Singer)
Chi Chi Chanel (Austrian Stripper)

Victoria Palace/Old Vic Theatres Christmas Fund Raisers
Trilogy
Jimmy Saville, Keith Harris & Orville
Kenny Ball & His Jazzmen, Dave Ismay
The Hip Hooray Band, David Browne

Appendix III - Important People

Los Magicos, Alan Randall, Basil Brush
New Vaudeville Band, Joe Longthorne
Michael Vine & Karen

All Change (1978/1979)

Stephen Gold with Flame
Stephen Gold, Carole St.James, Lynne Lacey (1978)
Sandie Hill (1979)

Seaside Special, Cromer - 1978
Stephen Gold with Flame
Millican & Nesbitt, Denny Willis
Johnnie Mack, Billy Crockett, Ian Simpson
Lee Reynolds, Lisa Jarvis, Ros Murray, Julie Reynolds
(Dancers)
David Harper (Organ), Jack Brear (Drums)

Yogi Bear and Flame Tour - 1979
Stephen Gold, Carole St.James, Carol Hungerford
Jackie Thompson, Lynne Lacey
Dawn Harrison, Bob (JJ) Stewart
John Bell (Roadie)

A Smouldering Flame (1980/1982)

Bahrain/Cairo/Portugal - 1980
Stephen Gold, Carole St.James, Theresa Gallagher
Elaine Harrison, Jackie Thompson

World Tour - 1980
Stephen Gold, Carole St.James, Penny Hogan
Elaine Harrison, Carol Hungerford

Cologne/Barcelona/Isle of Wight - 1981
Stephen Gold, Penny Hogan, Carole St.James
Carol Hungerford, Christine Widdows
Jackie Thompson, Elaine Harrison

Unparallel Careers!

India - 1981
Stephen Gold
Penny Hogan, Jayne Longfield, Debbie Rawson

Flame Christmas Show
Blackpool Pleasure Beach - 1982
Stephen Gold, Penny Hogan, Carol Hungerford
Nina Sharpe, Jayne Longfield
Jacqui Butler, Beverly Murcheson, Derry James

Falkland Islands – 1982
Carole St.James, Carol Hungerford, Tracy Thompson

Island Hopping (1983/1985)

Flame in Jersey - 1983
Penny Hogan (Singer/Dancer)
Adam Daye (Impressionist)
Liz Izen, Fernando (Singers)
Cheryl Mortimer and Lesley Young (Dancers/Magicians)
Jacqui Butler, Nina Sharpe (Dancers)
Alan Frayne (Sound and Lighting)

Ryde Pavilion - 1983/1984
Tony Campbell and Brian Reid (Guitar/Vocals/Comedy)
Dave Mayberry – Sheriff (Actor/Singer)
Vanessa Bond – Saloon Hostess 1983 (Singer)
Ali Hawkins – Saloon Hostess 1984 (Singer)
Jill Gardner (Singer), Mike Partridge (Pianist)
Carole and Mark Crosby with Rupert Bear
Chris Bylett with Desmond Duck

Ventnor Winter Gardens - 1983
Carole St.James (Singer), Chris Wheeler (Impressionist)
Carol Hungerford, Beverly Murcheson
Louise Smith, Susie Bull (Dancers)
Tim Raffles & Dallas, Mark Raffles (Magic)
The Leaways (Acrobatics)

Appendix III - Important People

Second World Tour - 1983
Stephen Gold, Penny Hogan, Nina Sharpe
Cheryl Mortimer, Michelle Dawson
Tony Packer (Road Manager)

European Tour - 1984
Stephen Gold, Penny Hogan
Nina Sharpe, Jayne Longfield, Cheryl Mortimer
Tony Campbell, Brian Reid

Japan - 1984
Stephen Gold, Cheryl Mortimer, Dawn Harrison
Trudi Kingham, Debbie Rawson

The Shipwreck (1985/1988)

Ryde Pavilion - 1985
Dancers
Alison Kirrage, Tracy Porter, Rachel Lee, Alison Catterall
Nikki Cross, Rachel Smith, Clare Bonsu, Lorraine Crouch
Ron Martin (Comedy Fun Show)
David Andre (Impressionist), Bill Gore (Comedy)
Mandy Ann (Singer), Chameleon (Music Duo)
Penny Hogan (Choreographer)

Song 85
The Three Degrees, Dozy, Beaky, Mick and Titch
Sonny Curtis, Pinkertons Assorted Colours
Peter Powell, Gerard Kenny, Jan Francis
The Waltons, Fizzical, Rivera Duo
Geoff Ashford (Country Music Award)
Gillian Mason (Rock/Contemporary Award)
Dave & Helen Grounds (Best Pop Song Award)

New Delhi - 1986
Stephen Gold, Penny Hogan, Cheryl Mortimer

Unparallel Careers!

Sunlit Uplands
Thorpe Park 1989/1995

Actors, Singers and Dancers - just some of the many.
Ruth Goodwin, Antony Lee, Lucy Lloyd, Julie Clough
Robin Pascoe, Debbie Robbins, Lisa Best, Nicola Cull
Ruth Donaldson, Julie Robbins, Kevin Austin
Michael Blackledge, Debbie O'Hanlon, Roslyn Porcus
Jocelyn Hewlett, Jacqui Fox, Jane Earnshaw, Max Hutton
Phillip Arran, Michelle Musty, Johnny Scott
Andy Boughtflower, Chris Gosling, Lisa Williams
Richard Herd, Mark Nixon, Heather Whittam
Alex Paulton, Vikki Sparkes, Liz Langham
Emma Field, Gaynor Riopedre, Tony Tarrates
Troy Webb, Mathew Bowyer, Simon Finch
Tony (Movie Director), Clare (Miss Primrose)
Ian (Black Knight)

Street Entertainment
Chris Hare (Crazy Chris - Comedy Magic)
Adrian Kaye (Charlie Chaplin)
The Flannelettes, Bulbhead
Alpha Connection, Itsy Bitsy Band, The Rapiers
Solid Steel, Cathy Carlton (Singer/Guitarist)

Theatre Guest Artistes
Jimmy Tamley (Ventriloquist)
Adam Daye (Impressionist)
Bryn Peters, Ron Martin (Comics)

Pantomime - Babes In The Wood
Bruno Brookes, Gary de Carrington, Johnny Scott
Seb Craig, Antony Audenshaw, Ruth Donaldson
Robin Pascoe, Charlotte Plent, David Williams
David Robbins, Nicola Cull, Julie Robbins
Tracy Withers, Anita Reader

Appendix III - Important People

David Burt (Puppets)
Lawrie Bolton (Musical Director), Don Davies (Percussion)
Bob Bustance (Lighting)
Penny Hogan (Director and Choreographer)

Thorpe Radio
Mark Daniels, John Clayton, Glen Acton, Setch

Management
Stephen Gold
Head of Entertainments and Events / Producer
Stephen Gallagher
Assistant Head of Entertainments / Musician
Kevin Townsend – Technical Manager
Andrew Nu – Technician

Contracts
Jim Harrop – Scenery Design and Build
Chris Wilcox – Lighting Design (1990/1991)
Bob Bustance - Lighting Design (1992/1995)
Mike Coltman - The Rangers Character Costumes

The Glory Days
The Parkshows Years 1996/2003

The talented people who helped me make it happen.

Penny Hogan (Director/Choreographer)

Vikki Sparkes (Actress/Dancer)
Thorpe Park, Belgium, Office Admin., Costumes and more

Lisa Williams (Singer/Actress)
Thorpe Park, Belgium, Dubai, Alice The Musical,
Theatre Tours, Director's Assistant and more

Liz Langham (Actress)
Thorpe Park, Dubai, Popeye Theatre Tours, Office Admin.

Adam Daye
(Wizard in Sylvanian Families tour and the voice of Popeye)

Unparallel Careers!

Sander Van der Horst (Stage Technician)
Thorpe Park, Alice The Musical, Dubai etc.

Bob Bustance (Lighting Designer)
Thorpe Park, Dubai, Popeye Tours, Alice The Musical

Jim Harrop (Set Designer)
Popeye Theatre Tour, Lightwater Valley, The Lampies etc.

Marion Hutchinson (Graphic Designer)
Concept design for Belgium show and others

Bruce Cant (High Diving Consultant)
Thorpe Park and Dubai

Marvin Campbell (Acrobatic/Stunt Director)
Butlin's and American Adventure

Jonathan Howell (Fight Director)

*A few of the actors, singers, dancers
and costume character performers
who I was privileged to work with.*

Lucy Lloyd, Richard Herd, Roslyn Walsh
Kelly Randall, Alex Paulton, Kiersten Theakstone
Clare Rayner, Leah Cross, Kester Lewis
Pauline Gill, Clare Jarvis, Kirsty Pellant, Jon Sawyer
Heather White, Andrea Lewis, Annelly James
Andrea Condon, Steven Foster, Richard Boschetto
Heidi Johnson, Karen Turner
Emma Alexander, Nicola Peace, Natalie Clasper

Alice The Musical - 2001
Alison Lobley, Lisa Williams, Adam Hoffman
Richard Esdale, Nicola Lagan, Annie Lee Jones
Adrian Lloyd-James, Heidi Johnson, Emma McRae
Greg Arrowsmith (Musical Director)
Sander Van der Horst (Stage Manager)